MEXICAN AMERICAN WOMEN ACTIVISTS

Identity and Resistance in Two
Los Angeles Communities

MEXICAN AMERICAN WOMEN ACTIVISTS

Identity and Resistance in Two
Los Angeles Communities

MARY S. PARDO

Temple University Press
Philadelphia

Temple University Press, Philadelphia 19122
Copyright © 1998 by Temple University Press. All rights reserved
Published 1998
Printed in the United States of America

Text design by Nighthawk Design

Library of Congress Cataloging-in-Publication Data
Pardo, Mary S.
Mexican American women activists : identity and resistance in
two Los Angeles communities / Mary S. Pardo.
p.   cm.
Includes bibliographical references (p.   ) and index.
ISBN 1-56639-572-0 (alk. paper). — ISBN 1-56639-573-9 (pbk.
: alk. paper)
1. Women in community organization—California—Monterey
Park.   2. Women in community organization—California—Boyle
Heights.   3. Community power—California—Monterey Park.   4.
Community power—California—Boyle Heights.   5. Mexican American
women—California—Monterey Park.   6. Mexican American women—
California—Boyle Heights.   7. Montery Park (Calif.)—Politics
and government.   8. Boyle Heights (Calif.)—Politics and
government.   I. Title.
HN80.M66P37   1998
305.42'08968'72079494—dc21   97-13960

Contents

Acknowledgments

My teaching experiences in the Department of Chicana/o Studies at California State University, Northridge, motivated me to document urban contemporary Chicana experiences that would illustrate how women contribute to grassroots politics. I, along with my comadre Avie Guerra and other members of a Chicana collective, encountered great difficulty locating suitable readings for a Chicana class that we team taught in 1979. My friend Rudy Acuña encouraged me to pursue graduate study at UCLA that eventually led to the idea for this book. Along the way, many assisted me in the process of documenting and analyzing the experiences of women in the two communities. A few words of thanks are indeed in order.

Karen Brodkin Sacks's analysis of women's activism and her guidance provided a firm foundation at the early stages of my study; Melvin Oliver and David Lopez frankly reminded me that I must decide how women's grassroots activism not only challenges but also "fits" into mainstream sociological literature. Ruth Zambrana, helped me sort out ideas and develop a coherent story. Finally, John Horton steadied my course from the beginning to the end of the research—his wit, intellectual insights, and "democratic nature" made it possible to "get it done." He is a unique and gracious man. I participated in the Ford funded "Changing Communities Project" that John Horton directed and I gained an invaluable team research experience. The research of other team members, Jose Calderon, Yen Feng, Leland Saito, and Linda Shaw, helps tell the story of politics in Monterey Park.

Don Parson's research on social movements in Los Angeles represents what I think is a model analysis that incorporates the voices of women and Latinos. Knowing Don and his work have inspired me. Richard Chabran, "the wizard," an extraordinary librarian and anthropologist acknowledged in many other books by Latinas and Latinos, helped me to sort out sources and ideas. Maria Soldatenko deserves many thanks for being a *compañera*—I continue to share trials and tribulations with her and Mike Soldatenko. Gracias also to Marta López-Garza who took time to read portions of the manuscript while she was working on her own study of immigration in Los Angeles and to Jorge Garcia who shared his books and insights with me. My irreverent friends, Tom Gonzales and Frank Metz, made me laugh about the complexity of ethnic, racial, gender, and sexual identity. Talks with my comadre Irma Cross and my god daughter, Alegra, also confirmed my sense of how community context shapes ethnic identity.

Thanks to all the women activists who shared their stories and "archives" with me—the Mothers of East Los Angeles; Madres del Este de Los Angeles, Santa Isabel; and the Concerned Parents and Residents in Monterey Park and the City of Alhambra. Frank Villalobos allowed me to photocopy his collection of newspaper articles on the Eastside prison issue as did Juana Gutiérrez and Elsa Lopez. Erlinda and Valentín Robles helped me to understand the historical context of the contemporary political processes that form the core of the Eastside case. In Monterey Park, Dorothy Donath, Peggy Moody, Annie Rodriguez, Marijune Wissmann, and Cindy Yee also shared their files on the parole office. All the activists deserve recognition, for they have helped to improve the quality of urban life in Los Angeles.

During the last stages of work Kathy Blackmer Reyes, best friend and librarian at UC Davis, generously helped me to confirm references. Julia Curry Rodriguez helped me in every way imaginable, taking time from her demanding teaching and research schedule. She is an astute and gracious *hermana* and teacher. My family—my mother Blanche Ybarra Santoli and my aunt Josephine Ybarra who exemplify particularly strong, independent, honorable women, along with Marcella, Roy, Vanessa, Clarisa, Martin, David Robles, and Connie Gonzales—always offered the unconditional support and love that keeps work in perspective.

Aside from all the assistance of colleagues, friends, and family, one needs time to research and write. I was fortunate to receive a research expense grant from the American Sociological Association and to take time off from a busy teaching schedule thanks to funding from the UCLA Graduate Affirmative Action program, the Ford Foundation Dissertation Year Fellowship, and a sabbatical from California State University, Northridge.

Putting the book together represents another stage, and Elizabeth Johns's careful editing clarified more than I ever anticipated! Thanks for her patience. Beatrice Gutiérrez Mojarro's artistic talent graces the cover of the paperback edition; the design merges the personal and political because her mother, Juana, is in the photograph. Thanks to Carolyn Cole, director of the invaluable Photo Archives at the Los Angeles City Library, who helped me locate the cover photo. David Fuller, cartographer at CSUN, helped modify a map of the Los Angeles region that was originally composed by Manuel Moreno, and Rueyling Tsay and Victor Carrillo helped with a translation. My photographer friends Jim Velarde and Carlos Guerrero volunteered time and expertise in efforts to capture the different character of each community.

Although I have enjoyed much support and found a wealth of

information and wisdom in interviews and secondary sources, I know that errors may remain or my interpretations may be contested. I welcome the comments generated by the book. Producing knowledge is part of an ongoing dialogue and we all need to take part in the conversation.

MEXICAN AMERICAN WOMEN ACTIVISTS

Identity and Resistance in Two
Los Angeles Communities

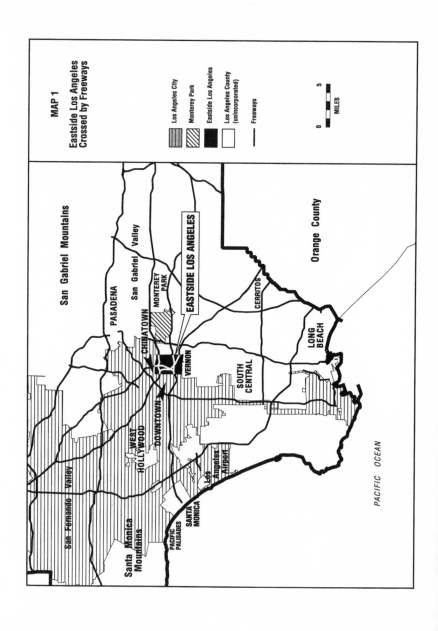

MAP 1

Eastside Los Angeles
Crossed by Freeways

Los Angeles City
Monterey Park
Eastside Los Angeles
Los Angeles County
(unincorporated)

Freeways

0   5
MILES

ONE

Introduction
Putting Women at
the Center of Politics

Yo como madre de familia, y como residente del Este de Los
Angeles, seguiré luchando sin descanso por que se nos re-
spete. Y yo lo hago con bastante cariño hacia mi comunidad,
y digo "mi comunidad" porque me siento parte de ella,
quiero a mi raza como parte de mi familia, y si Dios me per-
mite seguiré luchando contra todos los gobernadores que
quieran abusar de nosotros. [As a mother and a resident of
East Los Angeles, I shall continue fighting tirelessly so we
will be respected. And I will do this with much affection for
my community. And I say "my community" because I am
part of it. I love my *raza*, my people, as part of my family;
and if God allows, I will keep on fighting against all the government officials who want to take advantage of us.]

Juana Gutiérrez, Mothers of East Los Angeles (1986)

The parole office representatives, they think it won't be long
before the residents give up. I told them they would be hearing from us until it is moved. It is the little kids who suffer.
I'm sorry, I get emotional about it. It would be OK if it were a
high school a block away. But kids in elementary school are
still too young to defend themselves.

Annie Rodríguez, Concerned Parents
and Residents of Monterey Park (1989)

The words of Juana Gutiérrez and Annie Rodríguez express passionate commitment to the well-being of two different communities. Juana, who immigrated from Mexico to the United States over thirty years ago, lives in Boyle Heights, a densely populated, bustling, inner-city Latino barrio. Juana and her husband, Ricardo, raised nine children in the area. Boyle Heights, located in Eastside Los Angeles, lies only five minutes from the Civic Center, but few non-Latinos venture there because of its image as a dangerous place.

Annie Rodríguez and her husband, Nick, both U.S.-born Mexican Americans, grew up in Eastside Los Angeles. They moved to the suburbs after they married, settling in the ethnically diverse middle-class suburb of Monterey Park in 1975. The quiet neighborhoods, quality services, and proximity to Nick's employment appealed to them as a desirable place to raise their daughter. Ten years later, the positive image of Monterey Park promoted by a Chinese businessman had attracted thousands of new Chinese immigrants from Taiwan and Hong Kong, greatly changing the political, economic, ethnic, and racial composition of the city. In both communities, the struggle over community image is a struggle over power.[1]

Early one morning Juana stands with me on the porch of her two-story wooden house on Mott Street, two doors away from Whittier Boulevard, a lively commercial thoroughfare. Her street is so narrow that parking is permitted only on one side. Juana's front yard features an altar with a two-foot statue of the Virgin de Guadalupe, brightly flowering roses and cacti, and rock landscaping rather than a lawn. A six-foot-tall black wrought-iron fence surrounds the yard.

Directly across the street from her home stands the one-block-square Boyle Heights Park and Recreation Center. In 1986 she encouraged neighbors to join her in lobbying the city to renovate the neglected recreation center, which was being used as an informal dumpsite for stolen cars; the cars were often stripped, abandoned, and then set afire. After the city renovated the center, she shared cuttings from her rose bushes with the Latina gardener who landscaped the barren slopes of the park area. Juana has also acted as an advocate for Eastside Los Angeles, challenging the media portrayal of her barrio as a gangland battlefield teeming with tattooed "homeboys" and drive-by shootings. Stereotypical depictions of Asians, Latinos, and African Americans and their communities are often used to rationalize discriminatory practices. For this reason contesting degraded community images plays a key role in grassroots politics (see Chapter Three).

In 1985, with the encouragement of the local Catholic priest, Juana and other Mexican American women helped establish Mothers of East Los Angeles (MELA), a group that grew into a network of over four hundred families, mobilized four thousand people, and defeated the first state prison planned for an urban setting. Shortly thereafter, MELA stopped the construction of a toxic waste incinerator, established national political ties with other environmental groups, and emerged as a permanent community voice. In 1990 Mothers of East Los Angeles divided into two groups, roughly along parish lines. Both groups continued to advocate for community well-being and to inspire and affirm other women's community activism. In an adjoining parish Juana Gutiérrez and several other MELA members founded Madres del Este de Los Angeles, Santa Isabel (MELA-SI). In 1992 they created a nonprofit community-based organization. They promoted water conservation and generated jobs and funds that are reinvested in the community. They have also worked on a lead-poisoning and abatement program, immunization awareness, scholarships for high school and college students, and graffiti removal (see Chapter Five).

Age, birthplace, generation in the United States, regional context, and political views all influence one's choice of an ethnic or racial label. All except one of the women in MELA were of Mexican origin. The women used different terms to identify themselves, including "Mexicana," "American of Mexican descent," "Hispanic," and "Mexican American"; none identified herself as Chicana.[2] Out of respect for the women's choices and in the interest of consistency, I have used "Mexican American." In other contexts, I use "Chicana" for Mexican-origin women born in the United States, and "Latina" or "Latino" rather than "Hispanic" as an inclusive term for people of Latin American or Caribbean origins, both U.S. and foreign born. The diversity of ethnic labels emanates from ongoing political processes that pertain to us all. For the reasons I have just outlined, I use "Anglo" to refer to European American women who used Anglo and Caucasian interchangeably and I use Asian American as a general category to refer to persons of Asian ancestry. Wherever appropriate, I indicate national origin.

Later that week I spoke to Annie Rodríguez, a Mexican American woman who lives in the ethnically diverse middle-class city of Monterey Park, a suburb adjacent to the Eastside. Unlike Eastside Los Angeles residents, who are predominantly blue collar, Latino, and less likely to own their own homes, the Asian, Latino, and white residents of Monterey Park are predominantly middle-class, white collar workers. In a quiet and well-kept housing tract built in the 1950s, we sit in the living room of Annie's hilltop home, with its neatly trimmed front lawn, backyard pool, and view of the city below. In 1988, outraged by the presence of a state parole office serving felons a few blocks from the local elementary school, she helped to organize an ethnically diverse group of residents called "Concerned Parents and Residents of Monterey Park." On a smaller scale than MELA, the ethnically and racially mixed group of women and men in the middle-class suburban setting played a key role in mobilizing neighborhood opposition to the parole office.

Women much like Juana Gutiérrez and Annie Rodríguez have a long history of mobilizing civic action. Until the 1980s, however, little was written about the dimensions, let alone the dynamics, of women's grassroots political participation. We see children playing in a supervised park or hear about the renovation of a school, but seldom wonder who mobilized the community resources to upgrade the school or to staff the park. The places in which we live, learn, shop, and play are more than simply buildings; they represent outcomes of social relations that we take for granted. The quality of life in a community reflects unrecorded social and political processes, often originating in grassroots activism. Different from electoral politics, grassroots activism happens at the juncture between larger institutional politics and people's daily experiences. Women play a central role in the often unrecorded politics at this level.

This book focuses on the stories of Mexican American women from two Los Angeles communities and how they transformed the everyday problems they confronted in their neighborhoods into political concerns. These stories are more than fascinating human interest stories. They illustrate political processes at the local level. If we place women's experiences at the center of the analysis of local urban politics, we can see the gender, race, and class character of community networks. We can see how women and men help to shape the local urban environment as they create the resources for churches, schools, and community services. We also generate new questions and answers about collective action and the transformation of social networks into political networks.

Women's presence in local politics and their absence from conceptual discussions points to the analytic problem in defining and conceiving political participation. As conceived by male social scientists, narrow definitions of political participation have excluded women's contributions to grassroots political action. For many decades political participation meant taking part in electoral politics or holding office in a political organization. Despite much feminist research that challenges established political science concepts, feminist theories, questions, and conclusions have not been integrated into the field. The significance of politics occurring outside political institutions, and women's community activism particularly, continue to be largely excluded from conventional notions of political activity.[3] Since local activism takes place outside political institutions, many social scientists view it as unimportant, marginal, parochial, and therefore theoretically unimportant.

Theories of political action ought to help us to make sense of social relations—the repeated patterns of activity, and the direction of those repeated patterns—without eliminating the dynamic of human creativity and interpretation. However, the language of social science and the everyday language used to communicate information may exclude or include people. The words selected to describe a community may degrade or celebrate it.[4] Language and labels do more than simply reflect our realities; they shape those realities. These women's stories about moving from the personal problems of everyday life to collective action repeat patterns and themes and convey rich complexities about their gender, ethnic, class, and community identities.[5] Their activities show how gender and ethnicity and class shape each day of their lives.

Because of men's and women's differing social obligations to their families, group solidarity and local collective action emerge from neighborhood networks clearly organized by gender. Women's activities in the inner city and in the suburb differ over time and place; the ethnic and class composition of communities represent more than background or scenery. For example, most of the women activists in Monterey Park worked in white collar jobs and their children attended public schools; many of the women in MELA did not work for wages, but they had spent countless hours volunteering for the Catholic parish where their children attended parochial school. Finally, the ways women and men interpret their social identities—as mothers, fathers, wives, husbands, members of particular ethnic and racial groups, members of the working class or middle class—help them to devise creative strategies to solve community problems.

As a participant observer at rallies, meetings, and hearings, and as a recorder of life stories, I conducted field work continuously from 1987 to 1990, and intermittently during the years 1992–97.[6] I also used local newspaper and television coverage of community events to complement the women's accounts. I asked several questions emphasizing political participation as a process: How does one become a community activist? What is the course of women's grassroots activism, and how does their involvement begin? What is the character of their activism, and what strategies do they use to accomplish their work and convince others to join them? How do the answers differ for women in each community, which themselves differ by class?[7]

Additionally, what perceptions do women hold of their activism? Do they see conflict or congruence between their activism and their everyday lives? If they see conflict, how do they resolve it? In the resolution of conflict do they change their conceptions of social identity? Women's activism is rooted in the way they construct their social identity; conversely, women's activism also shapes their social identities. Women activists have implicit theories about power, and they test and reformulate their theories in relation to their mobilizing experiences. Women's narratives of grassroots politics not only make women visible; they illustrate as well as transform the concepts of political participation and urban change.

I interviewed core activists in each community but not every woman who became involved in different capacities in the community. Activists who had worked for extended periods of time on community issues offered rich observations of the mobilization process. Neither the women's stories nor my observations of their work represent the experiences of all women activists, or even of all the women politically active in these two communities.[8] But they do illustrate some of the fundamental ways women become community activists.

Different from many other social science studies of women of Mexican origin, this study is strength oriented rather than strictly problem oriented. It places women as actors in the center of a community controversy and follows the strategies they use to solve a problem. Patterns of occupational segregation and gang subcultures as experienced by Mexican American women warrant much scholarly attention and study (Melville 1988, Horowitz 1983, Harris 1988). Seldom, however, are Mexican American women seen as actors rather than as victims of poverty and injustice. Only in the last two decades have scholars of the Chicana and Chicano experience begun to document instances of how men and women have fashioned and gathered resources to attack social problems and empower themselves.[9]

The Importance of Latina Activism in Los Angeles

The size in square miles of suburban, multi-ethnic Monterey Park approximates that of the Eastside Latino working class neighborhood of Boyle Heights, but the two differ in ethnic, racial, and class composition, population density, and local governance. People are visible everywhere in Boyle Heights— women walking with their young children, people waiting for buses, adolescents playing ball and riding bikes in the middle of residential streets. By contrast, with half the population of Boyle Heights, the residential streets of Monterey Park seem calm and quiet. But in both communities, the quality of neighborhood life in relationship to urban development and land use drives grassroots activism. Mexican American women in both communities actively confront the consequences of urban growth.

By comparing the local political activities of Mexican American women in two such dissimilar communities, I hope to capture the character and trends in a heterogeneous Latino population. In this country the Latino population, even in what appears to be an ethnically homogeneous community such as Eastside Los Angeles, differs by citizenship status, language dominance, generation, and national origin. Mexican American women in Monterey Park represent the growing suburbanization of the Latino middle class. Different community contexts may result in differences in the types of work and strategies women use to solve community problems. There is no one homogeneous Latino population, and differential economic status and geographical dispersion generates differences and interconnections between Latina community activists.

Current demographic projections indicate that by the year 2010, 50 percent of California's residents will be Latinos. Latinos are more likely to reside in large metropolitan centers, where the public infrastructure—streets, transportation, services—is inadequate and overtaxed. While they are more likely to live in the large cities, they are also dispersed throughout many surrounding suburbs, which are not automatically protected against the problems of the inner city. This residential dispersal means that Latinos will play a significant part in the political processes affecting numerous California communities.[10]

New waves of immigration, particularly from Latin America and Asia, make Los Angeles an exciting and dynamic metropolitan context in which to study women's community activism. The size and ethnic diversity of the city's population define the conditions under which women activists do their work. The region's staggering growth complicates everyday activities associated with neighborhood and community life. Mobilizing others means communicating existing problems and constructing potential solutions even as commercial development, increasing density, inadequate waste disposal, and traffic gridlock destroy the quality of urban life. New international immigrants represent a diversity of ethnic and national origins that pose communication problems. Therefore, the ethnic and racial composition of the places women mobilize determines the material conditions of their work. In Eastside Los Angeles, the women mobilized others who were of the same ethnic origin; in the multi-ethnic suburb, women worked in multi-ethnic groups. Similarly, activists are affected by issues of economic class. In blue-collar communities, women's shared community work often compensates for an inadequate infrastructure. In suburban communities, women fight to defend existing conditions in their neighborhoods by subverting, modifying, or challenging unwanted projects.

"Insider-Outsider" Considerations

We researchers are no more "generic" than are the women and men on whom we center our inquiries. Each researcher brings a unique voice and a personal biography that shapes her interpretation of the places, events, and people she observes. The perspective I bring to my study has produced particular questions and interpretations of what I observed. As a second-generation woman of Mexican descent, I share the same ethnic origins and a similar immigration history with the women I interviewed. I grew up in a blue-collar family in neighborhoods similar to those in Eastside Los Angeles. I participated in the Chicano student movement of the early 1970s and worked in the Eastside. I was part of the 1970 Chicano Moratorium, when twenty thousand people marched down the middle of Whittier Boulevard protesting the Vietnam War. The event marked my growing political consciousness and left a lasting emotional impression. Consequently, I experienced the Eastside as neither dangerous nor foreign. By the same token, my college degrees and professional job as a college teacher made me similar to the middle-class women of Monterey Park.

But my educational, professional, and personal life story also differs significantly from the stories of both the women in the working class community and those in the middle-class suburb. I was not an objective observer at the hearings, meetings, and demonstrations I attended in the course of this study. I agreed with the women's opposition to the state-sponsored projects and assisted in their struggle in small ways—for example, by arranging two media interviews. Indeed, MELA's community concerns corresponded to my work as a Chicana and Chicano studies professor. Although shared ethnic origins and class background may have helped facilitate my entrée into circles of interaction and communication, I hesitate to say that the similarity of our backgrounds completely explains the ease of my entrée. In both communities, I observed that the women warmly welcomed non-Latino journalists who offered them an opportunity to gain more media coverage and possibly more support for their causes.

One incident helped me to think about the ways a researcher's own familiarity with a community will shape research questions. Women from MELA, an Anglo woman journalist, and I were sitting in the dining room of Juana Gutiérrez's home enjoying a dinner of chile rellenos, rice, and beans that Juana had prepared. The journalist asked how the women might mobilize around a hypothetical case of false imprisonment of an alleged gang member. A momentary silence engulfed the discussion.[11]

Earlier in the evening, the journalist had confided to me her apprehensions about driving out to what she understood to be a rough neighborhood. Her question about the alleged gang member reflected the media assumption that gang activity constituted the most significant problem facing Eastside Los Angeles residents. But the women from MELA were longtime, stable homeowners, most of whose children had already graduated from college. They had all worked in cooperation with the police and in Neighborhood Watch groups in order to discourage drug dealing in the neighborhood. They had also directed collective efforts at getting summer jobs for youth. Gangs had never been the focus of their efforts. Rebuilding a neighborhood park and opposing the prison and a toxic-waste incinerator consumed most of their time. Consequently, they were temporarily at a loss for an answer. The exchange reinforced my understanding of the women's social location in the community and their activism. It also showed me how the

journalist's own perceptions of the women and their community had shaped her questions just as my perceptions were no
doubt shaping mine.

Locating Activists

In order to carry out the study, I identified Latina community
activists in different ways. In Eastside Los Angeles, the barrio
setting, I contacted Father John Moretta, an Italian American
priest who was the pastor at Resurrection Parish in Boyle
Heights. He referred me to two women who were core activists in MELA; one was Juana Gutiérrez. After Juana and I
talked, she called another woman in the group and actually set
up the next interview. The following day, I was on a busy
schedule, driving from the Eastside to Monterey Park, attending meetings, hearings, demonstrations, and conducting interviews. I was added to the "telephone tree" of people to notify
about demonstrations and meetings. I continued to identify
other women activists who neither held official leadership positions nor acted as spokeswomen by asking each woman that
I interviewed for other names. I used pseudonyms at the request of some of the women that I interviewed.

My entry into the suburban community of Monterey Park
was different. First, I had the good fortune to be part of a research team and worked as an assistant to Dr. John Horton,
principal investigator for a study, supported by the Ford Foundation, of the changing relations in the community between
newcomers and established residents.[12] In that capacity, I assumed the primary responsibility for following the role of
women (not exclusively Latinas) in city politics. As I began attending community and city council meetings, I discovered a

grassroots community conflict—resident opposition to a parole office located within half a mile of an elementary school.
Although the protesters were not recognized as a women's
group, women activists outnumbered men. Two Latinas and
one Anglo woman were named as key organizers of the Monterey Park neighborhood opposition efforts, a newly formed
and loosely organized group of about thirty-five concerned
parents and residents and a Parole Advisory Board composed
of four men and nine women. I introduced myself to one of the
Chinese American women who made a statement about the
parole office at the city council meeting, and subsequently began attending their meetings and interviewing Mexican American, Chinese American, and Anglo women in the group.[13] The
controversy in Monterey Park was centered in one neighborhood of the city and began in 1988 and ended in 1991. It differed in magnitude and duration from the Eastside Los Angeles state-prison issue, which began in 1985 and ended in 1992.
Aware that events in the field seldom fit tidy, neat categories, I
decided to follow the issue because, like the Eastside controversy, it constituted a quality-of-life concern for the women
and both groups were opposing a state-sponsored project.
Speaking to women *in action* in the suburban and inner-city
settings meant I could draw comparisons.[14]

Organization of the Book

Although the stories of women's activism in each community
could be told separately, I have chosen to tell the stories in a
comparative way to highlight how the class, ethnic, and racial
composition of each community affected women's activities
and options. The case studies are organized around three main

themes that represent different dimensions of the political process: the politics of community images, becoming an activist, and creating community. Chapter Two, "Community Contexts: The Barrio and the Suburb," contextualizes the process of becoming a grassroots community activist, by which I mean putting the types of work women do and the ways they do it into specific sites, within concrete material conditions, and with specific historical legacies. The chapter provides a demographic overview of ethnicity and immigration in Eastside Los Angeles and Monterey Park and synthesizes the history of grassroots community activism and women's participation in each community.

The heart of the book addresses the themes of ethnic, gender, and class identity and resistance to state-sponsored and commercial projects in each community. Chapters Three and Four examine the politics of community identity by looking at physical and cultural surroundings and presenting the women's visions of their communities. The women weave ethnic, racial, and class contexts throughout their accounts of becoming long-time residents and recall how class, ethnic, and gender identities have shaped their choices for residential location. The chapters also illustrate how women transformed their experiences, observations, and problems into collectively defined interests and solutions. Chapters Five and Six present case studies of the specific conflicts that engaged women's activism—in the Eastside Los Angeles case, a proposed state prison, in the case of Monterey Park, a state parole office. The chapters explore the course of women's involvement and the ways social identities shape and legitimate the strategies they used to oppose the projects.

Chapters Seven and Eight move back in time to examine the women's routine work in neighborhood sites and the antecedents to their involvement in the community conflicts as a way of understanding the unpaid work that preceded their period of activism. Chapter Nine, "Women Transforming the `Political,' " concludes with a comparative analysis of women's community work in the working-class, predominantly Mexican American, inner-city Los Angeles barrio and in the predominantly middle-class, multi-ethnic suburb. The differences and similarities illustrate how communities of different classes resist and challenge the state's definition of social justice. The chapter also addresses the politics of writing about women in urban politics. As a Chicana professor with graduate training in sociology, teaching in an interdisciplinary field, Chicana and Chicano Studies, I draw from feminist studies, ethnic studies, and social science studies. While knowledge is increasingly interdisciplinary, mainstream disciplines slowly and begrudgingly change and acknowledge gender and ethnicity as meaningful categories of social organization (Klein 1996, 121). Crossing disciplinary boundaries enriched my understanding of women's community activism.

T W O

Community Contexts
and Controversies
The Barrio and the Suburb

Demography carries the weight of histories of struggle . . .
community is the product of work and struggle, inherently
unstable and contextual.

Biddy Martin and Chandra Mohanty,
"Feminist Politics: What's Home Got to Do with It?"

On a mansion-lined residential corner of Sunset Boulevard
near the UCLA campus and not far from Hollywood, one
can usually find a young immigrant Latino man dressed in a
worn T-shirt and jeans who regularly sets up a folding chair
and a large cardboard sign announcing "Maps to the Stars
Homes." His patrons are middle-class visitors from all over
the country, anxious to enjoy the balmy climate and palm trees
and hoping for a glimpse of movie stars. In Los Angeles, as in
other large cities, the informal economy operates alongside the
formal one. The former includes street vendors, garment
workers sewing in their homes, and anyone whose work takes
place outside of official regulation. The formal economy in-

cludes the prosperous Century City lawyers along with an expanding poor, Latino immigrant population.

Whether Latinos participate in the economy as poor immigrants or established middle-class citizens, they live in close proximity to wealth and luxury in a city whose film industry often produces negative images of their status. International immigration and investment have dramatically affected the life conditions and quality-of-life issues that the women portrayed here confront in their respective communities. Poor Latino immigration and a lack of investment in jobs and services have affected life in East Los Angeles. Chinese immigration and a corresponding influx of capital have revitalized Monterey Park. Nevertheless, from the viewpoint of established residents, neither community has escaped state attempts to locate undesirable development there.

International Immigration and Investment

California has experienced the most dramatic population growth of any state in the history of the United States. Between 1960 and 1990 the population doubled. At 30 million residents, the population exceeds that of any other state.[1] Immigration, primarily that of Latinos and Asians, accounted for half the growth, and the state's birthrate (20.4 per 1,000 persons) surpassed that of the United States (16.7 per 1,000 persons) by 22 percent.[2]

About one-third of the state's new residents live in the Los Angeles area, also making it the largest county in the nation.[3] Proportionally Los Angeles County has received more international immigrants between 1965 and 1980 than any other metropolitan area in the country.[4] Between 1950 and 1980 foreign-born residents increased from 10 percent to 22 percent of the county's population (García 1985, 74). By 1990, foreign-born residents composed 33 percent of the county's population, which totaled 8.8 million residents, eclipsing the populations of every state except for New York and Texas.[5] The increasing number of new immigrants and city growth are intertwined, mutually dependent phenomena.[6]

Los Angeles is currently the point of entry for both immigration and financial investment from the "Pacific Rim" countries. Geographic proximity, economic growth, and the low wages paid to immigrants create mutually reinforcing conditions. The large pool of low-wage, politically vulnerable immigrant labor attracts light industry that is labor intensive; the promise of jobs that do not require English-language fluency attracts new immigrants. Apparel manufacturing expanded in Los Angeles because of the growing supply of low- and semi-skilled immigrant women (Allen and Turner 1997: 185). The growing service sector also relies on immigrant workers.

Southern California competes with Third World areas in having low production costs and a disciplined, low-wage labor market (Sassen 1988: 185). Anyone driving along selected major thoroughfares is reminded of the economic barriers faced by many of the newest Latino immigrants. Groups of twenty to fifty Latino men line the curbs waiting to be chosen for casual or day labor in construction, landscaping, and unskilled work. Increasing numbers of immigrants from Central America, particularly El Salvador, join Mexicans, who compose the largest immigrant group in Los Angeles.

This mass international immigration resulted from the reform of the U.S. immigration policy, civil war and economic disarray in Latin America, and from the political transitions taking place in Asia. In 1965, the U.S. restructured its immigration policy abolishing restrictions that limited the number of immigrants coming from southern and eastern Europe and from Asia. It also created two main criteria for those who wished to immigrate to the United States: family ties with permanent residents or U.S. citizens, or the possession of scarce or needed skills. The advocates of the immigration reform expected southern and eastern Europeans, especially refugees fleeing Communist countries, to take advantage of the opportunity to immigrate. Instead those from Asia, Latin America, and the Caribbean countries used the liberalized immigration policy (Waldinger and Bozorgmehr 1996: 9). The collapse of the U.S.-supported regime in South Vietnam compelled a large number of refugees to seek immigration to the United States. The long anticipated return of Hong Kong to the Peoples Republic of China in 1997 also stimulated tens of thousands of Chinese to immigrate from Hong Kong and Taiwan. Fifteen years after the passage of the reformed immigration policy, the Chinese population in New York, Los Angeles, and Chicago more than doubled (Salter 1984: 18).

In the midst of the economic boom in Los Angeles, the income gap grows between the "haves" and the "have nots" (Ong 1989). According to economists, this reflects a national trend in which rising employment levels are failing to lift the poor out of poverty or boost the middle class.[7] Service jobs now account for 56 percent of the total jobs in the city. Electronic and labor-intensive manufacturing are also growing sectors of the economy, but both are predominantly nonunionized; gone are the relatively highly paid unionized jobs in the auto industry and steel plants. In Los Angeles County the proportion of unionized workers dropped from 25 percent in the 1950s to 15 percent in the 1990s (Acuña 1996, 180). Latinos typically earn their wages in the low-paying sectors. For instance, in the last decade nonunion cleaning companies hiring mainly immigrant Latino workers have cut the average janitor's hourly pay from $7.00 to $4.50 and have eliminated overtime and health insurance. Two weeks pay amounts to $329, not enough to pay for shelter and food.[8]

Racial and Ethnic Residential Patterns

The city of Los Angeles has a long history of racial and ethnic segregation, and the 1990s ethnic composition of communities reflects past discrimination. South Central Los Angeles, although experiencing a rapidly increasing Latino immigrant population, is perceived by some as an African American ghetto.[9] Since the 1940s, the Eastside has been predominantly Mexican American. The westside of Los Angeles and the San Fernando Valley are predominantly Anglo, with small pockets of African Americans and large enclaves of Latinos in the Northeast Valley and to a lesser extent in the West Valley. In 1929 the California Supreme Court upheld the right of property owners to refuse to rent or sell housing to nonwhite ethnic groups. A decade later, in 1940, an African American family challenged racial restrictions. By 1948 the United States Supreme Court declared restrictive real estate covenants invalid and unconstitutional (Bunche 1990: 114–19); but the practice continued well after the 1968 Fair Housing Act, and in the 1990s discrimination in housing remains widespread (Allen and Turner 1997, 44, 87).

The economic restructuring and new immigration to Los Angeles have further altered patterns of land use and de facto racial segregation. In low-rent areas, residential density and substandard housing have increased as multiple families share single-family homes or apartments. Central City harbors a contrasting mix of occupants: poor Latino immigrants living in substandard housing and affluent Anglos, seen only by day, who inhabit expensive high-rise condominiums and work in the palatial financial center. Tax monies allocated for urban renewal projects subsidized the land and costs of construction of the financial center, which swallowed up space previously occupied by low-cost housing. The contrast within the inner city reflects the economic polarization and attendant social consequences that are typical of the city as a whole. Increasing density and development unmatched by investment in social programs, services, and infrastructure erode the quality of urban life beginning in the center of the city.

The housing shortage of the 1990s surpasses that following World War II, when returning veterans protested by camping out in MacArthur Park with signs that read, "Fox Holes in '45—Rat Holes in '47."[10] Then, the politically acceptable solution was to offer federal subsidies for middle-class suburban development, a few public housing developments for the very poor, and mass subsidies for urban business development. Los Angeles actually spent only a small percentage of its share of federal monies allocated for public housing. Forceful opposition from the building trades and real estate interests, coupled with racial and ethnic hostilities, brought a halt to the city's use of the funds (Parson 1982). Now, subsistence-level wages coupled with a shortage of low-income housing have created increasing homelessness and caused families to double up in single housing units. Poor households scramble to meet rents of $600 and more and spend three-fourths of their income for shelter (Ong 1989).

Los Angeles shares characteristics with other major metropolitan areas, albeit on a much larger scale. The Los Angeles metropolitan region is almost twice as large as those of New York and San Francisco, and its cars, multiple freeway interchanges, new immigrant populations from all corners of the world, and economic and physical growth reach overwhelming proportions (Waldinger and Bozorgmehr 1996, 5, 14). As with many other large cities, the quality of life—measured by pollution, residential density, employment opportunities, and such services as schools and police, parks, and cultural attractions—varies from community to community.

The Eastside and Monterey Park represent some of the variation in status and residential patterns. Eastside Los Angeles is predominantly Latino, low-income, and working-class. In Monterey Park Latinos live in a multi-ethnic suburb where Chinese immigrants predominate, followed by largely U.S.-born Latinos and Anglos. In both communities, the quality of neighborhood life with respect to urban development and land use has become the rallying point for grassroots activism.

Eastside Los Angeles: The Latino Barrio

In this country the Latino population, even in what may appear to be an ethnically homogeneous community such as Eastside Los Angeles, differs by citizenship status, language dominance, generation, and national origin. The Eastside has traditionally been the port of entry for new immigrants as well as the home of second-generation Mexican Americans, who make up a significant number of long-time residents. Among Latinos, a popular assumption is that moving from Eastside Los Angeles to Monterey Park is indicative of upward mobility (Escobedo 1979). A number of Monterey Park residents once resided in Eastside Los Angeles and many have relatives living there. The distinctions between the communities are economic and class based; the connections are family ties and ethnic identity. Both the continuities and the differences help construct a distinctive, many-faceted identity for women to use in their efforts to shape community.

The Demographic Context

In 1990 Boyle Heights had an estimated population of eighty-nine thousand. Some say this figure is too low and excludes many recent arrivals who may be undocumented immigrants. With twice the density of Los Angeles as a whole, Boyle Heights averages twenty persons per acre, and half its population is under twenty-five years of age. Residents are primarily low-income blue-collar workers who rent their homes. About half the population is foreign born, and 89.8 percent speak Spanish. More than 30 percent of those who speak Spanish report that they speak English not well or not at all. Long-term residents give stability to a neighborhood; however, from one block to the next, the proportion of homeowner-occupied units may vary from 3 percent to 75 percent.[11]

Only 30 percent of Boyle Heights residents own their homes. The median family income for the Boyle Heights area for those the 1980 census designated as of Spanish/Hispanic origin was $12,767, with 25 percent of the residents receiving incomes below the poverty level. Women are concentrated in operator/laborer jobs (36 percent), followed by technical/sales (35 percent) and service positions (18.8 percent); the smallest number of women work as managers and professionals (6 percent) (see Phillips 1986: 129–30). Over 43 percent of the women participate in the labor force, and women head 19.5 percent of the households. Two to four people live in 51.4 percent of the households, while 35.8 percent of households contain five or more.

From Delicatessens to Panaderías

Boyle Heights was built in the late nineteenth century as a "streetcar suburb," the first neighborhood outside the center of the city. In the early 1900s, Jewish families began moving into the predominantly upper-class Protestant neighborhood. Cosmetics millionaire Max Factor and gangster Mickey Cohen resided in the once stately neighborhood. By 1938 more than eighteen hundred Jewish households had become established there, and it had become the first large, visibly distinct Jewish community in Los Angeles: "On the main streets of Boyle Heights were stores where Jews bought and sold, Yiddish was freely used, and Saturdays and Jewish holidays were marked by festive appearances and many closed businesses" (Phillips 1986, 129–30). Now, at the end of the century, synagogues remain scattered throughout the community, but "Latino" replaces "Jewish" and "Spanish" replaces "Yiddish" in the neighborhood portrait. *Carnicerías* and *panaderías* replace Jewish delicatessens and bakeries. Albeit in a much altered form, ethnic distinctiveness persists.

By the 1940s the Jewish exodus for the newer suburbs had begun as the Mexican population increased. Although some oral histories suggest that Mexicans and other groups easily intermingled, this may have varied by situation (R. Romo 1983; Acuna 1984). Residential areas remained segregated for more than a decade (Escobedo 1979). As late as the 1950s, privately owned housing tracts such as Wyvernwood denied rental units to Mexicans. Some of the barber shops on Brooklyn Avenue refused service to Mexicans for fear of head-lice infestation.[12]

The 1940s also marked the internment of a large number of Japanese American residents of Boyle Heights and the beginning of intense construction of public projects and industrial development. The completion of five freeways took up over 12 percent of the land; federally funded housing projects occupied another 2 percent; and industry, which developed along the railroad lines, occupied an additional 26 percent of the area while providing jobs for over eleven thousand people. Freeway construction uprooted ten thousand residents, but noise, air pollution, and traffic congestion disrupted the lives of the rest (Escobedo 1979). Painfully embedded in the collective memories of residents, the displacement experience was recalled and reconstituted to represent the political vulnerability of Eastside Los Angeles (see Chapter Three).

Community Organizations and Women's Activism

In the 1940s, and to some degree today, the troubled history of Eastside Los Angeles has included declining city services, police brutality, housing discrimination, and inadequate infrastructure such as paved streets, traffic lights, and street lighting. Several Mexican American organizations emerged between the 1940s and the 1990s, but the Community Service Organization (CSO) and the United Neighborhood Organization (UNO) gained the largest family-based constituency. Both groups used a model developed by Chicago-based grassroots organizer Saul Alinsky. Alinsky viewed churches as an ideal organizing base because they are an existing community structure whose members share values related to basic human dignity; further, they have funds available for organizing.[13]

The role of the Catholic Church in Eastside social activism has varied over time and from one parish to another, depending on the inclination of the pastor and the resources available. While the Catholic Church endorsed the CSO, it did not sponsor it. Less based in neighborhoods and families and more reliant on youth and students, the Chicano movement of the late 1960s challenged inferior education and racism and also criticized the Church's reluctance to support social activism. By the mid-1970s, the Church had modified its stance and sponsored UNO (United Neighborhood Organization); the Chicano movement contributed to a church position more receptive to community advocacy. Chicanas played key roles in organizing activities, although they were less likely than men to hold official leadership positions.[14]

Later, through interviews that I conducted with the core activists in Mothers of East Los Angeles, I learned that experiences in groups such as the CSO and UNO crisscrossed their life stories. The most active women had gained leadership and organizational skills as volunteers in the parish fundraising activities (see Chapter Seven). All the core activists whom I interviewed had a long and rich community commitment that informed their contemporary grassroots activism.

Community Service Organization. Mexican American veterans returned from World War II with high hopes for a better life. Edward Roybal, a UCLA graduate and veteran, exemplified the heightened expectations for an improved quality of life in Eastside Los Angeles. In 1947, Roybal along with twenty other residents, organized what came to be known as the Community Service Organization (CSO). That same year, Fred Ross, a field organizer for Saul Alinsky's Chicago-based Industrial Areas Foundation (IAF), assisted Mexican Americans in the development of the organization. The CSO addressed low voter registration, inferior schools and housing, unpaved streets, and widespread police brutality.[15] Women and men participated in equal numbers, but men generally held the position of president while women chaired many committees (Rose 1994, 180).

For East Los Angeles and other poor communities throughout the United States, the Industrial Areas Foundation, founded
in Chicago in 1940 by Saul Alinsky and Catholic Bishop Shiel,
became one of the nation's most influential models for political
empowerment in poor communities. Alinsky believed that
community organizing should build on traditional community
institutions such as churches and labor unions, rather than
compete with them for membership (Alinsky 1946: 101). In
working-class Mexican American and other Latino communities, the Catholic Church as a local institution has tremendous
potential for advocating community betterment. The realiza-
tion of that potential varies from region to region. Compared
to the role taken by the Catholic Church in some Mexican
American communities such as San Antonio, Texas, the Los
Angeles archdiocese has been less willing to adovocate for the
social needs of its constituency (Ortiz 1984).

Alinsky anticipated parish support in Los Angeles, but Fred
Ross advised Alinsky that "while Mexican Americans came
out of Catholic traditions, an organizer could not expect much
leadership from the young priests as Alinsky had enjoyed in
Chicago."[16] Cardinal McIntyre, who determined the activities
of all the parishes in the Los Angeles archdiocese, recognized
the new aspirations of returning veterans, but he discouraged—some suggest he even persecuted—priests and nuns
who engaged in community activism. Instead, Cardinal McIntyre promoted community school building and "Americaniza-
tion" programs.[17]

Critics accuse the church of perpetuating a paternalistic and
patronizing attitude toward Mexicans and not developing
Mexican American leadership (Dolan and Hinojosa 1994, 175).
Defenders of the Church position argue that in the era before
Vatican II (that is, prior to 1962), "the prevailing model of [the

Catholic] Church in the United States insisted that the church's primary goal was the preservation of the immigrant's faith and the salvation of souls, not the transformation of society" (Burns 1994, 175–76). While the official Church in the pre-1960s era may have been reluctant to endorse parish-based activism, in the 1940s Chicago's Polish immigrant community built a strong parish-based grassroots organization often led by young priests.

In Los Angeles the Church endorsed the CSO but did not initiate it through the church parishes. Instead, Roybal and Ross developed the idea of nightly house meetings, inviting friends and neighbors to gather to discuss community concerns. Women as well as men participated in the committees, and María Durán, one of twenty persons who initiated the group, set up CSO headquarters in her home. The members developed committees to address housing conditions, voter registration, public health, and civil rights. The civil rights committee handled community police brutality complaints (Boyte 1980, 93–94).

The quality of police-community relations often reflects the status of a community; poor relations suggest that a community occupies a subordinate status. In the 1940s, as in later decades, the abrasive relationship between the Los Angeles Police Department and the Mexican American Eastside community generated enough tension to become one of the key issues addressed by the CSO. Police employed racial stereotypes emphasizing criminality of Mexican American youth to justify daily harassment.[18]

By 1951 the CSO membership grew to three thousand and included unskilled workers, college students, and union members. The civil rights committee successfully organized to demand justice for seven young Chicanos who were arrested in a barroom scuffle on Christmas Eve, taken to the police station, and nearly beaten to death by drunken officers. Dubbed the "Bloody Christmas" case, it was one of the rare occasions when law enforcement officers have been prosecuted for assaulting Mexican Americans (Morales 1972, 21), and it represented a significant victory for the community. Referring to police-community relations, Fred Ross commented in 1950, "Three years ago [in 1947], Eastside streets were the scene of the blaring siren, the sidewalk shakedown, the pinch on suspicion of littering, the firing by police upon residents on the average of once a month."[19] After the CSO mobilization efforts, the monthly police shootings declined.

Although less dramatic an issue than police brutality, Eastside Los Angeles neighborhoods lacked the simple amenities taken for granted in other areas of the city. The Mexican American population had grown faster than the public infrastructure, and the absence of paved roads, drainage systems, street lighting, and stoplights at intersections created safety hazards for residents. Members of the CSO recalled conditions before they began organizing: "Suppose your neighborhood had so few street lights that your wife could not step out to the store after dark?" said one member. Another added, "Or, suppose you lived in a place where a rainstorm made all the guys hop out of their cozy beds and move their cars out of the mud to the end of the pavement blocks away?"[20]

Safety issues continued to draw the CSO's attention well into the 1960s, when the state built underpasses or tunnels under streets with heavy traffic. While intended to permit safe crossing for schoolchildren, the dimly lit tunnels instead became a danger. After several incidents involving the molestation of young girls by adults hiding in the underpasses, mothers from several neighborhoods joined to draw attention to the

problem and demand the removal of the tunnels. They advocated replacement of underpasses with overpasses covered
with chain-link fencing so that anyone using them could be
seen. Erlinda Robles provided me with a newspaper clipping
referring to the women as "Marching Mothers":

> In honoring the "Marching Mothers," Anthony P. Rios,
> CSO president, stated, "we present this plaque for your
> outstanding grassroots leadership in the CSO tradition,
> which brought about the decision to do away with the
> underpass and a definite decision by the California Divi-
> sion of Highways and the L.A. County government to
> build the overpass." This, said Rios, "was accomplished
> by these 'Marching Mothers' through two months of
> picketing the underpass and withstanding winter cold
> and rains, finally bringing about public awareness and
> pressure to the responsible governments."[21]

The CSO attributed its success to involving entire families. By
the 1960s the CSO had lost its lead in advocating for social
change, but it had offered practical training experiences for
women, some of whom went on to help implement War on
Poverty programs of that era.[22]

The Chicano Movement: ¡Que Viva La Raza! The Chicano
movement emerged in the context of national and international politics: the civil rights, antiwar, and feminist movements in the United States, and the decolonization movements
in Latin America, Africa, and Asia. Chicano student movement activists developed a more critical view of electoral politics than that of the CSO and charged that institutions such as
the Catholic Church and the educational system had neglected
and oppressed the Mexican American community. Opposed to

cultural assimilation, activists challenged racism in the schools by promoting militant mass demonstrations. They initiated high school walkouts and large antiwar demonstrations (Muñoz 1989, 52).

Similar to some conditions still present in the 1990s, overcrowded classrooms, poorly maintained facilities, and inequitable testing practices and policies plagued Eastside schools in the 1960s.[23] In 1968 ten thousand young people demanding quality education walked out of Eastside high schools. Although the students' demands were never completely met, the walkouts and subsequent organizing activities led to educational reforms, including the restricted use of IQ tests and the development of bilingual and bicultural curricula.[24]

Young women participated in all the activities, but men held most of the official leadership positions. At times women disagreed with men, but they seldom did so publicly (Hernández 1980). Chicana student activists came to political activity as single young women who were away from their families for the first time. Their organizing activities often collided with the traditions they had grown up with. They questioned the moral authority of the Catholic Church, and in some cases they also directly challenged the dominance of young men.

When Chicanas expressed disatisfaction with sexism in the movement, Chicanos would label them "women's libbers and lesbians." Intended to be derogatory, the labels served to discredit the women and the issues that they raised (Marin 1991, 135–36). Gloria Santillán, a CSULA student, observed, "Chicanas were there from the ground floor, but the guys took the leadership roles, they were always the most vocal. But if women weren't around to organize and coordinate everything, we [MECHA; see below] would have fallen apart." Santillán continued, "We did things like typing and cleaning because it was something that we were supposed to do . . . at first we didn't question . . . the more confident women challenged traditional roles" (quoted in ibid.).

Also different from the CSO and UNO (discussed below), the Alinsky-inspired grassroots groups, Chicano movement activists used historical and ethnic symbols—heroes from the Mexican revolution and the Mexican flag—in an oppositional way. The Chicano college-student group, the Movimiento Estudiantil Chicanos de Aztlán (Chicano Student Movement of Aztlán, or MECHA) displayed an eagle on its logo styled after the one on the Mexican flag; however, in place of a serpent, the MECHA eagle carries a lit stick of dynamite in its talons.

The Brown Berets, another Chicano youth group somewhat patterned after the militant Black Panthers, demanded social change "by any means necessary." Notwithstanding their militant rhetoric, they focused on reform in education, health care, and police-community relations (Marin 1991, 143–69). Although police authorities considered them dangerous, they initiated social projects such as preschool programs, and, most importantly, in 1969 they created the Barrio Free Clinic. Two women, Gloria Arellanes and Andrea Sánchez, cofounded the first free health clinic in East Los Angeles; the professional staff volunteered its services.

Much like some women in MECHA, women members of the Brown Berets expressed resentment when they felt men limited their participation. One former member complained, "At fundraisers, the girls did all the cooking and always got stuck with the cleaning, and the guys would just be there hanging around. . . . for the Brown Beret conference, we were slaving away, but we couldn't give an opinion or anything (Marin 1991, 163). Weakened by internal conflicts and police infiltration, the Brown Berets disbanded in 1972.

While women activists of the post–World War II era held leadership positions in local community efforts, as did young women activists in the 1960s, men were more likely to hold the top leadership positions. The women of the 1960s differed from their predecessors in several ways. The neighborhood-based CSO relied on family networks. Women used skills and resources within traditional family structures and worked with committees and organizations composed of women and men. They accepted the pattern of male domination in the highest positions of leadership. The Chicano movement coincided with the feminist movement, when women were beginning to reexamine their histories and question traditional expectations of women and men. A generation after the development of the CSO, women in the Chicano movement questioned the male-dominated organizations and began reexamining Chicano histories in search of the Chicana story. They continued to work alongside men in Chicano organizations but also began to develop Chicana organizations where they could focus on gender-specific issues, develop leadership skills, and examine the relationship between the white feminist movement and the Chicano movement.[25]

United Neighborhood Organization (UNO). A combination of circumstances resulted in Catholic Church sponsorship of the United Neighborhood Organizations (UNO), a grassroots group trained by organizers from Saul Alinsky's Industrial Areas Foundation. The changed philosophy of the Catholic Church placed emphasis on personal faith *and on the transformation of society,* and young priests and nuns became involved in the antiwar effort and joined civil rights groups. At the same time, Chicano student activists joined with others to develop Católicos por La Raza, a group advocating the church's active involvement in social change. They asked the church to sponsor leadership training for community residents and to assign priests and nuns to work actively with community projects.[26]

UNO, sponsored by the Catholic Church, developed in East Los Angeles in 1976. Los Angeles Archbishop Juan Arzube was inspired after attending a meeting of Communities Organized for Public Service (COPS), an Alinsky-style group of Mexican Americans in San Antonio, Texas, and he promoted the concept in East Los Angeles. In San Antonio, COPS members challenged prevailing patterns of power by working for the well-being of families. One depiction of COPS observed "hundreds of West Side [San Antonio] housewives who keep COPS going" (Ortiz 1984).[27] Similar to COPS in San Antonio, UNO began with a confederation of five parishes centered in the Boyle Heights and City Terrace neighborhoods. UNO identified issues similar to those that concerned the CSO, such as the need for street lights, reduced auto insurance rates, better community-police relations, and a crackdown on gang activity (Ortiz 1984, 572). Other UNO projects addressed a home improvement plan and in 1987 city-wide promotion of an increase in the minimum wage.

I interviewed the first president of UNO, Gloria Chávez, and two women who were activists at the time of UNO's inception and one who was part of the founding federation. I asked them about their initial entry into UNO, their experiences, and general observations about the group. Gloria Chávez's entry into grassroots politics follows a pattern I observed among other women community activists. Her involvement began through the PTA and her children's school-related events. She explained how she began working specifically with UNO:

At that time I seldom went to church and I was not involved in it. A priest, Father Sole, got my name from someone and called and asked me if he could visit me. I thought, Oh no, I am going to have to bring out all my [religious] statues to show I am Catholic. But he wanted to know if I wanted to do something about bettering the conditions in City Terrace. I knew what City Terrace looked like in the 1950s and 1960s, and then it started deteriorating . . . the streets were not being swept . . . it was dirty. So I was invited to a community meeting and that was the beginning. We started getting trained and it was fun. Then I said, If I say I represent St. Lucy's, I am going to have to start attending church again.

The creation of UNO also strengthened the parishes and in some cases "revived" parishes and contributed to a "tripling of the Sunday collections."[28] New leadership developed out of UNO as many of the members were initially inexperienced in grassroots politics. I asked Gloria if she recalled the gender breakdown in the group or any differences in the way men and women work. She answered,

I tend to believe that the women have more commitment to the organization. Men come in . . . but they like to "have their table served" and come in when we have done a lot of the work. When we say we are going to do something, we do it. As homemakers we know if you don't do it, it is not going to get done. I guess when we come out into the community we bring that same feeling . . . if we don't get it moving no one else will. Some men, not all, tend to feel . . . "go ahead, have your regular

meetings, and then when you have the large meetings
with the politicians, I will come to the meeting."

Gloria was not working for wages at the time, and she held
leadership for four years. Like the women in MELA, to avoid
domestic disruption she continued to meet her household responsibilities. When I asked her how she managed to balance
her household work with her activism, she acknowledged that
it was difficult. Her strategy was to take care of household
chores either very early or very late in the day:

> To avoid conflict at home, I would get up at 5 o'clock in
> the morning, clean house, prepare dinner if I knew I had
> day meetings. I would come home from meetings and be
> ironing at 11:00 at night, just to prevent my husband from
> complaining. My kids sometimes complained. Before I
> ran for president [of UNO] I asked them for their sup-
> port, and they said, Go for it! My husband does not get
> that much involved, but he goes to the conventions and
> some meetings.

When I asked Gloria about her election as the first UNO president, she stated, "First I was elected as chair of this local, then
as part of the five-chair federation. I remember the night of the
voting, I asked one of the nuns at another parish if she was going to support me, and she told me, `Oh, no. Our parish de-
cided we needed a man to represent us.' I always felt the organizers promoted the men for leadership. But I won anyway."

Many, but not all women, entered community work as
mothers and wives. But two women's cases illustrate variety
in the relationship between women's family situations and

community activism. Changing family circumstances released them from a home-centered focus at the same time that UNO began its formation. One woman, Rosa, divorced her husband of many years; the effects of his alcoholism had become intolerable. According to Rosa,

> I was always very sheltered and had everything done, but my husband was an alcoholic and I joined ALANON and then came UNO. After I got divorced, I started living with my sister and attending Our Lady of Victory. I was looking around for something to keep me occupied . . . and so I started teaching catechism. Then one of the nuns pulled me aside and got me into UNO. I met Jessica and we became close friends. We were going to meetings five nights a week.

The second woman, Jessica, unmarried and very close to her brother, sought an outlet for her grief when he died. She recalled the passing of her brother as a turning point in her life and the start of community activism.

After UNO became a recognizable force, some initial community members dropped out. Part of the Alinsky philosophy is to avoid taking on unwinnable issues (Moore 1966). Eventually some community residents found fault with this philosophy and questioned who could decide what is winnable and what issues are to be addressed. Some of the former UNO activists continued their community involvement in other groups or in other ways. For example, Gloria Chávez, the first president of UNO, left the group when she felt local issues were not being addressed. She organized the City Terrace Community Council and the East Los Angeles Property and Homeowners Association and served as president of both groups. In the 1990s she works in conjunction with Father John Santillán at St. Lucy's Catholic Church in City Terrace.

In Eastside Los Angeles, women participated alongside men in community organizations; however, in most instances, their activities reflect a gendered division of labor. Depending upon their ages, generation, the political context in which they were raised, and marital status, they responded to the division of labor in varied ways. By the mid-1980s, women activists began developing a cooperative working relationship with their elected officials, particularly Gloria Molina, who left her position in the assembly when she won election to the city council, and Lucille Roybal-Allard, who was elected to Molina's former assembly position. They joined forces to oppose the proposed state prison.

Monterey Park: The Multi-Ethnic Suburb

Monterey Park is an attractive suburb of mainly single-family homes, located close to downtown Los Angeles and accessible to freeways, which surround rather than intersect it, as they do the Eastside. Since the 1980s the community's changing ethnic composition has attracted national media attention, evoking such labels as the Chinese Beverly Hills and Little Taipei (Horton 1990), and a reputation as a community fraught with ethnic conflict. Its rapid demographic changes are also reflected in the disordering of meanings and ethnic and racial categories. By 1990 Asian residents had become the majority population (60 percent), while Anglo residents were the minority population (12 percent) and the Latino population remained stable (at 31 percent) (Horton 1995, 11). In a racial/ethnic survey used by the local school district, the "other" category refers to anyone who is *not* American Indian, Asian, black, or Hispanic. The "total minority" category is the sum of the whites (Alhambra School District 1987)! Now, the one-time minorities are the majority and the "others" are white.

Incorporated in 1916, Monterey Park was first settled by Anglos and Mexicans. Early in its history, Japanese Americans planted potatoes and developed nurseries in the hilly regions. As an incorporated city, Monterey Park funds its own services and operates its own form of local government, the council-manager system. Five low-paid, part-time council members take turns serving as mayor while the city manager, a full-time employee, attends to the city's day-to-day operations. The city expanded its boundaries in 1951 when it annexed three hundred acres surrounding East Los Angeles Community College despite opposition from East Los Angeles. In a carefully drawn plan, Monterey Park took land from East Los Angeles up to, but not including, the Maravilla public housing projects. The Monterey Park city government argued that they were annexing the land in an effort to stop the granting of a dump site permit. But as soon as the land was under their jurisdiction, they granted the permit (Acuna 1984: 35).

Monterey Park residents have tended to become involved politically through participation in Democratic Clubs and other local, electorally based political groups, in contrast to the Alinsky-style community activism in Eastside Los Angeles. Before the 1980s, Monterey Park's local politicians (for example, George Brown, Al Song, and Matthew Martínez) moved into state office. Grassroots activism in Monterey Park emerged in the early 1980s in response to Chinese immigration and investment in land development.

Demographic Context

Monterey Park remained a sparsely populated suburb for several decades. In 1940 the population numbered only eight thousand; many of the current housing tracts were not built until the 1960s. At that time, its residents were predominantly Anglo (85 percent) followed by Latinos (12 percent) and Asians (3 percent). By 1986 Latinos from East Los Angeles and Chinese immigrants from Hong Kong, Taiwan, and mainland China had changed the city's population to 20 percent white, 1 percent black, 50 percent Asian, and 30 percent Latino.

The community is generally middle-class with a median family income above the county average of $22,568. But there are ethnic and racial differences in income, education, occupation, nativity and languages spoken, home ownership, and the labor force participation of women. Asians earn the highest median family incomes ($30,119), followed by Anglos ($28,242) and Mexican Americans ($21,595). Asians also have the highest levels of home ownership (66.5 percent), followed by Anglos (61.8 percent), and Mexican Americans (42.8 percent). The majority of residents are employed in professional, technical, and service work, with only about 10 percent employed as operators and laborers. Poverty levels for each group differ, but the overall poverty rate for the city is approximately 10 percent.

Among Mexican American households 17.6 percent are headed by women; for Asians the comparable figure is 7.4 percent and for Anglos 8.8 percent. Most Monterey Park residents live in households numbering two to four persons. The labor force participation for Mexican American women is 53 percent, for Asians 54.3 percent, and for Anglos 45 percent (with a greater proportion of elderly workers than for the other groups). Occupationally Mexican American women are concentrated in the technical and sales category, which includes clerical workers (54 percent); 20 percent of Mexican American women are service workers, and 18 percent are managers and professionals.[29]

The residents of Monterey Park are by no means segregated, but ethnic and racial groups occupy particular sectors of the city in a pattern that is closely related to the income of each group. A large Spanish-surnamed population resides in the southern sector of the city bordering East Los Angeles; many Asians reside in the hilly sections of the city and the mid-region. Anglos are dispersed throughout the city, but the highest percentage live in the northern section. The aging Anglo population represents 54 percent of the elderly.

From Lettuce to Bok Choy

In the 1960s and 1970s, the membership of civic clubs and political organizations was primarily white with occasional Latino and Japanese American participation. Successful council candidates depended on the clubs for political support, and campaigns were run out of the Lion's Club by white males representing the local business establishment power structure (Horton 1990). By 1985 hostility directed at the commercial activities of Chinese newcomers became a key issue for the Monterey city council and community.

The fact that in grocery stores and restaurants throughout the city, bok choy and tea could be found more readily than hamburgers and coffee annoyed established non-Chinese residents (Fong 1994, 62). Recent Chinese immigrants have built a thriving ethnic economy; they own two-thirds of all the restaurants and banks and three-fourths of all the supermarkets (Horton 1995, 29). The Chinese immigrant investment in commercial establishments transformed the appearance of the city, and the changes became points of contention. Signs written in large Chinese characters identified businesses only to Chinese-speaking residents. City council members debated how to best regulate English- and foreign-language usage on signs. They revised architectural guidelines directing new business structures to conform to "general style and colors," making an implicit objection to "Chinese style" buildings. Plans for a new shopping mall recommended a "Mediterranean" architectural style" (Saito, forthcoming). Council members also blamed immigrants for social problems such as crime, disease, and excessive use of government services.[30] City council meetings erupted in heated debates as the community became polarized around growth and anti-growth issues, infused with racist attacks on Asians and Latinos.

Residents expressed their anti-immigrant sentiments by calling for an ordinance mandating English as the official language, even though two-thirds of new immigrant Chinese and Vietnamese report that they speak English well (Horton 1995, 19). It should be noted that similar movements occurred in Miami, Florida, in 1980 and in two small northern California towns in 1975 (Fong 1994, 118). With the assistance of a national group committed to making English the official language of the United States, two white residents filed a legal notice of intent to circulate a petition: "English is the language we use in Monterey Park when we want everyone to understand our ideas. This is what unites us as Americans, even though some of our citizens speak other languages. Let us make English our official language as a symbol of unity" (cited in Fong 1994, 112). Anglo city council members passed Resolution 9004, which called for support of English as the official language and the cooperation of Monterey Park police with the Immigration and Naturalization Service in deporting "illegal aliens." While the ordinance won significant community support, it inspired opponents to form a group called the Coalition for Harmony in Monterey Park (CHAMP). Latinos, Asians, and whites joined the group. CHAMP gathered over five thousand signatures on a petition requesting that city council members rescind the ordinance, and they complied.

Many Latinos comment that race did not seem to be an issue until wealthy Chinese immigrants began arriving, a seemingly casual observation that carries important implications. Several Mexican Americans use the cliché, "We didn't make waves." They mean that many of the second- and third-generation Mexican Americans who moved into Monterey Park in the 1960s never belonged to ethnic organizations, although some kept up their social and political associations back in East Los Angeles. But they did not challenge the political and cultural makeup of the predominantly Anglo Monterey Park, as have the upper- and middle-class Chinese immigrants who arrived in the 1980s. As Leland Saito (forthcoming) observes, Anglos, Latinos, and Japanese Americans alike recite the immigration history of their own group by saying, "We tried to blend in and adapt; why can't they?" Compared to Japanese Americans and Mexican Americans, Chinese entrepreneurs created a virtual tidal wave in Monterey Park by internationalizing its economy (Tseng 1994).

Community Organizations and Women's Activism

Latinos and Latinas belong to established social and civic groups such as the PTA, the Boys and Girls Club, and the

Chamber of Commerce; leaders emerge from these groups to serve on city commissions. The absence of ethnic organizations should not be interpreted as an indication of total political assimilation because Latino voter turn-out rates are much higher when Latino candidates are running than when there are none. Ethnic identity in a multi-ethnic setting, while seemingly dormant, changes, becomes reformulated, and reappears depending on the situation (Horton 1989). During the 1980s, three grassroots groups developed in Monterey Park in response to the community's rapid growth, demographic changes, and resulting expressions of ethnic, racial, and immigrant tensions. Women participated in each group, Anglos becoming active in RAMP and Mexican Americans in LULAC and the Hispanic Roundtable (each discussed below). Women's accounts illustrate how their social identities, both gender and ethnic, led them into these groups.

Residents Association of Monterey Park (RAMP). In 1986 three city council members—two Mexican Americans and one Asian—lost bids for re-election largely through the efforts of a grassroots organization called RAMP, an Anglo-led group in which a few Japanese Americans and Latinos participated. Dissidents cited a litany of complaints. Some pointed to lost tax revenues caused by the exodus of lucrative businesses such as department stores, car dealerships, and large chain supermarkets and the growing number of small Chinese businesses targeting an ethnic market. Other grievances focused on heavy traffic, parking shortages, and oversized buildings that encroached on residential areas and obscured views (Horton 1989). The group expressed dissatisfaction with the existing city council's position on growth and began campaigning for candidates selected from within its membership. Two Anglo women, neither of whom had held political office previously, won city council seats as a result of RAMP's support. Both had been founding members of the group. One traced the events leading to her political involvement:

> The first RAMP meeting was held in my house, and I was on the board until I got elected to city council. I was spurred into it when they [developers] began building the condos in the lot behind my back yard. They tore down my fence and dug thirty feet into a natural hill. My kids were young then and could have fallen in. So I called the city, and they told me that unless someone fell in and got hurt there was nothing they could do! I was furious! I walked the streets weekends and nights with two other women getting signatures on Q & L [a slow-growth ordinance], and then I ran for council and got elected.

One of the women who walked with her was also elected to the city council in 1988. The two women advocated slow growth and "English as the official language" politics. During this election, a voter's ethnicity was a more significant predictor of preference among the Chinese American, Anglo, and Latino candidates than age, sex, education, or income (Horton 1989).

One Latina whom I interviewed opposed development and attended a few RAMP meetings. However, she stopped attending, she said, because she was the only Latina there and felt "uncomfortable." "Discomfort" became a recurring theme in many of the stories of locally active Mexican American and Chinese American women. They often used it to describe situations where ethnic and racial identity became an issue and they felt indirectly under attack by Anglos.

For example, at city council meetings RAMP supported Councilman Barry Hatch, who was active in national groups and often made impassioned, impromptu mini-speeches advocating restrictive immigration laws and stringent border patrol "to control the hordes of illegal aliens ruining America." Once he angrily chastised the city for opposing his proposal to build a George Washington monument "to teach immigrants about American heroes." Among those testifying against his proposal was an established Mexican American woman who felt compelled to preface her remarks by affirming her own patriotism. "I oppose the statue and mean no disrespect for George Washington. Being an American is not wrapping yourself in a flag but having two brothers and uncles buried in a veterans' cemetery." As the woman walked back to her seat, Hatch indignantly challenged her comments: "What do you mean patriotism isn't wrapping yourself in a flag? Hispanics from all over can say 'Viva La Raza,' but they are not going back home. I am appalled by these views!"

The exchange illustrates how ethnicity and race, previously not the topic of polite conversation or public discussion, became a political issue. Mexican Americans had arrived in Monterey Park gradually and quietly in the 1960s and 1970s, fitting in with the established (that is, Anglo dominated) social and cultural structure. In the 1980s established residents of all ethnic and racial backgrounds responded to Chinese immigrants with antagonism ranging from annoyance to active grassroots organizing.

Mexican American Organizations. José Calderón, who lived in Monterey Park and organized its residents, observes that Mexican Americans have a history of joining ethnically and racially diverse neighborhood civic and sports groups.[31] The city government reflected the ethnic diversity of its constituents. In 1985 two Mexican American men, a Filipino man, an Anglo woman, and one Chinese American woman served on the city council. One year later, an electorate incensed over what they perceived as reckless development—massive hotels built in residential neighborhoods, cluttered minimalls, and large condominiums that generated traffic congestion and parking problems—voted the Mexican Americans and the Chinese American woman out and elected three Anglos into office (Horton 1995, 81). The electoral backlash punished the incumbents for not taking a aggressive stand against the rapid Chinese immigration and land development.

For the first time in Monterey Park, a small group of Mexican American residents began forming their own political groups and discussing how to organize Latinos to play a significant role in city politics. Two groups developed, and each discussed how best to work with other ethnic groups. One favored supporting only Mexican-American candidates, while the other argued for building multi-ethnic alliances. The Hispanic Roundtable expressed little interest in coalitions with other ethnic groups. An organizational pamphlet stated that its objectives were to provide leadership in the Hispanic community, to develop a united Hispanic network, and to perpetuate the power of the network through the election and retention of Hispanic public officials (cited in Calderón 1991, 144). In contrast, the League of United Latin American Citizens (LULAC) sought to promote the appreciation of Mexican American culture and build coalitions with other ethnic groups, particularly with Chinese immigrants and Asian Americans. LULAC organized along ethnic lines, but it emphasized supporting political candidates on the basis of their position on issues, rather than for their ethnicity.

LULAC began with twenty-six members evenly divided between men and women. About half the members are second-generation Mexican Americans who have resided in Monterey Park for most of their lives. They successfully participated in political campaigns of Latinos running for Monterey Park city council and the local school boards, and they endorsed non-Latino candidates and invited regional Latino leaders to speak on political and educational concerns. They also sponsored cultural events such as Cinco de Mayo festivities (a traditional Mexican holiday marking the 1862 defeat of the French army), which they reconfigured into a multicultural event (see Chapter 8). The Hispanic Roundtable met for a short time and then disbanded. The emergence of both groups illustrates the expression of ethnic politics in a suburban setting. The success of LULAC's multi-ethnic strategy of coalition building affirmed and worked with, rather than against, the changing ethnic and racial composition of the community.

Since suburban community conditions differ so greatly from those of East Los Angeles, grassroots protests had been minimal until the last decade. Women participate in the city commissions, and three women served as city council members in 1988–89. In the suburban, small-city setting, women's civic activism may lead into conventional electoral politics and possibly a political career. The small city government made it possible for residents to influence the decisions of elected officials and hold them accountable. A resident could successfully seek political office with a relatively small camapign fund and extensive community networks. One of the first Anglo women to be elected to city council, Louise Davis, reached the position through her children's school networks. She raised seven children who attended local schools. One Mexican American woman who worked on her campaign stated, "She did not have much money for her campaign. But she worked with the PTA and was always volunteering, so she was known for that. She got more votes than the other candidate, who spent four times as much as she did."

Comparative Contexts: The Barrio and the Suburb

Comparisons between Eastside Los Angeles and Monterey Park in terms of family income ($12,767 versus $21,595), occupational distribution (service versus blue collar), female heads of households (19.5 percent versus 17 percent), and home ownership (30 percent versus 42.8 percent) clearly show the economic status of those who live in Monterey Park. Mexican Americans in the Monterey Park setting are clearly advantaged compared to those in Eastside L.A., but in contrast to the other ethnic and racial groups in Monterey Park they are at the bottom of the socioeconomic hierarchy. In East Los Angeles, specifically Boyle Heights, the ethnic residential profile gradually changed from Jewish and middle class to Mexican American and working class; now it is predominantly a Latino immigrant community. Monterey Park changed from an Anglo middle-class, native-born community to a middle-class, multi-ethnic, native-born community and then to a multi-ethnic community that is predominantly Asian.

Grassroots activism and the institutions involved in political activity also differ between the two communities. In some instances, the community-based Catholic Church holds center focus. In the 1950s the Industrial Areas Foundation based on the Saul Alinsky model organized the Community Service Organization; the United Neighborhood Organization, also a church-based, Alinsky-inspired group, developed in the 1970s. In the 1980s Mothers of East Los Angeles, a lead group in a larger coalition of organizations against the prison influenced but not directly based on Alinsky's model, gained much recognition. Women are important and visible members of each group.

In Monterey Park, the Chamber of Commerce, service clubs, PTAs, Neighborhood Watch, but *not the church* occupy center stage as meaningful associations that sometimes lead to grass-roots mobilization. Women, visible and not so visible, have entered grassroots struggles in the community in ways very similar to women in Eastside Los Angeles. In the latter women's activism finds expression through church, school, and community groups focusing on ethnic organization; in the 1980s, women developed a cooperative relationship with elected officials. In Monterey Park women work in school-based groups and directly with the local city council and commissions. The massive size of Los Angeles (city and county) dilutes the Eastside residents' influence on political units, in comparison with that of a Monterey Park resident. The fifteen-member Los Angeles City Council represents 3.5 million people and decides on thousands of issues each year. The five-member Monterey Park City Council, in stark contrast, represents approximately 60,000 people, making the ratio of council members to residents 1 to 12,000, compared to 1 to over 200,000 in Los Angeles. The theme of social identity and its relationship to the character of women's civic membership winds subtly through the stories. At the neighborhood and at the city level, Monterey Park is reconstructing the definition of community in a period of rapid demographic change.

California's Community Controversies: Prisons, Parole Offices, and Pollution

Like residents in Eastside Los Angeles, residents in Monterey Park felt very tangible outcomes of the increasing rates of incarceration and concomitant increase in the numbers of parolees in California—a proposed state prison for the Eastside and a parole office in the midst of a Monterey Park residential area. Crimes newly punishable by prison terms, longer sentences, and the restricted discretion of judges to send prisoners to local jails instead of state prisons contributed to an escalating prison population. Following from California's enactment of stiff mandatory sentencing laws in the 1970s, the state's prison population had risen to more than 87,000 in the 1990s, forcing the state to build seven new prisons and expand existing facilities.

The shortage of prison space has also ballooned the parolee population. In 1990 the state released prisoners in record numbers. Statewide, the number of parolees jumped 100 percent since 1984; in Los Angeles County the number doubled. Those convicted of drug-related crimes drive the increasing prison population. According to the Department of Corrections, the shortage of community-based substance-abuse programs is responsible for a large proportion of the high recidivism rate: around 60 percent of all parolees are sent back to prison within two years of release for violating parole guidelines or committing new crimes.[32]

Under Republican governor George Deukmejian, California embarked on an ambitious prison-construction program in the early 1980s. Deukmejian attempted to rush the process in order to solve severe prison overcrowding and meet legislative mandates. A law passed in 1982 required approval of the Los Angeles County site before other California prisons could be built. Prison construction lagged behind prison population growth, and prisons were being packed beyond 190 percent of their capacity.[33]

My focus on the prison, and later a toxic waste incinerator proposed for Eastside Los Angeles, and the parole office in Monterey Park reminded me that all communities must face the discouraging failure of our criminal-justice system and our management of hazardous waste. Government officials and others have characterized communities fighting to keep out prisons, parole offices, and toxic-waste incinerators as parochial and self-interested, unable to see the general interest or accept the official solutions to the problems. Single-issue politics have certainly characterized much about U.S. politics in the twentieth century. But each community questioned the site selection process, and each community criticized the failure of state officials to adequately inform them of the projects. Eastsiders demanded better schools instead of more prisons. Indeed, prisons, parole offices, and toxic-waste incinerators are metaphors for larger concerns that demand citizen intervention and solutions that address the sources of the problems.[34]

The Proposed State Prison in Eastside Los Angeles

In March of 1985, Governor Deukmejian and the Department of Corrections (DOC) announced the site for the first of the new California state prisons. The location they chose was a five-minute walk from Boyle Heights in Eastside Los Angeles.[35] The state legislature had to approve the selected site and authorize funds to buy and prepare it for construction, but Governor Deukmejian and the DOC foresaw little difficulty in the approval process. To their surprise, the California State Assembly blocked the bill after the Senate passed it in 1985.[36]

The selected site raised several issues. It would set a precedent as the first California state prison built in a downtown urban location. (Other state prisons had been built in rural areas.) Moreover, the DOC bypassed its own procedures when it selected the expensive parcel of industrially zoned land. It failed to test for hazardous waste, provide adequate public notice, or develop an environmental impact report (EIR) (Gutiérrez 1994, 226). Environmental impact reports, customarily compiled even for relatively small proposals such as apartment buildings, provide a detailed study of a project's socioeconomic and environmental effects on an area. The reports anticipate a project's possible repercussions on population density, traffic, water usage, and pollution.

Because the governor thought any delay might result in the Eastside property being purchased by someone else, he insisted that the DOC waive the EIR and they agreed.[37] Corrections officials argued that the site was more suitable than others for two reasons. First was its proximity to the courts in downtown Los Angeles. Second, the majority of state prisoners, about 40 percent of the state's 90,400 inmates, come from Los Angeles County (not necessarily the Eastside). Officials assumed that inmates families lived in the area and that prisoners could more easily continue communicating with them (Blonian 1986).

Assemblywoman Gloria Molina, familiar with uphill battles, vehemently opposed the Eastside site. Considered an aggressive community advocate and an outspoken feminist, she had opposed a male-dominated Latino political network to win election to the Eastside Fifty-sixth Assembly District in 1982.[38] Later she became the first Latina elected to the Los Angeles City Council (1987–91) and the first woman and the first Mexican American elected to the five-member Los Angeles Board of Supervisors, which oversees an annual budget of $13 billion. Molina did not object to the construction of a prison in Los Angeles County; instead, she argued that the chosen site was too close to the long-established Boyle Heights neighborhood, and she pointed out that it was also within two miles of thirty-four schools. She pointed out that 75 percent of the county's prison population was already housed in her district;

thus, another prison would add to the over-concentration of penal facilities in the East Los Angeles area (Molina 1986). Downtown Los Angeles houses twenty-five thousand prisoners, the largest inmate population of any city in the nation. Five inmate facilities, including a county jail, a federal prison, the men's city jail, and a juvenile detention center, also lay within a six-mile radius of the site.[39]

When the DOC brushed aside Molina's objections, she explored the possibility of grassroots mobilization. James Vigil, Jr., a field representative in her office, and later Martha Molina (no relation to Gloria Molina), who became the deputy field representative for the assemblywoman, began informing the community about the proposed prison. They anxiously gauged residents' sentiments about it shortly after the state announced the site selection. Vigil stated that without organized community opposition, there would be no chance of stopping the project. The field representatives used two strategies—direct mailings to residents and calls to leaders of community organizations and business groups.

In the spring of 1986, after much pressure from the Fifty-sixth Assembly District office and the community, the DOC agreed to a hold a preliminary informational meeting at Lincoln High School. People filled the auditorium and listened intently and responded emotionally, cheering Molina's statements and booing the DOC's representative. Later, about six hundred people attended the first official public meeting, which was held at the proposed prison site on Santa Fe Street near Olympic Boulevard. From this moment on, the community mobilized and, according to James Vigil, Jr., the "tables turned and the community began calling the political office to attend hearings and meetings."[40]

By the summer of 1986, the community, now well aware of

the prison site proposal, began weekly protest marches on Monday evenings. Mothers of East Los Angeles (MELA) became an important focus of community activism. Through the summer months of 1986 and 1987, the group helped to organize weekly marches on the Olympic Boulevard bridge leading from downtown into Boyle Heights, emphasizing the proximity of the prison site to their community. In 1987 the legislature agreed to a compromise by passing what some called a "pain for pain" bill. The legislature agreed that the East Los Angeles prison would be built as planned, but a companion institution would also be built in the white, middle-class, and Republican Antelope Valley. But even after the legislature passed this bill, additional delays resulted from lawsuits challenging the environmental impact report that had finally been completed. The final defeat of the proposed prison resulted from eight years of community solidarity, sacrifice, and sustained political battles at several levels—mass community protests on the streets, litigation in the courts, and lobbying in the legislative bodies.

At the end of 1989 a panel certified the environmental impact report after DOC officials testified the prison would have no effect on property values and the community's character. Lawyers representing the Eastside appealed the certification of the EIR. Until July 1992, when the California Supreme Court rejected the appeal, the community continued to stall the prison construction.[41] At that time, California's fiscal crises provided additional pressure on newly elected Republican governor Pete Wilson, who finally signed Senate Bill 97, eliminating the Eastside prison project and redirecting funds to expand existing prisons in other parts of the state.[42] The hard-won victory helped to create a new political image for the Eastside.

The marches marked the beginning of one of the largest grassroots coalitions to emerge from Los Angeles's Latino community in the last decade. Newspaper accounts document an eight-year battle in the courts and in the legislature. Women's life stories tell how they became community activists by employing their experiences and perceptions of the East-side community to counter the negative image implied by Governor Deukmejian and the media (see Chapter Three) and how they transformed social networks into political networks (discussed in Chapter Five).

The Parole Office Controversy in Monterey Park

Without notifying residents in either city, the Department of Corrections (DOC) signed a lease to open a parole office in Al-hambra, on the border of Monterey Park, and provide counseling and drug testing to over a thousand paroled ex-felons. The lease was signed one month before passage of a law requiring the DOC to notify local residents before opening parole offices.

Residents in the quiet Monterey Highlands residential area, unaware of the parole office that had opened a few blocks away from an elementary school, began noticing unfamiliar men standing outside the modest white building located on the corner of Garvey Avenue and Casuda Canyon Drive. Meanwhile, the high school and grammar school students' bus continued to stop directly in front of the facility.

In early July 1988, four months after the parole office had opened, the brutal beating and robbery of a woman living in the Monterey Highlands neighborhood prompted neighbors to begin asking questions. Women took the lead, and they soon discovered the parole office. They began a door-to-door information campaign that led to an unusually large community presence at the next Monterey Park city council meeting. Over 250 Alhambra and Monterey Park residents packed the city hall to offer testimony about increasing crime, loitering, and graffiti near the parole office. Residents questioned the appropriateness of a parole office so near an elementary school and residential area. They lobbied the city council, who then passed a resolution to take action against the parole office.

Department of Corrections representatives asserted that the office was appropriately located since most of its parolees lived in a three- to four-mile radius of the facility. They denied that parolees were committing crimes in the area and assured residents that they had nothing to fear. Statistics from the Monterey Park Police Department registered an increase in crime, but the chief of police could not prove that the crimes were being committed by parolees.[43] By September 1988 the DOC considered moving the office "just to appease citizens." The two cities planned to split the $100,000 cost of relocating the office. Meanwhile, the cities would have to wait for the state to find an acceptable site, sign a lease, and secure the cooperation of the city where the office was to relocate.

DOC representatives observed that they had never had such concerted community opposition to any other parole office in Los Angeles County. The DOC agreed to move the Garvey Avenue office in response to organized daily pressure from residents—letter writing and petition campaigns, testimony at city council meetings, lobbying in Sacramento. They also set up a parole advisory board with representatives from the community, the elementary school, and the DOC. The board would not have any special powers; it would simply monitor the progress of relocation. But the controversy was far from settled. The office could not be relocated until the DOC secured an alternative site. Suggested sites in nearby Pasadena, where most of the parolees resided and where there was no parole office, drew opposition from residents. Monterey Highlands residents grew increasingly frustrated as the difficulty of finding a site stalled the move for almost three years, until April 1991. During those three years they diligently lobbied local political representatives, the city council, and officials in Sacramento.

The speed, intensity, and persistence of residents' opposition led to their success. As I observed the daily, behind-the-scenes activities of the campaign, I found that both women and men worked together, but women outnumbered men in the day-to-day communication of meetings and strategies. Twice as many women as men served on the parole advisory board. From 1988 until 1991, when the state finally relocated the parole office to Pasadena, women continued to be the driving force behind the opposition.

Comparative Conrtroversies:
The Prison and the Parole Officer

The state prison proposed for the Eastside in 1985 and the parole office located in Monterey Park three years later drew strong community opposition and the untiring efforts of women and men activists. Compared to the Eastside antiprison coalition, the community campaign against the parole office spanned a shorter period of time and addressed a smaller concern, but the two cases shared the striking presence of women who were long-time residents. Also similar to the Eastside case, Monterey Park's women activists had a history of volunteer work in the local schools. Different from the Latino composition of Mothers of East Los.Angeles and the Eastside community, an ethnically diverse group of women in Monterey Park managed to convince a largely new Chinese immigrant population to endorse their efforts.

As I attended meetings and demonstrations and conducted ongoing conversations with the women activists in both communities, I reflected on the differences and similarities between them. I became part of the process of community mobilization, and as I drove the approximately six miles back and forth between the two communities, I felt and observed the differences in the population density and services between them. I also experienced the contrast between the active street life of the barrio and the serenity (and to some degree, isolation) of suburban living. The economic status of each community expressed itself in the availability of public services, accessiblity of political representatives, and the quality of everyday life.

THREE

The Politics of Community Identity in Eastside Los Angeles

"We Got Everything Nobody Else Wanted"

The Fourth Street exit off the Santa Ana Freeway leads into the Boyle Heights neighborhood in Eastside Los Angeles. Immediately after the exit lies Hollenbeck Park—a large green park graced by a lake, a bridge, and tall shade trees, and disturbingly bordered by a freeway.[1] The busiest in Los Angeles, the Eastside Freeway exchange carries half a million cars and trucks daily (Pitt and Pitt 1997, 161). Throughout Eastside Los Angeles, six-lane freeways criss-cross neighborhoods composed of modest housing. On my trips into the community for meetings and interviews, I often lost my way in the maze of dead-end streets that stop at a freeway and pick up somewhere on the other side. Freeway overpasses tower above several main intersections and interrupt the low skyline. The freeway construction in the 1960s displaced thousands of residents, compelling some families to move more than once.[2] The freeways brought noise and air pollution as they divided neighborhoods without consideration for residents' loyalty to extended family and parish church. The freeways invading Eastside neighborhoods linked Anglo suburbs to the civic center. Freeways had been planned for other sections of the city, but residents' opposition stopped their construction. Similarly, the decision to locate Los Angeles County's first state prison in the Eastside was reached after several other communities had opposed its placement within their boundaries.[3] People told the tale of displacement by freeway construction and repeated it as a lesson well learned. Juana Gutiérrez, for example, moved two times to make way for the freeways. She and other activists transformed this experience into a springboard for resistance to the state prison, which represented an additional encroachment. The ensuing eight-year political battle between Eastside residents, the Department of Corrections (DOC), and Governor George Deukmejian pivoted around the debate over the appropriateness of building the prison in Eastside Los Angeles—in essence, a debate over community identity.

A careful observer would be struck by the internal differentiation in the neighborhoods of Eastside Los Angeles; blocks with reputations for being quiet, clean, and well kept may be adjacent to blocks considered untended, noisy, and dangerous. Inner-city neighborhoods appear to have greater diversity in this respect than do suburban ones. In Eastside Los Angeles, a block of neat, single-story homes built in the 1930s or 1940s— newly painted, surrounded by manicured lawns and gardens—appears fresh and inviting. An immediately adjacent block may be in disarray. Graffiti proclaiming rivalry between gangs cover fences and garages. Trash-strewn streets and sidewalks, and homes that appear battered and worn, send a message to outsiders, leading them to believe that Eastside Los Angeles harbors crime, poverty, and apathy. Women activists place high on their list of grievances the primarily negative reflection of their community in the media. The women repeated this concern throughout our conversations, and while I agreed with the criticism, at first I set their comments aside. The issue of stereotypical community images seemed to me so commonplace that it would not contribute anything new to understanding the women's activism.

Later, I recognized that the women emphasized the "outside" image of Eastside Los Angeles as poor, crime ridden, and politically powerless for good reason. They stressed that it was used to justify "dumping" everything no other community wanted in Eastside Los Angeles. The women quickly acknowledged the poverty of many residents and the existence of gangs, but they argued that the community had a redeeming social life and culture. They fought their battles around an image of Eastside Los Angeles that competed with the one they saw in popular films, the news media, and in the policies and comments of elected officials.

Contesting Community Identity

Governor Deukmejian's comments to the media regarding the community's opposition to the state prison illustrate the dialogue with state officials about community identity. Throughout the debate about the state prison site, he argued, "L.A. County now exports all of its 36,000 convicted felons to our state prisons. There is not one single state prison in this county. It is irresponsible to throw up roadblocks when it has been debated for years and decided. NIMBY [Not In My Backyard] attitudes are with increasing frequency hampering problem solving policy making and the completion of public works projects."[4] The other public works projects proposed for the Eastside included a toxic waste incinerator and an oil pipeline (see Chapter Five). The governor and Department of Corrections representatives also consistently argued that the prison should be close to the downtown areas where the inmates' families could easily visit.

Characterizing a community group's concerns as "NIMBY" politics seeks to brand the group with a derisive and simplistic political label and to discredit its opposition to projects it perceives as potentially injurious.[5] The term grew out of efforts to counter the ability of small grassroots groups to influence the decision making process. Opponents charged that such groups were narrow, self-interested movements opposing projects that would benefit the public as a whole. NIMBYs characteristically "organize to block a specific facility, are ad hoc in origin, focus on stopping rather than changing, and refuse to accept the imperative of building the contested facility" (Blumberg and Gottlieb 1989: 77).

The governor's statements set in motion counterarguments about the community's identity. Eastsiders never objected to the construction of a prison in Los Angeles County. They acknowledged that 40 percent of the state's prisoners originated in Los Angeles County, but they resented the implication that most of the felons and their families resided in the inner city, which is primarily Latino and African American. They emphasized that the county stretches over four thousand square miles. Neither the governor nor the DOC specified the geographic distribution of the state prisoners' families.

Opponents of the prison contended that the site should be shifted to an area less densely populated than Eastside Los Angeles and far from schools. In the case of the toxic-waste incinerator, Mothers of East Los Angeles argued against incineration as a waste-disposal strategy. When the governor accused Eastsiders of harboring "NIMBY" attitudes, he took for granted political decisions made by the state as if no alternatives were available: The state selected incineration over recycling and reducing trash problems at the source. The solutions placed the burden for solving Los Angeles County's trash-disposal and prison problems on the Eastside Latino community. Ricardo Gutiérrez commented, "We don't want the incinerator in *anyone's* backyard" (Christrup and Shaeffer 1990).

Noting that journalists researching articles on the prison and incinerator battles invariably asked about gangs, Juana Gutiérrez commented, "Some people think that East L.A. is the worst area with nothing but gangs and people with tattoos, and that is not true!" Ricardo also observed,

We were interviewed by a reporter from the *Sacramento Bee*. He was telling us that we were so lucky, that there were so few families like us that had children who went to college. I said whenever you want to meet more like us, tell me and I will get a dozen families around here. Because their kids are professionals and went to school with my kids. We have educated people in the community, but the press always gives the bad news the coverage.

The Gutiérrez family, central in the Coalition against the Prison in East Los Angeles and in the Mothers of East Los Angeles, recognized the community has problems associated with poverty.[6] However, they constructed a positive community identity alternative to that suggested in the media and implied by Governor Deukmejian's public statements. They see the upward mobility of their children as representative of others born and raised in East Los Angeles.

One *Los Angeles Times* journalist observed that Los Angeles is divided by race, income, attitude, and geography. Although Eastside Los Angeles is no more crime ridden than the western section, Westsiders perceive the Eastside as dangerous after dark.[7] Eastsiders felt that siting the prison in their area further reinforced that negative criminal image emphasized by outsiders.

The media's projection of an image of the Eastside community as undesirable and dangerous has persisted over the last three decades and touched the lives of the women activists. Erlinda Robles, another long-time resident, lives on Bernal Street, a place her childhood friends called "the gully." At the end of Bernal Street, tall, arched gray columns rise to support the Fourth Street bridge, which crosses the gully. Her block, lined with small, single-story homes, begins at the foot of the bridge. The expansive space under the bridge presents a strikingly familiar scene. This scene, or one very much like it, appears in numerous films that focus on gang violence in East Los Angeles. She recalls the behavior of film crews during the mid-1960s, when she was raising her three children: "They did a lot of filming near the bridge where I live. They would come and throw trash and write on the walls to make it look terrible. The films they make are all about gangs and shooting, and it is not like that."

Upset by such unfair representation of the community, the women on the block first tried individual resistance strategies. Erlinda explained how she and one other woman attempted to disrupt the work of the filming crews: "We would come by honking the car horns. And you could hear them saying, 'Cut, cut!' I would go out and call real loud, ARMANDO! DANNY! EDUARDO' [the names of her three sons]. Some women would yell, 'Why not put something good about us?' "

Erlinda's observations and the women's opposition illustrate how the media arrives to construct a preconceived image
of the Eastside community. As Erlinda noted, the area under
the bridge was not sufficiently dirty for the image the director
was seeking of the Eastside Mexican American community.
The film crew intensified a negative image of the barrio by
scrawling more graffiti and dumping more trash underneath
the bridge. Film crews also disrupted the neighborhood's
daily activities as their long equipment trailers occupied all
the parking on the block.

Residents finally turned to their city councilman at that
time, Art Snyder, objecting that the fees paid to the city for permits to film in the streets did not compensate for the resulting
disruption and litter. According to Erlinda, none of the payments benefited the immediate area; instead, the money went
into a general city fund. For a short time Snyder was able to
curtail the filming; but when he resigned from office in 1985,
film crews resumed using the area (Acuña 1988, 424). In a similar vein but across the country, a Latino elected official in New
York protested the filming of a movie based on a best-selling
novel *Bonfire of the Vanities*. Filmmakers wanted to apply graffiti to the walls of the Bronx County Courthouse, which had
been free of graffiti since the official had been in office.[8]

Elsa López, project director for MELA-SI, confirms that film
crews continue to seek out a preconceived image of Eastside
Los Angeles. One early summer morning in 1997, she was out
with a group of youths who work for the graffiti-removal program that she supervises. They had just finished painting over
an entire wall of graffiti when a man drove up, surveyed their
work with great dismay, and began angrily accusing her of ruining his plan to film that day. He complained that he had
spent considerable time scouting the area and locating his vision of an Eastside inner-city image.

Films that focus on Los Angeles's Mexican American community continue to project ethnic stereotypes. Examples are the gang film *Colors* (1982), *Mi Vida Loca* (1990), a film about girl gang members in a community adjacent to downtown Los Angeles, and even *Stand and Deliver* (1988), one of the few movies about "good kids" in East Los Angeles. Press reviews of these films differed according to the publication in which the review appeared. Noreiga (1988: 23) observes that with little exception, the reviewers who published in the mainstream press mistranslated the word "barrio" as "a problem space denied a culture and a separate point of view, not to mention internal complexity." Reviewers who published in the Hispanic or alternative press identified the barrio as a cultural space, a neighborhood, or *nuestra comunidad* (our community), a place with pride and achievement despite institutional racism and neglect" (Noriega 1988: 19).

The example illustrates a pattern that has also occurred in the African American community of South Central Los Angeles. Those who work to preserve a neighborhood—often long-time, middle-aged residents—remain unseen. Strangers to the inner city have their views shaped by media coverage of police actions, drive-by shootings, gangs, and "crack" cocaine.[9]

Journalists see the world through eyes that filter and re-create reality. Selected images may exaggerate certain elements of a community to produce a distorted picture. Degraded images of minority communities, intended or not, have a history of serving political purposes. For example, the demeaning images of Chinatown as rife with corruption contributed to discriminatory treatment of Chinese immigrants.[10]

Urban planners and policy makers both shape community images and respond to them. Degraded community images have served the interests of urban renewal under the auspices of the Los Angeles Community Redevelopment Agency (CRA). Created in 1948, the CRA has the power to acquire, sell, and lease property, issue bonds, and collect taxes. The pattern is well worn: allow conditions of disintegration to worsen, label an area "blighted," condemn property, purchase it with federal urban-renewal funds, sell it inexpensively to developers, and allot mass federal subsidies for its improvement.[11] The term "blight," borrowed from the plant world, describes the conditions that make a place a slum. Statutes generally require that an area be blighted before it is eligible for urban renewal, but what constitutes blight is open to interpretation and often manipulated by public officials. In most communities competing images exist, and no one image presents a complete picture of a community. The class status and in some cases the creativity of a community greatly affects its power to promote a particular image.[12]

Becoming a Long-Time Resident

Listening to women's observations of change over time helps one understand how the social construction of community identity and long-term residency influence women's activism. They reflect on changes over time within the community and give meaning to their experiences and observations to bolster their challenge to the state's definition of "the common good."

How does any person select a residential community? Certainly people have notions of what makes an ideal neighborhood—the proximity of work, schools, and churches; cultural attractions; adequate city services. All these features, however, must be available at an affordable cost, and there may be other restraints such as ethnic or racial covenants and other forms of discrimination.[13] Thus incorporation into a community can be seen as a process much like incorporation into the labor force. That is, people make their choices within a web of social and economic constraints. The women's stories about how they came to be long-time residents illustrate this point.

One of the most striking facts about the core activists in Mothers of East Los Angeles is their long history in the Boyle Heights community. Erlinda Robles is now in her mid-sixties, married, and the mother of three grown sons. Her sons, one of whom is a bilingual teacher, live and work outside of Eastside Los Angeles. Erlinda's case is illustrative of many other second-generation Mexican Americans who grew up in Los Angeles. She has lived most of her life where she was born and raised. Her life story intertwines with the history of the community and the rise and decline of community organizations. She knows local political representatives and the history of the community from having lived it. For example, she knew Fred Ross, the first Alinsky organizer to come to Los Angeles, because her mother was an active member of the CSO; she knows Congressman Roybal and his family because Mrs. Roybal's family grew up in the same neighborhood. She also worked in many local political campaigns and community events.

Erlinda describes the social relations in the neighborhood and shares community history from an insider's view:

Our neighbors were really close. In the evenings the kids would play together. Some of the mothers would sit on one of the women's porches and talk and keep an eye on us. We [children] would build a big bonfire on the hill across the street and sing songs and tell stories. By nine o'clock we had to go in, and they would call out, "Ya! Vamos!" [Now! Let's go!] People in the neighborhood spoke Spanish until we went to school. Then we spoke both English and Spanish. My mother was bilingual. I married when I was twenty-eight years old in 1954. My husband was in the Navy, and we had been living in Port Hueneme in the late 1950s. In 1958 Wyvernwood would not rent to us, and they sent us to look for a place in Estrada Courts [a large federally funded housing project for the poor]. Can you imagine that? My husband even went to Wyvernwood in his Navy uniform. The place was really kept nice. A doctor and his wife lived there and I had babysat for them, so I had seen the apartments. Then we went to Montebello and Monterey Park, and they wouldn't rent to us because we had kids. Since we couldn't find a house we stayed with my mother.

My oldest boy used to miss my husband when he left for his duty with the Navy, so when we saw a house for rent here [Bernal Street], we rented it so we could be close to my father. My father was very good. If I had to go to a meeting, my dad used to take care of the kids. I [already] owned this property [where her parents lived]. My mother kept telling us to build on it and we did.

Erlinda's comments illustrate the closeness and familiarity of Boyle Heights residents in the 1940s, as well as their ease in moving between two languages and cultures. She finally returned to the street on which she was raised as a result of residential discrimination against Mexicans, especially those with children. Until the late 1940s, Wyvernwood generally refused to rent to minorities. By the 1980s, recently immigrated Latinos made up the majority of Wyvernwood residents (Acuña 1984, 14).

Angie Flores, also U.S. born, was forced to move out of Boyle Heights when the city began building public housing projects in 1941. She married shortly after World War II, and her husband asked where she wanted to live. She said, "Take me back to where I feel comfortable—East Los Angeles." But she noted changes over time:

> Everything was decaying and getting worse and worse. When I moved here, there were Japanese and Jewish. It was really a Jewish community. Everything was so green. We had everything—the theater, the drug stores, the little post office in the drug store. But since the Jewish people went, that was the end of the post office. Now, no more post office, no more banks. So we have to go to the one on Brooklyn or go downtown. I said I want to go [oppose the prison] because if I don't I will feel guilty. It is not enough that our community is already dumped on; it is going to be wiped out.

Angie's recollections connect the declining services to the changing ethnic composition of Boyle Heights. She tells how daily chores such as going to the post office became more difficult. Prompted by a sense of civic responsibility (what she calls "guilt") to defend the community, she began attending the Coalition against the Prison meetings.

As long-time residents, all but one of the core activists shared the experience of losing a home and having to relocate to make way for a freeway. Juana Gutiérrez refers to the community response at that time,

> Una de las cosas que me caen muy mal es la injusticia, y en nuestra comunidad hemos visto mucho de eso. Sobre todo antes, porque creo que nuestra gente estaba más

dormida, nos atrevíamos menos. En los cincuenta hicieron los freeways, y así, sin más, nos dieron la noticia de que nos teníamos que mudar. Y eso pasó dos veces. La gente se conformaba porque lo ordenó el gobierno. Recuerdo que yo me enojaba y quería que los demás me secundaran, pero nadie quería hacer nada.

One of the things that really upsets me is injustice, and we have seen a lot of that in our community. Especially before, because I believe our people used to be less aware, we didn't assert ourselves as much. In the 1950s they put up the freeways, and just like that they gave us notice that we had to move. That happened twice. The people complied because the government ordered it. I remember that I was angry and wanted the others to back me up, but no one wanted to do anything.

The freeways that cut through communities and disrupted neighborhoods remain as a tangible reminder of shared injustice and the vulnerability of the community in the 1950s. The community's social and political history thus informs perceptions of its current predicament; however, today's activists emphasize the progression toward political empowerment rather than the powerlessness of the community.

Rosa Villaseñor, born in Cuba and raised in Eastside Los Angeles from the age of nine, is fifty-one years old. One of the few fluently bilingual residents in Wyvernwood, she is an activist in the rental complex that houses many new Central American immigrants. Her husband explained that they could have afforded to move up until 1970, but were content with Wyvernwood at the time. Rosa's recollections of the Wyvernwood Apartments also offer her a way to think about what is possible:

They were all Jewish and Mexican people from here—born and raised here. Hollenbeck had a lot of Jewish people and Mexicans. Brooklyn Avenue had nothing but Jewish people. When we were small they had guards, and they would not allow the Mexicans to walk through here [Wyvernwood]. And still there are a lot of French, English, German people. There is a German lady still living there, and her kids went to Santa Isabel. They kept this community just for themselves. And then if you went past Vernon toward Huntington Park, you were in trouble. All that area over there was nothing but Anglos. The police would harass them [Mexicans].

So that is why I say this. The people that come from Latin American countries should appreciate what the Mexican people did before now. Because the Mexicans had it rough.

Rosa's observations reinforce the other women's comments and refer to another bit of socialization work that she performs as she tells new immigrants about past injustices. She sees the tensions between new immigrants and the *pochos,* a colloquial term meaning "faded" that refers to Mexican Americans who have lost Mexican culture and assimilated the dominant white culture. Rosa says many new immigrants ridicule Mexicans Americans who do not speak Spanish. By describing how people had to struggle for bilingual services, she tries to dissipate some of the negative conceptions of *los pochos.*

Taken together the three women represent the diversity among residents in Eastside Los Angeles. All three are lifetime community members. Their stories show how economic circumstances and racial covenants structured their residential choices. As Erlinda Robles observed, "I was born in East L.A.

and lived here all my life, and everybody was always afraid to say anything. We saw everything nobody else wanted put here. We decided to get together to stop that!"

They had to translate their objective material conditions and experiences into group interests. Part of that work entails contesting the media's and the state's images of the community and making their own versions known and recognized. In an artful way they say that negative images fail to capture the full range of social relations in the community. At the same time, they recall a better time when community services and cohesiveness were greater.

In some cases, convincing other residents required more than simply providing information. According to one woman, the U.S.-born residents sometimes resisted invitations to join meetings and marches. I asked Erlinda Robles why that might be, and she suggested one explanation: "I think we have more immigrants involved than citizens. A lot of the ones that are citizens take it for granted. They were born here and for so many years they have looked down on us, and it is hard for them to believe that they count and that if we get together it will work. The others haven't seen these things because they haven't lived here so many years."

Erlinda's comments synthesize an important concept: Life's experiences may be interpreted in various ways. As the activist women saw it, the history of neglect and the series of negative projects in Eastside Los Angeles justified their moral indignation and their militant opposition. These defeats could just as easily be interpreted, as Erlinda observed, as justification for doing nothing. Discrimination based on ethnic identity may provide a reason to resign oneself to subordination, or conversely serve as a source of pride, unity, and resistance (Spelman 1988).

Ethnic Identity: What Are We Now, Anyway?

Just as the women contested the degraded community identity imposed from the outside, they questioned ethnic labels and the meanings attached to them. As the second largest ethnic/racial group in the United States, Mexican Americans have used varying labels to designate themselves, labels that differ between regions, by length of residency in the United States, and across class. This diversity reflects the lengthy and contested history of Mexican Americans in the United States.

Assuming that one's preference for a particular ethnic label constitutes a measure of ethnic identification misses the complex situational, contextual, and political genesis of ethnic classifications. Since the 1960s, Mexican American youth active in civil-rights issues have preferred "Chicano." It signified a politically conscious act of self-determination, just as the switch from "Negro" to "black" did. Older generations adamantly rejected the term "Chicano" as used by the 1960s youth. Prior to the 1960s, some working-class Mexicans used it as a colloquial self-designation, and others used it in referring to "low-class" Mexicans (Acuña 1988, 1996).

People arrive at preferred ethnic labels through their interpretations of life experiences and in contradistinction to other ethnic/racial groups, state policies and practices that discriminate against them, and internal class differentiation. What may seem to be vacillation, confusion, or suppression of ethnic and racial identity represents ways people resist discrimination and, in some cases, retain ethnic identity.

I asked the women how they preferred to identify themselves. The only women who responded with no hesitancy were those born, raised, and educated in Mexico. Juana Gutiérrez answered, "Pues [Well], Mexicana!" No identity confusion here. Alexandra Dávila also spontaneously responded with enthusiasm: "Mexicana!" For women raised and educated in the United States, both the question of ethnic/racial classification and their choice of an answer are "loaded," or rich with their life experiences in the community and the meanings they derive from those experiences.

I asked Angie Flores how she liked to be identified. Her answer reconstructs the dialogue she has had with the state during her lifetime in Los Angeles. She shared her efforts to make sense out of the multiple ethnic designations, ending by laughing at the complexities:

> Hispanic is something different. It sounds like South American. I am not South American. Why do they [the state] separate us? Even if we are born here, we are still Mexican American? Since I was born here, am I American? Like for jury duty, they asked me if I was Spanish. If I was Spanish, I would be from Spain. I speak Spanish, so I would probably say I was Spanish speaking. I was born here, so what am I? I think I am American of Mexican descent. I could say I was American because I was born here, but I am of Mexican descent. So I told them, You take it however you want!

I joined in her laughter because she captured a history of changing designations in her brief, humorous, internal dialogue. Angie's last statement ("You take it however you want!") does not mean she is confused about who she is but only that she is not sure of the intent of those who need to classify her and of the consequences attached to the selection of a label.

Another woman stated that school and hospital records

made distinctions based on ethnicity and race for Mexicans only. In the schools during the 1940s, a U.S.-born child of Mexican descent would be designated Mexican, while a second-generation Irish child would be designated "white." In 1950 similar discriminatory practices led the CSO successfully to oppose the Pentagon's practice of designating Americans of Mexican descent "Mexican" on enlistment forms and segregating their names in the Armed Forces files.[14] In the 1940s and 1950s, many Mexican Americans opposed ethnic/racial designation. In some instances, the opposition has been wrongly interpreted as a denial of ethnicity. It is more correctly seen as resistance to discriminatory policies and practices. In the 1990s, the political implications have changed; being "counted" can help to establish a base of power.

Gloria Chávez, a U.S.-born Mexican American woman who is fifty-six years of age expressed ambivalence, not about her own sense of ethnic identity but about the changing currency of particular labels: "I don't know anymore! We were always Mexican Americans, and all of a sudden it's Hispanos and Chicano and whatever. I think most of the time we use Hispano. I think I prefer Mexican American. I feel that I am of Mexican descent and I am American because I was born here. I am not so much for the term 'Chicano,' maybe because of my age."

The chronology of changing ethnic labels used by the U.S. Census reflects the continuing search for a generic, acceptable term for persons of Latin American origin living in the United States. In 1930 census coding instructions stated, "all persons born in Mexico, or having parents born in Mexico, who are definitely not white, Negro, Indian, Chinese or Japanese, should be listed as Mexican."[15] In this case, the census fused place of birth or nationality with race. The 1940 coding instructions stipulated that Mexicans were to be listed as "White, unless they were definitely Indian or some race other than White." The census taker would determine a person's race by observing their physical characteristics. The census of 1950 reported that there were three major races: "White, Negro and Other: persons of Mexican birth or ancestry who were definitely not Indian or other non-White race were classified as White"; there was also a category for "White person of Spanish surname." The federal government created the term "Hispanic" in 1970 and, after much criticism, modified it in 1980 to "other Spanish/Hispanic," which was listed among other choices that included Mexican, Mexican American, Chicano, Puerto Rican, and Cuban. Surprisingly, the 1990 census categories are generally comparable with the 1980 census. In 2000, the U.S. Census will allow respondents to check off more than one category. Criticisms from those of mixed racial heritage prompted the revised policy.[16]

In the context of the last four decades, the political and economic significance of ethnic and racial classification persists. The meanings and consequences attached to particular designations also continue to be a dialogue between the state and ethnic and racial groups. The repercussions of ethnic and racial classification and counts are felt through social service allocations and the mapping of electoral districts for purposes of political representation.

Discussion

What do the ways in which women contest their community's identity and their own ethnic and racial designations by the state reveal about activism? They illustrate the process by which the women recognize the contradictions inherent in the way the community is defined by the media, the state, and others. They have experienced the consequences of those socially constructed identities, and they use that lived experience to justify militant opposition and to redefine their community. The women observed that the integrated, middle-class Jewish community of the 1930s received adequate services, and they concluded that the community suffers from ethnic, racial, and class discrimination. In Eastside Los Angeles, a Latino community with internal differences, expressions of opposition to the state are shaped by social constructions of the community. The way women construct the community history reflects their social positions not simply as women who are working class but as women who are Mexican Americans.

A particular community identity only arises in contrast to other communities. MELA's collective representations of community identity became part of their work as activists. Community identity can be conceived as a dialogue among community members and between community members and outsiders, including the mass media (Suttles 1972: 51). The community images that result from the dialogue either denigrate or complement the places they represent. In either case, the community identity may be contested in the interests of different political purposes. The ethnic and racial composition of the community, the economic status of the community, and length of time people have resided in the community help shape residents' perceptions of where they live in relation to other places. For example, black women have organized across class differences when they perceived outside racial discrimination. Long-time residents who hold visions of better times and an emotional attachment to the community may use these visions to guide their activism (Gilkes 1980; Saegert 1989). As in the case of black women's organizing, many of the Mexican American women activists who were long-time residents associated the poor condition of their community with discriminatory practices on the part of elected representatives. Women used their life experiences in the neighborhood and the relationship of those experiences to outsiders to build positive collective representations of the community. Constructing community identity became a key element in defending Eastside Los Angeles.

FOUR

The Politics of Community Identity in Monterey Park
"Things Looked Better over There"

As I reach the freeway off-ramp to one of the main commercial streets in Monterey Park, I wait for what seems like an interminable three minutes to exit. At one o'clock in the afternoon, cars line Atlantic Boulevard. The street offers the usual services—gas stations, restaurants, and banks. I consider whether a stranger could determine the ethnic makeup of the city simply by careful observation.

The block begins with a large commercial chain selling automobile tires. The one-story, unadorned white stucco building houses a row of open stalls equipped with hydraulic lifters to facilitate changing tires. Raised white letters on a red background identify the business: "Firestone"; directly underneath is written "All American Auto," and immediately adjacent are Chinese characters that I am unable to read. The next business is a grocery store located in a two-story mall, an identifiable and distinct, if not authentic, version of Chinese architecture. Glazed forest-green clay tiles cover the gently sloping roof. Bright red letters written prominently across the front of the building say "SHUN FAT" (approximate translation: Everything goes smoothly—prosperity and growth). Large ceiling-to-floor windows reveal burlap sacks of rice and flour stacked up about five feet high. Across the street is a Hughes supermarket, identified by large red letters on a revolving sign; this store's windows are covered with sheets of white butcher paper announcing sale items. No merchandise is displayed for view from the outside, and no advertisements are written in Chinese.

On the next large commercial street, signs by a large medical center suggest the mixed population it serves. The concrete slab at the entrance to the six-story complex communicates in three languages from top to bottom: "Garfield Medical Center," "Garfield Centro Médico," and Chinese characters. Directly across the street is the Yan-Yan Pharmacy. On its sign a cartoonlike line drawing of a chubby Chinese man accompanies the name of the pharmacy; underneath the name, in red letters, is written "Se habla español" (Spanish spoken).

Even a visitor unconcerned about Monterey Park's ethnic or immigrant composition would rightly guess the demography of the city. What the commercial strip tells us is that the population is multi-ethnic—Anglo, Chinese, and Latino, and the Chinese population has the largest new immigrant numbers. Some large business establishments seem oblivious to the community's ethnic makeup; others have sought to appeal to the changing population. Chinese immigrants own most of the small family-operated businesses.

Monterey Park's established residents are currently adapting to physical, social, and cultural transformations in their community in a period of rapid demographic, ethnic, and economic change. Media accounts sensationalize the city, calling it the "first suburban Chinatown." Some residents regard ethnic change in the neighborhood—predominantly the recent arrival of Chinese immigrants from Hong Kong, Taiwan, and the People's Republic of China who have university educations and enough capital to purchase homes upon arrival—as the root of uncontrolled growth and a "foreign takeover."

How is the demographic change significant for Mexican American women's ethnic identity and community activism? The heightened racial antagonism and struggles over development that centered on Chinese immigrants forced the issue of ethnic identity into the community's public discourse.

Moving from the Barrio to the Suburbs

Women in Eastside Los Angeles battled negative community images from the media and other "outsiders." In Monterey Park residents also contend with the media, in this case contesting its representation of community identity in response to a set of class and ethnic/racial conflicts different from those in the predominantly Latino Eastside. Since about 1985, the media has highlighted Monterey Park as a hotbed of racial hostility toward new Chinese immigrants. In most instances, the Latino community faded into the background as the dialogue involved Anglo and Asian residents and the media.

"Things Looked Better Over There"

A second-generation Mexican American woman who is fluently bilingual, Josie Howard moved to Eastside Los Angeles from New Mexico with her family of nine when she was thirteen years old. She lived in East Los Angeles for twenty years. A single parent of two young sons at the time of her first community involvement, she recalls the mid-1960s, when gang violence and killings had begun to disrupt the family life of her friends and neighbors. For Josie the gang-related murders of her friend Rita Figueroa's two sons dramatically marked the beginning of her community activism in Eastside Los Angeles. As she said, "It is bad enough to lose a son, but then not even to have enough money to bury him? That was too much!"

Women in the neighborhood decided to go door to door requesting donations for burial costs. In addition they organized food sales and cooked traditional Mexican food. The group of women continued calling attention to gang problems.[1] As women talked to each other about their children and safety concerns, they decided to form a group to address gang violence. They called the group Concerned Parents. As I have discussed, Eastside neighborhoods vary, as does the presence of gang activity. The variations lead women in some neighborhoods to channel their energy into working with gang-related problems while other groups such as MELA address environmental issues.

She observed that "somehow the kids seemed to have some respect when parents were around," so they got permission to maintain a presence in and around the junior high schools. With police consent although not their assistance, they worked out what they called "patrols": two or three mothers walked around the vicinity of the school. Some of the women shared stories about how police released gang members into rival gang territory, exposing them to possible beatings and even murder.[2] Because of this, Josie explained, kids would not talk to them if the police accompanied them. By talking to the kids and simply being "around," they fended off potential gang confrontations.

Soon after Josie became a member of the Concerned Parents

group, she volunteered to work with other community groups. Through her community work she learned much about obtaining support from Chicano agencies, such as the Mexican American Legal Defense and Education Fund (MALDEF). Later, when she confronted other community issues in Monterey Park, she sought assistance from these and other public agencies created to fight discrimination and promote Mexican American political representation.

Despite her concern and volunteer work to deter gang violence in her neighborhood, she soon recognized that her son was being drawn toward the gang subculture. Shortly after his twelfth birthday, she noticed a change in his grooming, dress, and speech that expressed his attraction to gang styles: "He began wearing one of those hair nets, which are just ridiculous, walking that little walk, and I knew what that meant!"[3] She decided to move from the Eastside in order to separate her son from the gang activity. At the time she was married to an Irish American, and they decided to purchase a home in Monterey Park.

Monterey Park seemed the best choice for two reasons. First, the community was adjacent to Eastside Los Angeles, so she could easily visit her two sisters. Second, the schools appeared superior to those in East Los Angeles. "It looked pretty good over there, and I knew there were a few gangs but nothing like in East L.A.," she said. Following her move to Monterey Park, she continued to work a few years with the community center, "Bienvenidos," located in a nearby suburb. After a while Josie's community involvement declined, although she still communicated with her sisters and friends in East Los Angeles. Her son adjusted slowly and still experienced difficulties in school; however, he did terminate his budding gang affiliation.

"We Are Not Fighting for Our Daily Bread, As in East L.A."

Sally Castellanos, a woman in her mid-fifties who works in social services in Eastside Los Angeles, followed a path somewhat similar to that of Josie Howard. She speaks of her first experiences in a community-based group: "I was in my twenties and living in East L.A. I had never been involved in any groups. Then one day, I was reading the local paper and I saw an article on a preschool center being started by parents in my neighborhood. I went down to a meeting that was announced and met other parents who wanted to learn about child development." The timing of Castellanos's initial involvement coincided with the tumultuous era of the War on Poverty and subsequent California Supreme Court decisions bearing on the Mexican American community. She carried out extensive grassroots work around issues of bilingual education. In the mid-1960s community meetings and demonstrations were commonplace. During that time, she chaired the Mexican American Ad Hoc Education Committee, composed of activists and educators who identified with the "Chicano movement." The committee worked to publicize and agitate around educational inequality in the Los Angeles city school district. In 1971 the California Supreme Court held that the funding scheme based on local property taxes invidiously discriminates against the poor because the quality of a child's education becomes a function of the wealth of his or her parents and neighbors. The decision led to an equalization of school-finance formulas. Compensatory programs such as bilingual and bicultural education soon followed (Acuña 1997, 290–91).

Castellanos's husband, however, did not share her enthusiasm about community activism, and the conflict contributed to the end of her marriage. She reflected on the steady growth of her activism and awareness and the effect it had on her and her husband:

> The more I attended meetings, the more interested I became. But my husband just didn't understand. He couldn't see why I wanted to do anything but stay home and take care of the kids. He began questioning why I wanted to be involved. As time went on, I felt I was learning so much and growing more and more aware. Unfortunately, my husband didn't share my excitement. After a few years we divorced.

She then began working for War on Poverty programs. Her divorce and growing involvement in community projects expanded the range of her political activism.

Like Josie Howard, Sally Castellanos saw suburban Monterey Park as an ideal community: "When I first moved to Monterey Park, it was about one-third Latino, less than a third Asian, and one-third Anglo. Because of my past experiences with the multicultural issues, I wanted my children to experience growing up in an integrated community."

While she made no disparaging comments about East Los Angeles, inherent in her description is an image of the ideal neighborhood as a multicultural community that is ethnically and racially integrated. Her vision also anticipated that her children would be living their adult lives in an integrated community.

Sally Castellanos moved to Monterey Park in 1968, but she continued her activism in East Los Angeles rather than in her new suburban neighborhood. She noted the differing needs and material circumstances of the two communities: "It seemed to me that there was more of a struggle in East L.A. against unemployment, high-school dropouts, drugs, and gangs. I saw great need there. In Monterey Park we are not fighting for our daily bread. We have a certain amount of comfort, and residents have just about all they need."

The two women who began their political activism in Eastside Los Angeles moved to Monterey Park to provide a better education and safer environment for their children than they saw available in East Los Angeles. Similarly, they saw the suburb as a place where the intensive work they carried out in the inner city was unnecessary. Federal funding available for grassroots social programs in the 1960s led some Mexican-origin women into paid positions as community liaisons. Josie Howard and Sally Castellanos moved out of the Eastside barrio, but maintained some of their old community and social networks.

Lorraine Beltrán, who grew up in Eastside Los Angeles, has lived in Monterey Park since 1964, although her parents and two of her sisters remain on the Eastside. Her comments emphasize how she managed to meet two potentially conflicting concerns—a desire to live in a community with quality public services and a concern for maintaining close kinship and cultural ties.[4] She solved the problem by moving to Monterey Park, adjacent to East Los Angeles. She continues a daily commute to Eastside Los Angeles to work. On Sundays and some Saturdays she also commutes to attend mass with her parents and sisters at Resurrection Catholic Church in Boyle Heights.

Lorraine constructs her image of Monterey Park in contrast to that of her old community, offering the difference in police services as an example.

In my neighborhood [Monterey Park] you see one car that doesn't "belong," and you have a quick police response. On the Eastside, someone stole something from my car. A man jumped out of the bus and held the man, and you know that the police car came half an hour later

and the man escaped. It's just a totally different neighborhood. If they don't have the best of cars, you know they
don't belong here [in Monterey Park].

Lorraine, much like other suburban Mexican Americans,
solved the problem of inadequate services by moving. But
Monterey Park did not meet her social and cultural needs. The
Eastside still holds family and cultural attractions and fulfills
her needs in these arenas. She comments philosophically, "I
grew up in a neighborhood where the *comadres* [literally, god-
mothers, but often used colloquially in referring to close
women friends or neighbors who look out for each other] were
always sweeping their yard, so you would always talk to your
neighbors. But I cannot complain about the 'Orientals' because
they are good neighbors."

She came to terms with the culturally different context of
Monterey Park in order to enjoy better services. By commuting
from Monterey Park to the Eastside, she can maintain her cultural and familial ties through church activities and work. She
comments that inflation and changing economic circumstances
resulted in making it easier for her to move out than it is for her
younger sisters. The comment implies that her sisters would
move out of Eastside Los Angeles if it were economically feasi-
ble. Instead, her two sisters are actively involved in the Mothers
of East Los Angeles. The church pastor and her sisters have successfully encouraged Lorraine to participate in demonstrations.

Redefining Community and Ethnic Identity

Lorraine, who is bilingual, raised seven monolingual children
in Monterey Park. If language ability is a measure of ethnic

identity, her sons and daughters are now less identified with Mexican ethnicity than she is. But her experiences and those of her daughter, described below, show the ways a move to suburbia may not dictate a decline in ethnic identity. She discussed the need to communicate with her Spanish-speaking in-laws and with customers at work:

My parents spoke fluent Spanish, and we answered in English. But I couldn't do that at work or with my in-laws, who speak [only] Spanish. So I started speaking more Spanish at work and with my in-laws. My daughter does not speak Spanish. When I tried to speak to her in Spanish and teach her, she would say, "Don't talk to me that way. I am not a 'T.J.' " [from Tijuana, a poor city on the California-Mexico border].

A student at Cal State University in Los Angeles, Lorraine's daughter now scolds her, "Mom, you should have talked to me in Spanish."

I told her, "But you didn't want me to; you said you were not a 'wetback' or a 'T.J.' " "Well," she says, "you should have made me speak." I said, "Now you say that, but it was different then."

Lorraine's daughter's resistance to speaking Spanish before she entered college suggests how time and place affect one's ethnic identity. It also illustrates how Mexican American teens may link the degraded status of new and very poor Mexican immigrants with the act of speaking Spanish. Language and cultural differences contribute to the social distance between these groups, as does the physical separation of new immigrants into English-as-a-second-language classes. In 1997 some U.S.-born Latino high school students continue to use derogatory terms when referring to new immigrant students.[5]

The political activism of the late 1960s generated ethnic studies departments in colleges across the Southwest and other parts of the United States. Chicano student groups sponsored by ethnic studies departments continue to organize around cultural and political issues. Within these groups, however, one who is unable to speak Spanish may be perceived as ethnically unauthentic—a "Chicana falsa," or fake Chicana. Their inability may also be seen as a denial of ethnic identity or as evidence of assimilation. In the 1990s university setting, Spanish speaking ability signifies a whole new range of meanings and social relationships, including ethnic pride and political activism.

Throughout Los Angeles the new immigration from Latin America has added a new slant on Latino youth and ethnic identity. Until the late 1960s teachers punished Mexican American students for speaking Spanish in school. When they became parents they taught their children only English. The new immigration tipped the demographics so that foreign-born, fluently bilingual youth now outnumber the U.S. born, and Spanish fluency is now recognized as advantageous for many careers. In Los Angeles, for example, Spanish-language radio stations capture the largest audience.

Becoming a Long-Time Resident:
"We Didn't Make Waves"

Women who moved to Monterey Park in the late 1960s and early 1970s describe their rather uneventful incorporation into the community, which was predominantly white at the time they moved in. Mexican Americans who describe their entry into Monterey Park as "not making waves" meant that they moved in quietly and conformed to the dominant white culture. Whites did not react to Mexicans in overtly discriminatory ways.

One woman remembered ethnic name-calling among neighborhood children. She says when they first moved in during the late 1960s, she heard the neighborhood kids calling her kids "you L&Ms!" She asked her son what the term meant. He explained it stood for "Lousy Mexican." (The slur was probably borrowed from the name of a cigarette brand popular at the time). Another woman mentioned that her sons, playing ball in the front yard, had annoyed a neighbor, who muttered, "That is why we moved from the [Boyle] Heights." None of the women indicated that they had encountered discrimination in Monterey Park.

Josie Howard, who married an Irish American man and moved into the community in 1965, described her experience:

It's a funny thing. At the time we moved here, it was mostly Anglos. And I noticed that the few Mexican people living here tended to be Anglicized—like the food . . . the sandwiches and the roasts were "in," and the *enchiladas* were kind of forgotten [laughing]. I guess I kind of wanted to fit in with the group and be part of the community. That meant thinking like them, talking like them, saying their jokes. We lived here for twenty years really happy. The Anglos made you feel like you belonged. I didn't feel discriminated against until the last election and this racial thing.

The "racial thing" Josie refers to is the open hostility expressed by long-time residents against the recent Chinese immigrants. Hostility toward the rapid and sizable Asian influx was manifested in the city-sanctioned ordinance making English the "official language" and Resolution 9004 directing the Monterey Park police to stop and apprehend those suspected of being undocumented immigrants (Horton 1995). After the "official language" conflicts, Josie perceived racial antagonism on the rise. She describes an incident in City Hall that turned her away from a slow-growth group she had previously supported:

> [A]t the time I also felt the Chinese were invading us, and I would attend meetings with the RAMP [Residents Association of Monterey Park] group. They would call me up and tell me, You better come to the council meeting because the "chinks" will be there. I began to think, If they say that about them, what do they say about me? I was the only Latina. Then one day at a city council meeting, they started in on David Almada—jeering and laughing at him, the Latino on the council. That hurt me because he is Latino. So I broke away from the group. I agree there should have been better control of development, but it is too late in our area.

Another long-time resident of Monterey Park illustrates how ethnicity, race, and class weave in and out of her life experience and community activism. Ruth DeLeon is an active organizer of "Citizens for Property Rights against Downzoning." ("Downzoning" refers to changing the use of land by restricting use to single-family residences, rather than allowing two-family or apartment dwellings.) She has been a Neighborhood Watch block captain for ten years. Separated and currently unemployed, she supports herself and another family member on retirement benefits. Her small stucco home on Orange Avenue faces a street where the traffic sounds force her to keep her front windows and door closed. My tape recording of our interview picked up the sound of whizzing cars and rumbling trucks. As she says, it sounds like a freeway out there.

She is particularly upset because she feels what little investment she has is in her home, and she lives in a heavily developed area, so downzoning would lessen the property's value. A few years ago the city cut six feet off the sidewalk in order to widen the street. The widening increased traffic, dust, and noise, and brought traffic closer to her home. Residents on the block were not compensated; they did not protest at the time, thinking they had no option to oppose it. She concludes that Latinos and Asians who are concentrated in the center of the city will be hurt by any plans to downzone the area.[6] As mentioned in Chapter Three, Mexicans are not segregated, but they tend to be concentrated in the sectors of the community where some of the heaviest development has already occurred.

Ruth got a list of four thousand affected property owners in the area, ran off flyers listing her name and phone number and those of four other women, and called the group "Citizens for Property Rights." A multi-ethnic group of people showed up at a city council meeting and soundly argued against the proposal to downzone sectors of the city. During the meeting, Ruth walked up and down the aisles of the council chambers passing out flyers. She also made a statement during the open forum informing the city council that she had been advised to read the Brown Act to remind the council of citizen's rights.[7] She stressed that their homes were the only investment most people had, and concluded saying that she knew sixteen hundred homeowners who opposed downzoning. The city council defeated the proposed downzoning ordinance. Later she confided to me that she got the information on the Brown Act from the Mexican American Legal Defense Committee and Southwest Voters Rights, groups she knew as a result of her activism in Eastside Los Angeles.

As Chinese Americans, We Get All This "Asian Flack"

The way a Chinese American woman experienced the changing ethnic composition of the Monterey Park community builds on the argument that ethnic and racial identity is dynamic, contextual, and historically specific. Asian American women experienced the community changes differently from Mexican American and Anglo women. Some of their experiences illustrate that being "American" can have multiple interpretations and that it is often ethnically and racially qualified.

In Monterey Park most established residents do not share language or a cultural background with the new immigrants. This presents quite a different set of circumstances from those in Eastside Los Angeles. Some Chinese Americans resent what they refer to as the "Asian flack" they have received from Anglos in recent years. According to one Chinese American woman who has lived in Monterey Park for many years, Anglo Americans who "can't tell the difference" between U.S.-born Asian Americans and new Asian immigrants make snide comments about "an Asian takeover."

> We get this "Asian flack" as a consequence of the upper-class Asians here. You know that the upper-class Asians flaunt their money and drive around in Mercedes. Now, all the Asians look alike [to non-Asians], so they think every Asian they see is rich. See, I am second generation but they don't see the difference. The other day at the

grocery store a Caucasian lady turned to her friend and said, "They are even taking over our area." They didn't even lower their voices!

Asian Americans thus became perpetrators and targets of anti-immigrant Chinese sentiments (Saito, forthcoming). As a U.S.-born Chinese American, the woman makes a distinction between her own ethnic identity and that of the new immigrants. Her comments also point to class differences and suggest resentment about what she perceives as the conspicuous display of wealth. She grew up in the San Fernando Valley, where her parents spent long hours operating a small Chinese restaurant. She recalled difficulties growing up in a predominantly Anglo community and finds Monterey Park's ethnic mix a culturally "comfortable" community for raising her own children.

For Asian American women, criteria for a "good community" included quality city services and a delicate balance of ethnic and racial minorities that would dissipate racism. The perception is that "too many or too few" of any one group create an inhospitable context. Lucia Su, a middle-aged woman of Chinese origin, is a technician and the mother of four children. She immigrated to the United States over thirty years ago, first living in Salt Lake City. She chose Monterey Park to raise her children and compares it to Salt Lake City:

> I remember in Salt Lake City [in the late 1960s], my little girl said the other kids called her "flatnose" because there were only a few Chinese there. So all the kids were teasing her. You know how kids are when they are little.

> In Monterey Park [in the 1970s], there were more Chinese [than in Salt Lake City]. So the kids felt more comfortable in school here because there were all kinds of other peo-

ple. People were very friendly; only recently [in the 1980s] did we have racial tension. For a long time I felt we had harmony here.

There were about one-third Asian, one-third Caucasian and one-third Hispanic. Myself, I don't like living in a ghetto either. I really like the mixed neighborhood. But unfortunately, in the last ten years, all the Orientals with the same background I have landed here.

Lucia Su never taught her daughter to speak Chinese. Upon entering UCLA, her daughter sought out Chinese language classes and she is now bilingual—albeit with an American accent, according to Lucia. Lucia joined community groups— PTA, Boy Scouts, Little League—and followed American cultural "traditions." Apparently, she managed to settle in an ethnically mixed community without encountering any incidents of ethnic or racial discrimination.

She notes that the new Chinese immigrants do not conform to the "traditions of the community," as she did when she arrived. She explains how she can see them from the Chinese cultural perspective as well as that of the established Anglos:

Well, in the market sometimes I think to myself that the Chinese like to talk very loud, including myself. I know I don't talk very soft. When I get emotional, I talk very loud. So I have to tell myself, "Don't talk too loud." You can hear the Chinese in the market talk so loud! Because that is their cultural background; back home they talk like that. They don't pay attention or they don't observe the tradition here, and they get carried away with their emotions and talk very loud. And there are a lot of people around that they don't even know . . . I stand there, and I always want to tell them in a friendly way, "Please don't talk so loud."

Lucia's comments illustrate her understanding of two different interpretations of everyday behavior. She came into the community at a time when Anglos dominated. Some may label her strategy for joining the community assimilationist. From her perspective, she observed American traditions so her children would be well received. She continues to use her observations and perceptions to become active in events that bridge cultural differences. For instance, she participated in the last two Cinco de Mayo celebrations, which incorporated Chinese cultural entertainment.

Chinese Americans in Monterey Park observe existing community traditions and also create their own. Cindy Yee, who has been active in the community for many years, maintains ethnically homogeneous friendship networks and perpetuates her ethnic identity in various ways. She takes her daughters to perform a Chinese "flower dance" on International Day at Disneyland. She also works out rotating child-care arrangements with three other Chinese American women in the neighborhood.

In another attempt to maintain an Asian American identity, which differs from a Chinese identity, she enrolled her daughters in a girls' basketball league called the Jetts. Established after World War II by Japanese Americans in the nearby suburb of Montebello, the leagues (Jets for boys and Jetts for girls) were aimed partly at maintaining ethnic cohesion in a dangerously anti-Japanese environment. Cindy explained the group:

> The basketball league was formed a long time ago. It provided an opportunity for people to meet people of the same background. See, there is an effort to place only one or two non-Japanese on each team. I am counted as a non-Japanese. It is an effort to preserve something cultural.
>
> You know one time [while selling raffle tickets to raise

funds for the Jetts] I met a Japanese guy who was in his forties. His eyes lit up instantly as he talked about his boyhood experiences in the Jets. He and his brother were the first to be on the team. He was excited to hear it was still going on. He told me that he lived on a farm in Paramount, and his mother made him take the long drive to Montebello to play on the team. He said he was so surprised to see so many other Japanese Americans in one place!

The Jets sports leagues formed by Japanese Americans over fifty years ago now offer Cindy a place to meet other Asians, and not necessarily Japanese Americans. Given the declining number of Japanese Americans, more Chinese are joining the group and it has become an Asian network. It does not replace the specificity of Japanese or Chinese identity, but it provides a place to build ethnic and racial social networks that are also potentially political. The Japanese Americans who organized thet Jets and the Chinese Americans who later joined them created an Asian American network while pursuing two all-American pastimes. The case illustrates how people continually renegotiate and interpret their ethnic identity, rather than simply reproduce it.

Celebrations at Tamayo's

While the Asian Americans and Mexican Americans who settled in Monterey Park in the 1960s and 1970s conformed to the Anglo cultural context, they have also continued activities that expressed an ethnic identity and have maintained ethnic family and friendship networks. For Mexican Americans, this means traveling to the Eastside. Some also leave Monterey

Park for celebrations at a large Mexican restaurant named Tamayo's. Located in East Los Angeles, The restaurant is named after the internationally famous Mexican painter Rufino Tamayo, who began painting during the 1930s. Housed in a finely refurbished 1930s-era Spanish-style building, and distinguished by wrought-iron embellishments, tall arches, and a two-story-high ceiling, Tamayo's caters to white-collar Mexican American professionals.[8] One Sunday I happened to meet Dora Padilla there. She is a school board member and has been a community activist for over fifteen years. She had booked the banquet room for a wedding shower for her daughter. Later she told me that she often scheduled family and professional social events at the restaurant.

This is more than a casual choice. Monterey Park has some of the finest Chinese restaurants in all of Los Angeles County, and their banquet rooms could certainly accommodate large celebrations. People of all ethnicities patronize the Chinese restaurants, but more Chinese seem to gather in large groups than do members of other ethnic groups. Later, in casual conversations, several other Mexican American woman told me they planned social events at Tamayo's. They also regularly visit the Eastside to purchase Mexican food items such as *pan dulce* (sweet bread) and meat products.

In a similar account, John Horton tells about the symbolic significance of the ethnic and racial character of meeting sites in Montrey Park. A select group of politically active Anglos regularly met for many years at the Anglo-owned Paris Restaurant in the heart of the business district. The restaurant later became the Hawaii Restaurant, after it was transferred to Vietnamese owners who offered a wide range of Chinese cuisine (Horton 1995, 64). The Anglo group changed their meeting place. Now they travel to a non-Asian-operated restaurant in a neighboring suburb. For Anglos as well as for other groups, certain food choices constitute symbols of ethnicity. Restaurants specializing in particular ethnic cuisines represent the performance of ethnicity, which occurs when cooks use culturally specific ways of preparing and serving food. Language also enters into the presentation, prompting some to recall how a mother or grandmother prepared the dish.

The Politics of Community Identity: Comparative Contexts

The case studies of Mexican American women who became active in Eastside community politics and then moved to Monterey Park illustrate several important points. First, they indicate how material conditions influenced their activism in each community. One can see change in their activism as they moved from the barrio to the suburbs. In Boyle Heights women had long histories in the community. All but one was born and raised there, and one lived in the community over thirty years. Several of the women activists in Monterey Park grew up in East Los Angeles and moved to Monterey Park after they married. Thus, a simple but significant difference between the women in Boyle Heights and the women in Monterey Park lies in the continuity or discontinuity of their experiences in one community of the same socioeconomic status.

Women in the two communities diverged along other life paths: age, work histories, and marital status. For example, all but one of the women from Boyle Heights are married and have children; one is single and never had children. In age they range from forty to sixty-five. More of the Monterey Park community activists are younger than those in Eastside Los

Angeles, and more have worked for wages either full-time or part-time over the last twenty years. The women from Monterey Park also show greater differences in household organization and marital status. Two are divorced and have children; the others are married and have children. The two women who began activism in Eastside Los Angeles learned much from participation in War on Poverty programs of the 1960s.

Two of the Mexican American women activists grew up in East Los Angeles and experienced their first community involvement there. Much like the women who still live in Boyle Heights, the Monterey Park women entered grassroots activism when they perceived family well-being at stake; in contrast, their work did not begin with church-related activities. Instead, it began in the social and political context of the 1960s. These volunteer community activists for a short time became paid workers in the antipoverty programs.

Just as the women rooted their activism in Eastside Los Angeles in the wish to secure a safe environment for their children, they moved to the suburbs to accomplish a similar purpose. After moving to Monterey Park, they maintained contact with friends and community groups on the Eastside and initiated a limited degree of involvement in their new suburban neighborhoods. The women's stories reveal how the process of suburbanization can lead to different involvements and reformulations of identity in a multi-ethnic setting.

Activists in Monterey Park, a community in transition, faced many communication barriers. Even though it is a multi-ethnic community and people do have multi-ethnic acquaintances, their social lives may be concentrated among those of their own ethnic group. In the suburban setting ethnic identity may become less visible because it is practiced in less public ways. Living in Eastside Los Angeles is living in a reconstructed ethnic and cultural center. The women acknowledge that Monterey Park's ethnic identity is in transition, although it continues to be viewed as a safe suburban setting. The new Chinese immigrants are not all rich, but they are primarily professionals and middle class. Women did not have to op-pose a degraded image of their community, as did women in Eastside Los Angeles.

Simply assuming that suburbanization automatically leads to assimilation and acculturation ignores actual demographic changes. First, the 1960s vision of the suburbs as ethnically ho-mogeneous no longer exists. As the internationalization of American cities proceeds, many of the ethnically homoge-neous suburban communities of the 1960s are giving way to ethnic diversity in the 1990s. The largest concentrations of new Asian immigrants in the region live in Monterey Park. The move out of the barrio and "ethnic heartland" into the suburbs may lead to reconfigured ethnic identities. The changing eth-nic and racial composition of the community reshapes ethnic identification instead of obliterating it. Cultural identity is not unilinear and unidirectional. It is a dynamic lived strategy that may appear dormant and then resurface in changing circum-stances.

Erlinda Robles, Mothers of East Los Angeles, Sister Carmela Vieira (left), and Sister Arcadia from Resurrection Convent march to City Hall to protest the Eastside prison (March 1989). (Security Pacific Collection/ Los Angeles Public Library)

Mothers of East Los Angeles wearing white scarves protest prison (July 1986). (Security Pacific Collection/Los Angeles Public Library)

Multicultural Cinco de Mayo celebration in Monterey Park featuring Chinese Lion Dance and piñatas hanging above (May 1989). (Photo courtesy of the author)

Trilingual commercial signs represent diverse population in Montery Park (1994). (Photo courtesy of Jim Velarde)

Annie Rodriguez (left), Kate Kariya, and Rosemary Lopez, Concerned Parents and Residents of Monterey Park, get petitions ready (August 1988). (Ray Babcock/*Monterey Park Progress*)

Monterey Park Highlands School students, Vince Ramirez (right front), and Concerned Parents and Residents of Monterey Park write letters to move parole office (1988). (Ray Babcock/*Monterey Park Progress*)

Eloise and Lon Hardy and Members of Concerned Parents and Residents of Monterey Park protest parole office (February 1990). (Ray Babcock/ *Monterey Park Progress*)

Annie and Nick Rodriguez helped to organize against billboards in Monterey Park (May 1997). (Photo courtesy of the author)

Pastor John Moretta (seated left), Assemblywoman Gloria Molina, Field Representative Rosemary Lopez, Frank Villalobos (standing right), and other Coalition Against the Prison members hold press conference at proposed Eastside prison site (June 1986). (Photo courtesy of Jorge Garcia / *La Opinion*)

Over 1,000 protesters led by Juana Gutiérrez (right), Congressman Edward Roybal, Assemblywoman Lucille Roybal-Allard, Aurora Castillo, and Mothers of East Los Angeles protest the building of a toxic waste incinerator in Vernon, adjacent to East Los Angeles (November

Juana Gutiérrez, Mothers of East Los Angeles, her husband, Ricardo, their daughter, Veronica, and sons, Ricardo (top), and Martin (1989). (*Los Angeles Times* photo)

Mothers of East Los Angeles join the Cesar Chavez funeral march in Delano, California (April 1993). (Photo courtesy of Diana Martinez)

FIVE

Becoming an Activist in Eastside Los Angeles

"For My Kids, for My Community, and for My 'Raza'"

During the summer months of 1986 and 1987, between five hundred and three thousand people marched every Monday evening on the Olympic Boulevard bridge that links downtown Los Angeles with Eastside Los Angeles. They carried bilingual placards proclaiming "No Prison in ELA" and "No Cárcel en Este L.A." A broad-based community group, the Coalition against the Prison, eventually defeated the first state prison planned for construction in a densely populated urban area. The prison proposal symbolized the legacy of "dumping" unwanted projects on the Eastside. The community victory in 1992 marked the end of an eight-year struggle and illustrated the potential power of grassroots activism in working class communities.

From a conventional perspective, political activism assumes a kind of gender neutrality. This means that anyone can participate, but men are expected to be the key actors. In this case, gender, class, and ethnicity became visible dimensions of Eastside politics when Fifty-sixth District Assemblywoman Gloria Molina voiced opposition to the project planned for her district. Many viewed the residents of the Fifty-sixth—predominantly working class, with significant numbers of Mexican immigrants and noncitizens—as politically powerless and unlikely to raise organized opposition.

The media also entered into the debate over the prison. Editorials began appearing on a regular basis, with the influential *Los Angeles Times* initially backing the prison.[1] One radio editorial stated, "Gloria Molina likens herself to a drum major in a march against the East L.A. Prison. Few have fallen in line behind her."[2] *The Los Angeles Herald* questioned the fairness of the site selection, and *La Opinión* and local Eastside neighborhood papers opposed it.[3] When Molina met with *Los Angeles Times* editors in 1986, she convinced them that the Eastside deserved a public hearing, although they continued to support the site selection. Within a year after the community mobilization gathered momentum and wider support, the *Los Angeles Times* began changing its position.

In 1987, as the prison controversy continued, Eastside residents in conjunction with Lucille Roybal-Allard, now representing the Fifty-sixth Assembly District, challenged another large detrimental project: one of the first toxic-waste incinerators planned for California. Through a maze of complex political maneuvers, Eastside residents contested both projects in the legislature, in the courts, in hearings at the state and federal level, and at the grassroots, where women played a central role. In the process of fighting the prison, Molina strengthened her base of support as preexisting community networks, especially among women, became politicized.[4] As women became activists, they reflected on their experiences as mothers and working-class Mexican Americans, converting long-established social networks into political networks. In transforming their social networks, they expressed what were formerly individual concerns as collective community concerns.

Mobilizing the Community: "Whatever It Takes!"

The mobilization began by involving existing community networks. Different segments of the community contributed their resources, among them merchants, business people, and extended family members, including the grown children of Boyle Heights residents. Widening the opposition to the prison meant continuing to spread the news and appealing to ethnic and class solidarity. East Los Angeles, historically the first neighborhood with a large concentration of Mexican Americans in the city, is a symbol of an "ethnic heartland," so Mexican Americans from outside the community joined the struggle in solidarity. These outside supporters included individuals as well as representatives of Chicano student groups, such as MECHA (Movimento Estudiantil Chicano de Aztlán), and the chapters of state and national Latino organizations, such as the Mexican American Political Association, the League of United Latin American Citizens and the Mexican American Education Commission.[5]

Merchants and Business People

Shortly before the massive 1986–87 community demonstrations, merchants and professionals from three Eastside Chambers of Commerce unsuccessfully promoted the creation of an enterprise zone in the area.[6] An enterprise zone is an area specially zoned and subsidized by public funds intended to attract light industry, small businesses, and jobs. The business leaders had been meeting regularly, and had already begun to take issue with proposals for the community that they deemed detrimental. In 1984, for example, they stopped the siting of a junkyard in Lincoln Heights, across the street from a school for the mentally retarded. In August 1985 they brought two hundred people to testify at hearings over a Rapid Transit District proposal to curtail bus service to East Los Angeles. When members of the group found out about the prison, they were already primed for a political confrontation with state officials.

Frank Villalobos and other men from the group made many trips to Sacramento to lobby legislators to vote against the prison bill. Finally, Gloria Molina asked Villalobos, who had invaluable knowledge regarding land-use regulations, why there were no women traveling to Sacramento to speak against the prison. As he explained it, "I was getting some heat from her because no women were going up there."

In response to Molina's pointed question, Villalobos invited Veronica Gutiérrez, a law student who lived in the community, to accompany him on the next trip to Sacramento. (Gutiérrez later became a field representative for Gloria Molina when she served on the city council). Meanwhile, representatives of the business sector, particularly Steve Kasten, José Luis García, and Carmine Baffo, and the Fifty-sixth district office were continuing to compile arguments and supportive data against the Eastside prison site. Villalobos explained one of the pressing problems: "The Senators . . . didn't even acknowledge that we existed. They kept calling it the 'downtown' site, and they argued that there was no opposition in the community. So I told Father Moretta, what we have to do is demonstrate that there is a link [proximity] between the Boyle Heights community and the prison." Father John Moretta, the pastor at Resurrection Parish in Boyle Heights, and as many priests as he could persuade to join the effort announced the many hearings and demonstrations from the pulpit and mobilized hundreds of people. Less formal information networks complemented the parish bulletins. Information also traveled by word of mouth among families and in neighborhood shopping areas.

Extended Family Networks

Extended family networks greatly contributed to the mobilization efforts. When I asked Dolores Duarte how she went about encouraging more people to participate, she reminded me that she comes from a large family born and raised in Boyle Heights. "All my six sisters came to the marches with my mom and my brother. I have a sister who lives in Commerce, another one in Monterey Park, one in Hacienda Heights, and two sisters that live here in Eastside L.A. Then, my sisters started bringing their daughters to the marches."

Although some of her relatives no longer lived in Boyle Heights, they commuted weekly to the Eastside from their suburban communities to attend church and visit their parents. They added the demonstrations to their agenda. In fact, some news about the Department of Corrections came through Dolores's sister before Dolores heard it at the meetings: "My sister works for the employment office in the area. So whenever anything came in on the prison she would let me know. She told us when they were accepting applications for the prison. She read all the qualifications [a high school diploma] to me and if you are an immigrant [and not yet a U.S. citizen] it is not that easy [to get a position]." Another women added that some neighborhood people had believed the promise of jobs until she mentioned the qualifications they would not be able to meet.

Because East Los Angeles holds a powerful symbolic meaning for the larger Mexican American community, Chicano student groups began joining the marches. *La Gente,* a UCLA-sponsored Chicano student newspaper, ran an extensive article on the issue.[7] In turn the women in MELA came to the UCLA campus in West Los Angeles, a substantial distance through congested traffic, to join a student demonstration against campus discrimination. MELA and Chicano student groups developed a relationship of mutual support. Later I found out that several of the women in MELA had children or grandchildren attending UCLA. So it was a combination of family and ethnic ties that formed the social networks for political action.

The Parish Networks

Another woman, Juana Gutiérrez, active in the neighborhood for many years, found out about the prison issue when she received a call from Assemblywoman Gloria Molina's deputy field representative, Martha Molina. Juana stated, "You know, nobody knew about the plan to build a prison in this community until Assemblywoman Gloria Molina told me. Martha Molina called me and said, 'You know what is happening in your area? The governor wants to put a prison in Boyle Heights!' So I called a Neighborhood Watch meeting at my house, and we got five people together. Then Father Moretta started informing his people at the church, and that is when the group of two to three hundred started showing up for every march on the bridge."

Juana had an established information network in the community that ranged from local political offices to the Neighborhood Watch group to the parish; she commenced to link up these networks. Her husband, Ricardo, and a group of five women collected nine hundred signatures on petitions that Gloria Molina took to Sacramento to illustrate community opposition to the prison.

While capitalizing on her extended family networks, Dolores Duarte also used her work site as a place to disseminate information. She has been an employee for fifteen years in a large Boyle Heights pharmacy. Once the demonstrations began, she came to know her customers in a different way: "I have lived in this parish all my life and I have gotten to know so many people through my work in the pharmacy. But it was nothing until this prison march. If there would be a day I didn't go, they would call me at work and tell me they missed me. Everyone got close."

Father Moretta requested that priests in other parishes announce the marches after mass. In addition, the women would visit other parishes and make the announcements. Dolores did some of that work: "I met people from other parishes, like San Antonio de Padua, that I never knew. At Assumption, we would go out there on Sunday to invite them. Different people would go to other parishes every week."

Preexisting networks formed the core of the first groups of people who participated in the marches. After that, they took the marches through the Estrada Courts housing project, chanting "No Prison in East L.A." as they made their way through the small walkways separating the hundreds of housing units. Dolores tells how they called people to join them: "We would march past the houses and invite the people to join us. We used to yell come and give us your *apoyo* [support] in English and in Spanish." Dolores felt that often people didn't fully understand what the protests were about, although they gained some people as they marched through the housing projects.

She particularly recalls one woman yelling back at the marchers, telling them to "shut up and get out of here." She recalls the incident with quite a bit of energy: "One day, that same woman brought her kids to enroll in school at Resurrection. She talked to me and said, 'I remember that day you were yelling for us and I told you to shut up. Now that I see what you are going through and how things are getting really serious, I am sorry.' And I just 'ate it in myself' [suppressed any comment]. I thought, Now she knows. She says please call her and she would get involved. When she hears what is going on she is here."

Dolores attributes the negative responses to people not "really understanding" and thinking they were "just a bunch of *viejas* [old women or women in general] making a bunch of racket in the street." But important to the incident is the fact that the woman who turned her back on the rally had to confront Dolores when she brought her child to register for school. Dolores volunteers many hours every Saturday to work on school activities. Much like a web drawing in other people, the parish networks served to widen the basis for participation.

Politicizing Motherhood:
Mothers of East Los Angeles (MELA)

The women's activities and stories illustrated how they crafted oppositional strategies from gender, ethnic, class, and community identity. Feminist analysis often speaks about the "intersection" of race, class, and gender, but the term fails to capture the fluid dynamism of the women's interpretations and actions. Social identity may be interpreted and used in innumerable fashions; it is not predetermined. Below I discuss incidents that show how the women creatively crafted their expressions of identity and used them to confront the state's agenda. These situations also illustrate the subtle way that women modified the social identity Father Moretta created for them and successfully used at the beginning of community mobilization.

"You don't have to have children to belong"

Perceptions of gender-specific behavior set in motion a sequence of events that brought women into the political limelight. One Sunday after mass, Father Moretta decided to ask all the women parishoners to meet with him. He told them about the prison site and asked for their support. I had assumed that Father Moretta assembled the women because they attended church more regularly or in greater numbers than did men, but he described his rationale differently:

> I felt so strongly about the issue, and I knew in my heart what a terrible offense this was to the people. So I was afraid that once we got into a demonstration situation we had to be very careful. I thought the women would be cooler and calmer and easier to control than the men. The bottom line is that the men came anyway. The first times out the majority were women. Then they began to invite their husbands and their children, but originally it was just women.

Father Moretta met with the women and named the group. He also selected a woman to be president and spokesperson for MELA. Thus bolstered by the authority of the church and by a mother's responsibility to protect her children, the women coalesced into a group. The name of the organization, "Mothers of East Los Angeles," clearly communicates gender identity and the metaphor of mother as protector of the community. Not all of the core activists, however, came to the issue as mothers or directly through the church. Two women responded to the appeal by Father Moretta. Four others took their first step into the eight-year struggle by responding to other information sources—a neighbor who is related to one of the first women involved, the local free newspaper, and the state assemblywoman's office.

One of the core founders of MELA, a self-described senior citizen, is unmarried and has no children. She discussed the pastor's appeal to the group of women who stayed after mass:

> He wanted the mothers to get involved. You know if the safety of one of her children is jeopardized, she turns into a lioness. That's why Father John got the mothers. We have to have a well-organized, strong group of mothers to protect the community and oppose things that are detrimental to us. You know the governor is in the wrong and the mothers are in the right. After all, the mothers have to be right. Mothers are for the children's interest, not for self-interest; the governor is for his own political interest. Father Moretta told us on a Sunday. Lo and behold, on Monday following we were on the bridge.

Her statement indicates how some of the women legitimated their involvement and bolstered their authority to enter the battle. She also modified my emphasis on the predominance of women: "Of course, the fathers work. We also have many, many grandmothers. And all this is with support of the fathers. They make the placards and the posters; they do the security and carry the signs; and they come to the marches when they can."

When the women explained their activism, most of them linked family and community as one entity. In the statement that opens Chapter One of this book, Juana Gutiérrez identified family, community, and ethnic identity as the impetus for her involvement: "digo 'mi comunidad' porque me siento parte de ella, quiero a mi raza como parte de mi familia" (I say "my community" because I am part of it. I love my *raza*, my people, as part of my family). She clearly uses motherhood and family as a metaphor for civic responsibility and action. She has expanded her responsibilities and legitimized militant opposition to projects she assesses as detrimental to the community.

The women also manipulated the boundaries of the role of mother to include social and political community activism, and they redefined the word to include women who are not biological mothers. At one meeting a young Latina expressed her solidarity with the group. Almost apologetically, she qualified herself as a "resident" but not a "mother" of East Los Angeles. Erlinda Robles replied, "When you are fighting for a better life for children and 'doing' for them, isn't that what mothers do? So you don't have to have children to be a mother."

All the examples show that gender identity and responsibilities may blend together, as do the parish and community boundaries, and the notion of civic responsibility is not lessened by the connections.[8] Working class women activists seldom opt to separate themselves from men or from their families. In this particular struggle for community quality of life, they are fighting for the family unit and thus are not competing with men. Of course, this fact does not preclude different alignments in other contexts and situations.

Angie Flores, a senior citizen and mother of two sons in their thirties, read about the prison in the local free newspaper, the *Belvedere Citizen*. She recalls her first reaction to an article about the demonstrations on the Olympic Boulevard bridge. The article was accompanied by a picture of Mexican American women with white scarves worn over their heads and tied under their chins.

> I saw a picture of the women with the scarves and I wondered who are these ladies? I thought they were nuns! Then I read that they wanted help in the demonstrations on the bridge. When I went, I told them that I want to help in any way I can because some of them [other residents, primarily recent immigrants] don't know how to be heard, and I want them to learn how to defend themselves and not get this prison. I used to be active in the PTA and in the parish and community clubs. I went because I would rather be with them instead of feeling anxious and not knowing what the outcome is.

Some women found out about the issue through various family networks. Several have sons and daughters who attend college and participate in ethnic student groups, and thus knew of MELA's activities. Several of MELA's core activists have sons and daughters who work as lawyers, teachers, or community organizers in Los Angeles and continue to take a political interest in the community. The women also had strong preexisting associations and a civic consciousness that is historically rooted in Boyle Heights.

Clearly, the Catholic Church, and in particular one priest—Father John Moretta from Resurrection parish—served as a primary catalyst in disseminating information. Most newspaper accounts of Mothers of East Los Angeles include an interview with Father Moretta. However, it is significant to note that the women entered into the struggle not only as good Catholics at Father Moretta's behest but also as good citizens.

Las Abnegadas (The Self-Sacrificing Ones)?

Father Moretta named the group Mothers of East Los Angeles and asked them to wear white mantillas for deliberately calculated reasons. He believed the name and the visual image the women would present could help generate sympathy and support for the cause. Inspired by the film *The Official Story,* about the courageous Argentine mothers who demonstrated publicly for the return of offspring who "disappeared" (that is, were kidnapped and, in many cases, assassinated) during a repressive right-wing military dictatorship, he adapted their name (Las Madres de la Plaza de Mayo) for the Boyle Heights group. Following the example of the Argentine women, who wore mantillas, Father Moretta bought yards of white cotton cloth and had them cut into scarf-sized squares for the Eastside women to wear during demonstrations (Fisher 1989, 54).[9]

Hundreds of Mexican American women wearing white scarves at the demonstrations did attract media interest. However, the media's response seemed to mix curiosity with a reiteration of stereotyical perceptions of East Los Angeles women. Even some of the women agreed they looked like "poor homebodies"; another laughingly said, "We are supposed to be *las abnegadas,*" a word with connotations of submissive or selfless behavior, often used in reference to the role of motherhood.

The women accepted the scarves in the beginning out of respect for Father Moretta, but as time went by fewer wore them. One woman commented on the difference between a real mantilla, which is made of lace, and the "pieces of white rag" they were asked to wear. Women began to balk; some would say it was "too hot" or they "forgot" them. The explanation for the women's dislike for the scarves may be that their identities as Mexican American women in a U.S. setting departed from those of the Argentine women. Or it may be that they had not made the initial decision to wear them, as had the women in the Argentine case.

One woman indicated a vague awareness of the origin and significance of the scarves: "I didn't like wearing the scarves. They look like a religious group to me, and it really wasn't that. The idea came from women in South America." Another woman agreed that the scarves successfully attracted media attention. But for many, they represented something different from what Father Moretta intended. Said one: "I used to rebel against wearing those white rags because frankly I associate wearing a scarf with doing housecleaning! I think the scarves are a symbol that we are 'homebodies,' [but] we are dignified people. Of course, the young girls don't like wearing them tied under their chins." Another interpreted the white as a sign that they were "protesting, but protesting peacefully."

At the demonstrations, I observed scarves worn in a variety of ways. Some of the young men and women twisted them and wore them tied across their foreheads as headbands. Others wore them tied around their necks or around their upper arms. The women's responses show that symbols of struggle may not be so readily transported across national and cultural boundaries.

Ethnic Identity and Language: Tools of Protest

Ethnic identity and language can be viewed as bases for discrimination or for solidarity. Some view the inability to speak

English as a barrier to active citizenship; others see ways to include those with limited ability to speak English. Discussed below are small dramas revolving around ethnic identity and language that occurred at official meetings and in community settings. At each community meeting, women had to work with the varied language facility of the Eastside residents. At public forums they also advocated for interpreters so that Spanish-speaking residents could follow the proceedings and participate in them. In order to mobilize the community, women had to communicate with immigrants who are predominantly Spanish-speaking and with the English- and Spanish-language media. Humor certainly entered into the ways women devised to address the complexities of communication in a bilingual community.

Language

According to Dolores Duarte, from the onset of the community mobilization, the local newspaper, the *Belvedere Citizen*, the Spanish-language newspaper, *La Opinión*, and the now-defunct *Herald Examiner* covered the marches and demonstrations when the group called them. Channel 7 (ABC) and the *Los Angeles Times* also covered the controversy, generally orienting their coverage toward the need to build new prisons and address inmate overcrowding.

Spanish-language media, both print and electronic, provided crucial information for the community. *La Opinión* covered the prison issue on a regular basis, featuring not only the legislative news but extensive coverage of community sentiment. The *Los Angeles Times*, in comparison, focused on legislative decisions and seldom noted the sentiments of community residents. At least half of the core activists were second-generation Mexican American women, and many felt insecure about their Spanish-language facility and hesitant about communicating with Spanish-language media. But they did it. One woman commented, "I don't like to do it [be interviewed] in Spanish. For the speakers in the media Juana's good in Spanish. I will do it with *La Opinión* sometimes because I started getting confidence with the reporter that covers it. I had Channel 52 come out and interview me, but it was kind of hard. I get nervous in Spanish and say the wrong words. In English it is different. I don't have any hesitation." Her comment points to a common issue for second-generation immigrants: While they are capable of speaking in Spanish, they often have had no formal language education and feel uncomfortable speaking in an official capacity, where their lack of facility may prevent them from adequately explaining the issue.

At meetings of the Coalition against the Prison, the president of MELA often made short announcements to the predominantly Spanish-speaking group. A second-generation Mexican American woman, she had to struggle to translate her ideas into Spanish. As she spoke, she would hesitate before a word, and then laugh and say, "I am learning as I go!" The language facility of the women in the group varies; some are fluently bilingual, some are Spanish dominant but understand English, and others are English dominant and speak Spanish with some effort.

For some core activists, speaking out was not a novel experience. For instance, Angie Flores noted, "I am not afraid to speak because I had my club meetings and senior citizen meetings." All the core activists are bilingual to varying degrees, but only a few were born and raised in Mexico. When one of the latter is available for the Spanish-language interviews, she is called on to act as the group's spokesperson. The women used bilingual skills to mobilize others by phone and to communicate with both Spanish-language and English-language media.

In public hearings held to allow community input and participation, language turned into a focus of protest, an act of resistance, and a critique of the city's disregard for the often cited but seldom respected multicultural and multilingual population. One example was a hearing held in the state office building auditorium, which was filled beyond capacity by Eastside community members. Councilwoman Gloria Molina approached the podium to speak against the prison project. She looked from side to side, seeking an interpreter. There was none. Facing the audience, she asked, "Who needs a Spanish translation of the hearing proceedings?" The audience was silent for a moment; no one responded. Then someone called out, "Ask that question in Spanish!" She did. About three-fourths of the audience raised their hands. She read her entire statement in Spanish and then again in English, dismaying the hearing panel with the extra time that was required to deliver her comments twice.

At the next hearing, again translators were not provided. The issue was raised at meeting after meeting. Some residents gave testimony in English and Spanish demonstrating bilingual ability and unsubtle criticism of the absence of translators.

Ethnic Identity

One rainy morning, about 150 women demonstrated at a recreation center in East Los Angeles where the Department of Corrections was holding a job fair for people interested in working in the proposed state prison. Rectangular tables lined the walls of the large recreation room. Several DOC representatives staffed the tables, which contained information leaflets and job announcements neatly arranged in stacks. The women filed in, some wearing white scarves.

Juana Gutiérrez held a small bullhorn and led the women in a march, chanting, "No Prison in E.L.A.! No Prison in E.L.A.!" A woman from the DOC stood up and, seemingly oblivious to the protesters, began speaking to the crowd about job opportunities. Other protesters began calling out as the DOC representatives attempted to quell the demonstration: "¡Pues, yo no quiero trabajar en prisión! ¡Mejor mándeme hacer pan!" (Well, I don't want to work in prison! Better have me bake bread!) Another woman called out, "¡Yo quiero hacer pan dulce o tortillas!" (I want to make sweet bread or tortillas!) The other women began to laugh. Juana picked up the bullhorn and in Spanish told the crowd to pick up the pamphlets and take them out and throw them away. They followed her directions.

Dolores Duarte approached the only Latino Department of Corrections representative and began scolding him: "You know you are on the wrong side of town. You have nerve to sit here in a Hispanic area and let them do that to YOUR people. You say you want to give jobs to people who don't want the prison here—your OWN people. And you support these gringos. You go along with them after the way we have been treated. You want to dump everything on us!" The representative made a feeble attempt to explain that he was from San Diego, where the community had willingly accepted a large prison. As she walked away, two women who had been listening to the exchange cheered, "Give it to him, Dolores!" Dolores expressed satisfaction that her efforts deterred the man from attending meetings because she never saw him again. The job fair ended in chaos, the intention of the demonstration achieved.

Continuity and Change:
New Activities in the Public Sphere

The women's accounts illustrate how the struggle to mobilize a community and to sustain the mobilization is also played out within the family. Core activists tell about personal change and a new sense of entitlement to speak for the community. But at the same time that women assert themselves in public forums, children and husbands may resent the time and energies they spend on activism. An environmentalists' support group, the Citizens Clearing House for Hazardous Wastes, has recognized that family conflicts and tensions are common among activists and has prepared materials that suggest ways of managing such stresses. These suggest that women involve their children and husbands as much as possible.[10] The women in MELA were unaware of the suggestions, but like other women who are environmental activists, they have found ways to manage sources of potential household conflict.

Personal Empowerment

For one of the core activists, speaking in front of people or to the media was particularly intimidating. Her previous work in the community had centered on parish work, and she recounted her initial apprehensions:

> I was afraid to get involved. I didn't know what was going to come out of this, and I hesitated at first. Right after we started, Father John came up to me and told me, "I want you to be a spokesperson." I said, "Oh, no, I don't know what I am going to say." I was nervous. I am surprised I didn't have a nervous breakdown then. Every time we used to get in front of the TV cameras and even

interviews like this, I used to sit there and I could feel myself shaking. But as time went on, I started getting used to it.And this is what I have noticed with a lot of them [other women activists]. They were afraid to speak up and say anything. And now, with this prison issue, a lot of them have come out and come forward and given their opinions. Everybody used to be real "quiet like."

She also recounted a situation that brought all her fears to a climax. She confronted and resolved them as follows:

When I first started working with the coalition, Channel 13 called me up and said they wanted to interview me, and I said OK. Then I started getting nervous. So I called Father John and told him, "You better get over here right away." He said, "Don't worry, don't worry, you can handle it by yourself." Then Channel 13 called me back and said they were going to interview another person, someone I had never heard of, and asked if it was OK if he came to my house. And I said OK again. Then I began thinking, What if this guy is for the prison? What am I going to do? And I was so nervous, and I thought, I know what I am going to do!

Since the meeting was taking place in her home, she reasoned that she was entitled to order any troublemakers out of her domain.

If this man tells me anything, I am just going to chase him out of my house. That is what I am going to do! All these thoughts were going through my head. Then Channel 13 walked into my house followed by six men I had never met. And I thought, Oh, my God, what did I get myself into? I kept saying to myself, If they get smart with me, I am throwing them *all* out!

In fact, the situation proved to be neither confrontational nor threatening when the men were introduced as other members of the coalition. This woman confronted an anxiety-laden situation by relying on her sense of control within her home and family—a traditional source of authority for women—and transforming that control into the courage to express a political position before a public audience in one of the largest metropolitan areas in the nation.

Between Home and Community: Lobbying in Sacramento

The summer of 1986 was one of great legislative and community activity around Senate Bill 904, which would authorize $31 million for the initial costs of the 1,750–inmate prison. The bill was expected to pass the Senate easily.[11] The first week of July 1986, MELA members traveled to Sacramento on chartered buses. Hundreds of women marched with signs reading, "Our children need schools, not prisons—MELA." They also lobbied representatives.[12]

As the issue was debated, about two hundred members of MELA wearing white bandannas converged on the capital. It was clear that the strong show of community opposition to the prison had a major impact on the Senate debate. The governor's administrative aides tried to delay the vote until the following week, hoping the Eastside residents would have left Sacramento by then. But Democratic senator David Roberti convinced Republican senator Robert Presley to bring the bill to a vote. Partly at issue was the environmental impact report; Senator Presley assured the legislators that the EIR would be completed once the land for the prison had been purchased.

MELA held up signs chiding Senator Richard Polanco, the newly elected Eastside representative, for casting the vote that released the bill from the assembly committee. Passage had been all but assumed, but that day the Senate reversed itself and rejected the plan to build the prison in East Los Angeles by a four-vote margin.[13] The Senate now rejected the bill that it had passed 35–0 and then sent to a Senate-Assembly conference committee in 1985. Surprised by the Senate's vote, Deukmejian offered a compromise to sway the senators, agreeing to a limited environmental impact report to be completed before the purchase of land for the prison.[14] The Senate voted down the bill a second time in as many weeks. Democrats cast all the opposing votes, with Republicans providing all the votes in favor. The governor was stunned by the rejection. According to news sources, he had underestimated the effect of strong lobbying efforts by Latino organizations. Several senators were up for reelection, and they feared antagonizing the Mexican American community and had voted against the bill.[15] In 1987 the legislature reached a compromise and passed a bill authorizing two prisons to be built, but challenges to the environmental impact report and legislative debates over the funds for prison construction further stalled the start of construction.[16] The compromise made by Governor Deukmejian resulted from the concerted efforts of Latino legislators, grassroots community pressure, and formal challenges to regulatory procedures.

The newspapers reported the legislative debates and maneuvers. Unseen by the media were the practical organizing concerns with which women had to contend. Meeting places and demonstration times had to be planned, keeping in mind the household and family responsibilities of everyone concerned. While all community activists must sort out the logistics of organizing, these are often not recognized as intertwined with family concerns. Dolores Duarte speaks about the importance of meeting places: "We [used to have] coalition meetings every Wednesday at the Occupational Center. Now we have them here [at Resurrection parish] because we found that a lot of the people wouldn't go because they didn't have transportation. Only the members of the Chamber of Commerce would come. A lot of our ladies get around by using their bus passes. Now more of the people come because they can walk to the church."

The women's demonstrations in Sacramento also represented financial and personal sacrifices. The cost of airfare was out of the question for working class women who live in a community where the median annual family income is under fifteen thousand dollars. To minimize transportation costs and involve the greatest number of people, buses were chartered. The next concern was food and lodging. When approximately 160 people travel nine hours by bus, logistics and costs escalate.

Resurrection parish held a large breakfast to help pay for the hotel rooms when the demonstrators went to Sacramento. People also donated food for the women to take on the bus rides. According to one of the women went,

> I was even surprised that some of the women from Mexico came on the bus trips to Sacramento. I know them from around here, and I know how there husbands are . . . very *celosos* [jealous]. They said, "Tengo que cargar a los niños" [I have to bring my children]. And we did not reject children on those trips because we were fighting for them and we wanted them to see what we were fighting for. We made sure they got us a motel that had a pool for the kids.

I asked, if their husbands were that jealous, how the women managed to get away for a weekend trip alone. Several women speculated that the husbands accepted the women's trips because they had come to the marches and were well informed about the seriousness of the issue. The political work of core activists in Mothers of East Los Angeles generated personal changes in the activists themselves as well as in the community. However, according to the accounts of both women and men, household and domestic relations changed very little. Core activists are recognized as grassroots community leaders. They have acquired public visibility; they are the focus of many newspaper interviews and popular magazine articles.[17] Now they are sought out by other organizations—parent education projects, such as the one sponsored by the Mexican American Legal Defense and Education Fund (MALDEF, a national organization established to pursue civil rights litigation and focused on the Latino community), and environmental groups such as Greenpeace—and by local political representatives.

"The women are carrying the flag for the family"

Far from what I expected and some other studies suggest, it appears that women activists kept pace with household duties most of the time. Juana Gutiérrez, one of the most active leaders in MELA, said she had time for all her housework: "I clean my house, I babysit for my grandchildren and other kids, and take care of my block because I am captain of the Neighborhood Watch program [laughing]—a lot of *metiche*." (*Metiche* is colloquial for someone who knows everyone else's business, from the Spanish verb *meter*, to meddle.)

There were times when she left things on the stove if someone called her outside, but her husband, Ricardo, agreed she managed to do it all: "She does her housework before she goes out there. She always does both things. I am so used to it that it just seems natural. I don't think it is anything out of the ordinary."

Ricardo Gutiérrez elaborated on how Juana's activism fits comfortably into the household routines: "See, we started when our kids were very young. We have always been involved with their education. To us education is the main thing. It is going to allow them to live on their own and have no one manipulate them. So it does not bother me that she goes out there and demonstrates. In fact, she tells me when she is on TV or the radio, and as soon as we come in we turn on the TV and tape it."

Ricardo's conception of his own family unit does not violate what he sees as conventional:

> The mother in a Latino community is the head of the household and the man is the supplier . . . but the woman runs the whole show. She is the one that takes care of the kids, she is the one that goes here and there whenever something happens to the kids when they are in school. The macho image is a little different when you put it into practice. Sure, she does not do anything against my will. We always talk about it and then she goes ahead and does it. She has always been vociferous; maybe that is why we have stayed together so long.

According to Ricardo, the women do what the men have wanted to do all along: "They are carrying the flag for the family." But because the men work during the day, they are unable to attend hearings and meetings. Most of the women attending the daytime hearings did not work outside the home. However, their children's schedules dictated when they could leave in the morning and what time they had to be home in the afternoon. As one woman observed, "They [most of the women who go to marches] are very concerned about their children. Say, if we go downtown and have a march, we can have it anytime when the children are in school. But if it is between 11:30 and 1:30, they can't go. If it is before 8:30, they can't go. In the evening the kids are out of school, and they have them with them."

At critical points, grassroots community activism requires many meetings and phone calls, and much door-to-door communication—all very labor-intensive work. In order to preserve domestic harmony, the core activists must creatively integrate family members into their community activities. I asked Erlinda Robles how her husband, Valentín, felt about her activism, and she replied quite openly:

My husband doesn't like getting involved, but he takes me because he knows I like it. Sometimes we would have two or three meetings a week. And my husband would say, "Why are you doing so much? It is really getting out of hand." But he is very supportive. Once he gets there, he enjoys it and he starts in arguing too! See, it's just that he is not used to it. He couldn't believe things happened the way that they do. He was in the Navy twenty years, and they brainwashed him that none of the politicians could do wrong. So he has come a long way. Now he comes home and parks the car out front and asks me, "Well, where are we going tonight?"

Whether men are too tired to attend meetings or see community activism as the work of women is not evident. But the fact that women who are core activists were not working for wages did allow them some flexibility in organizing their days. Valentín Robles, Erlinda's husband, explained his sentiments about MELA: "I'm part of the coalition . . .all I can do is back my wife up. I can't be a Mother of East L.A. since I'm a man. They should be in control. They have started this fight. I believe that no one priest or one man should be in charge" (quoted in Gutiérrez 1994, 231).

New Community Issues: Environmental Justice

As thousands of residents became politicized in the process of organizing against the prison, they learned about other undesirable projects planned for their community. Some felt they should concentrate on the prison issue rather than "spread themselves too thin." Nevertheless, when Lucille Roybal-Allard informed them of a proposed toxic waste incinerator to be built in the industrial city of Vernon, MELA decided they should fight it. Father Moretta supported them.

While the fight against the prison engaged other Latino groups on the basis of ethnic and class identity, few if any groups of other ethnic backgrounds joined the grassroots battle. But when the women decided to oppose an oil pipeline and a toxic waste incinerator, they began linking up with other environmental groups, particularly those calling for environmental justice. The environmental-justice movement exposed the racism inherent in the pattern of placing toxic waste sites in low-income minority communities. The pattern holds throughout the state and country: three out of five African Americans and Latinos live near toxic waste sites, and three of the five largest hazardous waste landfills are in communities with at least 80 percent minority populations (Sánchez 1988,

13). Greenpeace joined in at some of the meetings and provided testimony at the hearings.

The Oil Pipeline

MELA joined with another local group, the Coalition against the Pipeline, when oil companies proposed a pipeline to carry oil from offshore rigs at Santa Barbara, a wealthy coastal resort ninety miles north of Los Angeles, to the port of Long Beach, forty-five miles south of Los Angeles. The pipeline, to be located only three feet underground, would be routed close to many schools, presenting a safety problem in the event of a gas leak. Further upsetting residents, the proposed route detoured into East Los Angeles, bypassing affluent white coastal cities such as Pacific Palisades (Russell 1989a).

MELA noted that the detour around the Westside presumed the political vulnerability of the Eastside. At one community meeting, for example, representatives of several oil companies sought support for running the oil pipeline through the center of East Los Angeles. The exchange between the women in the audience and the company representative was heated, as women asked questions about the chosen route for the pipeline.

"Is it going through Cielito Lindo" (President Reagan's ranch)? The oil representative answered, "No." Another woman stood and asked, "Why not place it along the coastline?" Without thinking, the representative responded, "Oh, no! If it burst, it would endanger the marine life." The woman retorted, "You value the marine life more than human beings?" The man's face reddened with anger, and the hearing disintegrated into angry chanting. The proposal was quickly defeated. But one of the women acknowledged that it was not solely their opposition that brought about the defeat: "We won because the Westside was opposed to it, so we united with them. You know there are a lot of attorneys who live here, and they also questioned the representative. Believe me, no way is justice blind."

As they took on other issues, the women of MELA began meeting community activists from other sectors of Los Angeles. One woman commented on the issue of aligning with other groups.

And do you know we have been approached by other groups? [She lowered her voice for emphasis.] You know that Pacific Palisades group asked for our backing? But what they did, they sent their powerful lobbyist that they pay thousands of dollars to get our support against the drilling in Pacific Palisades. So what we did was tell them to send their grassroots people, not their lobbyist. We're suspicious. We don't want to talk to a high-salaried lobbyist; we are humble people. We did our own lobbying. Twice in one week we traveled on buses to Sacramento [to lobby against the prison].

The contrast between the often-tedious and labor-intensive work of mobilizing people at the grassroots level and the paid work of a "high-salaried lobbyist" represents a point of pride and integrity, not a deficiency or a source of shame. If the two groups were to construct a coalition, they would have to communicate on equal terms.

The Toxic Waste Incinerator

Soon after the defeat of the pipeline, Lucille Roybal-Allard, assisted by her field representative, Miguel Mendívil, notified MELA that the small industrial city of Vernon, three miles south of downtown and on the border of Boyle Heights, had granted permits to one of the first entirely commercial hazardous waste incinerators proposed for California. While the city of Vernon, with a population up from ninety in 1980 to 150 in 1990, constituted the smallest city in the county, 51,000 people work there daily (Pitt and Pitt 1997: 927). The smaller residential population and the dominance of industry result in city council decisions that favor industrial development. The incinerator would operate twenty-four hours a day and burn 125,000 pounds of waste daily. As with the prison site selection, no environmental impact report had been completed. Regulatory agencies at each level—the Southern California Air Quality and Management District (SCAQMD) at the regional level, and the California Department of Health Services (DHS) at the state level, and the Environmental Protection Agency (EPA) at the national level—had granted permits for the incinerator without requiring an environmental impact report (Russell 1989b).

Governor Deukmejian and the DHS argued that any health effects would be mimimal bcause no residential communities were close enough to the incinerator to be at risk (Russell 1989a). The company argued that conducting an EIR would increase their costs and delay construction. Opponents of the incinerator, including the *Los Angeles Times*, emphasized the dangers of locating the incinerator within blocks of dozens of food processing plants, including the Leslie Salt Company, across the street, and the Oscar Meyer and Farmer John meat companies, a few blocks away. Residents emphasized that the incinerator would worsen the already compromised air quality of the entire county and set a dangerous precedent throughout California.[18]

After opponents had collected more than four thousand petition signatures and staged marches and rallies at the Vernon site, the city of Los Angeles, MELA, and Assemblywoman Roybal-Allard filed suit against the DHS for approving the project. Further investigation revealed that the operator had a poor safety record and a long history of safety violations at its other facilities. Environmental groups such as Greenpeace supported the demonstrations and invited MELA to support other working class communities confronting environmental threats. In 1988 MELA members traveled to Casmalia, 150 miles north of Los Angeles, to join in a demonstration for the closing of a toxic dump site. They also visited Kettleman City, which was also fighting a toxic waste incinerator. Later that same year, grassroots groups from small northern California cities with large minority populations—Kettleman, McFarland, Casmalia, Richmond—joined the march led by MELA in opposition to the toxic waste incinerator (Christup and Schaeffer 1990, 14).

In 1991 the company abandoned the incinerator project, stating that the process had proceeded smothly until the community was alerted. Company representatives charged that political pressure had unraveled the six-year-old deal and that "interminable law suits led to their decision."[19] As a result of the community struggle, Assembly Bill 58 (Roybal-Allard), which provides all Californians with the minimum protection of an environmental impact report before the construction of hazardous waste incinerators, was signed into law. But the law's effectiveness relies on a watchful community network.

Juana Gutiérrez, along with some of the other women who formed the core group of activists, has taken the lead as a spokesperson on Eastside community issues. She is now invited to speak at conferences, demonstrations, and community meetings. While she does not see herself as political, she expresses herself forcefully as an advocate for social justice and the rights of the Latino community. She once commented, "I don't consider myself political. I'm just someone looking out for the community, for the youth . . .on the side of justice" (quoted in Gutiérrez 1990, 223). In August 1990, as a representative of the Mothers of East Los Angeles, Santa Isabel (MELA-SI), Juana spoke at the twenty-year commemoration of the Chicano Moratorium march against the war in Viet Nam.

Madres del Este de Los Angeles, Santa Isabel (MELA-SI)

In 1990, after establishing considerable community presence and a reputation for championing community causes, the Mothers of East Los Angeles split into two separate groups, generally along parish lines. Some confusion developed as to the reasons for the split and the relationship between the two groups. The separation occurred when women and some men began questioning who could decide which community issues to address, who was entitled to speak for the group, and the relationship of the pastor to the group.[20] One group continued to work with Resurrection parish and Father John Moretta. Juana Gutiérrez, a core member of MELA, established the second group at the adjacent parish of Santa Isabel. Because the split generated some confusion and tension, she wrote an open letter in a local newspaper to explain the groups' separate identities:

La señora Gutiérrez es una activista comunitaria de tiempo atrás, y su membresía con el grupo comunitario Mothers of East Los Angeles es relativa únicamente al grupo de Mothers of East Los Angeles que se reúne en la Parroquia de Santa Isabel. Este grupo no tiene presidente, pero sí un concilio de gobierno. Otros miembros de este concilio son Erlinda Robles de la Parroquia de Talpa, Lucilla Mendoza de la Parroquia de Dolores Mission, y Lucina Mendívil y Rosa Villaseñor también de la Parroquia Santa Isabel. . . . Los grupos Mothers of East Los Angeles de Santa Isabel y Resurrección, aunque tienen luchas en común, operan independientemente uno del otro.[21]

Mrs. Gutiérrez is a long-time community activist, and her membership in the community group Mothers of East Los Angeles is only related to the group of Mothers of East Los Angeles that meets at the parish of Santa Isabel. This group has no president, but it does have a governing council. Other members belonging to this council are Erlinda Robles from the parish of Talpa, Lucilla Mendoza from the parish of Dolores Mission, and Lucina Mendívil and Rosa Villaseñor, also from the parish of Santa Isabel. The Mothers of East Los Angeles groups from Santa Isabel and Resurrection, although they have common struggles, operate independently of one another.

At Resurrection parish the predominantly women's group continued to work closely with Frank Villalobos, an urban planner with a commitment to Eastside betterment, and Pastor John Moretta, who named and worked tirelessly with the first group.

After 1990 the newly formed Madres del Este de Los Angeles, Santa Isabel (MELA-SI) continued to attend community hearings on urban development issues that affected the Eastside, but the group developed a slightly different relationship with the pastor at Santa Isabel parish. The women keep the pastor informed of their activities, but they prefer a less direct relationship with him than the women have at Resurrection parish. Juana Gutiérrez continues to act as the spokesperson for MELA-SI. In 1992 she and other members developed the collaborative Water Conservation Project with the Metropolitan Water District, the Los Angeles Department of Water and Power, and Corporate Technologies Service International (CTSI). They offered free low-flush toilets and recycled old ones. The old toilets are crushed into a material that is mixed into the asphalt used to pave the streets. The joint effort allowed MELA-SI to generate funding to develop several community betterment programs.

In just one year the Water Conservation Project created twenty-seven employment opportunities, with medical coverage and salaries well beyond the poverty levels of many inner-city employment projects. The jobs were created during a national and (even more acute) state economic crisis, without any additional taxpayer foundation or government monies. MELA-SI's partnership with the Water Conservation Project also made possible other community endeavors, including a graffiti clean-up project run entirely by Eastside youth and a scholarship program for high school and college students.

During this period, Los Angeles County budget cutbacks led to drastic reductions in funding to clinics offering infant immunization and basic health care. Well aware of the dangers of the budget cuts, given that 75 percent of Eastside residents are uninsured, MELA-SI developed the Child Immunization Project in conjunction with the nearby White Memorial Hospital. MELA-SI coordinated a program that sent high school volunteers door to door to inform Eastside residents about the importance and availability of vaccinations and tuberculosis testing; they also offered free transportation to the hospital.

Discussion

What do these accounts tell about the dynamics of women's community activism in Eastside Los Angeles? First, assembly-woman Gloria Molina chose to seek grassroots mobilization in the face of a legislature and governor largely unresponsive to her concerns. The state violated procedures and disregarded the need for public information, so gaining widespread media attention provided a way to garner enough support to help disrupt, delay, and ultimately defeat the proposed prison and the toxic waste incinerator projects. The mid-1980s marked a turning point when Eastside residents developed a harmonious working relationship with their local elected representatives. The strong show of unity among residents complemented the efforts of elected officials who kept the residents informed of legislative developments. Women's success at community mobilization emanated from the daily face-to-face interactions that occur as they meet their social obligations to their families and construct the social networks that bind a community.

Second, the church, and particularly one Italian American pastor, Father John Moretta, centered the struggle, legitimated it for the entire community, and attracted media attention with the creation of Mothers of East Los Angeles. The group's image, as one woman described it, was at least initially one of "las abnegadas," the women in the white cotton scarves. As in other Latino working-class communities, the church continued to be a strategic place for the development of women's social and political networks and leadership skills, but individual parishes differ in their peceptions of and responses to community needs.

Third, although the women initially followed Father Moretta's lead, eventually they refashioned and reinterpreted the social identity he gave them. They accepted the metaphor of "mother as protector" but rejected the self-sacrificing *las abnegadas* image by gradually "losing" the white scarves Father Moretta had given them. The women also redefined mother to mean anyone who "does for" children. Family became a metaphor for community, and community identity was closely tied to ethnic identity or *la raza*. The women reinterpreted their identity within existing power relationships, including the church and the family, showing how gendered identities may constitute a source of authority as well as a source of limitation.

Fourth, women asserted and manipulated their ethnic identity through language and the symbols they used as oppositional tools. Instead of being shamed by lack of English facility, they demanded bilingual presentations. They successfully opposed institutional practices that keep limited English speakers in the periphery of active citizenship. Relying on the patience and acceptance of residents who were predominantly Spanish-speaking, some second-generation women struggled to communicate in Spanish. They called on ethnic identity and loyalty to berate state officials of Latino origin as "traitors." Extended family networks helped to widen opposition, as did ethnic networks that drew in Mexican Americans from other communities and socioeconomic groups.

The women used gender, ethnic, and class identities to understand the political situation and to question social injustice and the authority of the state. Women took on a public identity and became personally empowered to speak about community issues. According to their accounts, their activism represented an extra job and did not challenge the domestic relations and division of labor in the home. They redefined themselves in ways that incorporated their family and traditions. The victories over the proposed prison and the toxic waste incinerator now represent much more than success on isolated issues; they symbolize the Eastsiders' pride and willingness to struggle and successfully defend the quality of life in their community.

SIX

Becoming an Activist in
Monterey Park
"The Elementary School Kids Are Still
Too Young to Defend Themselves"

Gently rolling hills and curving streets lined with large, well-tended, single-family stucco homes framed by conventionally landscaped lawns and trimmed shrubs typify Monterey Park. The Highlands residential tract was built in the 1950s by a developer who donated land for a combination elementary school and park, the Monterey Highlands Elementary School. A daytime visitor to the area will probably find a few Asian American children playing outside the only town houses in the neighborhood. Gardeners' trucks filled with lawn mowers and other equipment rumble down from the tranquil hills. This multi-ethnic neighborhood is now predominantly Asian—some Chinese Americans and Japanese Americans, and many new Chinese immigrants from Hong Kong, Taiwan, and the People's Republic of China—and there are also Mexican Americans and Anglos.

In February 1988, an inconspicuous-looking white building on Garvey and Casuda Canyon, technically in Alhambra but bordering Monterey Park, opened as a state parole office. Over a thousand parolees were assigned to meet the conditions of their release from prison by visiting the Alhambra site for counseling and drug testing, and the office began to be visited by an average of fifty parolees daily. Meanwhile, the high school bus continued to stop directly in front of the office, and Monterey Highlands schoolchildren continued to purchase candy at the Hi-Ho Market across the street. Then, over the next few months, residents began noticing men loitering outside the building and panhandling at the market.

In early July the brutal beating and robbery of a woman living in the Highlands jarred the tranquil neighborhood. An investigating police officer remarked that he would check the description of the assailants with the "local parole office." The discovery of the parole office prompted Kate Kariya, the mother of school-age children, to begin asking questions. Annie Rodríguez, who had raised her daughter in the area, joined her, and they began a door-to-door information campaign that led to an unusually large public meeting. Over 250 people packed city hall, about 40 of them loosely organized under the name of Concerned Parents and Residents of Monterey Park.[1] Flyers announcing meetings listed four women's names and phone numbers.

Residents learned that no regulations governed the siting of a parole office and that they would have to lobby state officials to have the office relocated. After listening to two hours of testimony by residents, the city council formally resolved to take action, and shortly thereafter sent city officials to Sacramento to present evidence of increased crime in each community that surrounded the parole office.[2] City representatives met in Sacramento with State Senator Joseph Montoya and Assemblyman Charles Calderón, who represented the Monterey Park area. They presented petitions with thousands of signatures and a video of residents' testimony. However, the Department of Corrections (DOC) denied any connection between the parole office and increased crime in the area, and indeed no direct link could be made. Parole office representatives argued that parolees came from within five miles of the office, but residents had discovered that less than 10 percent of the parolees resided in Monterey Park. Most lived in the nearby city of Pasadena, which had no parole office.[3] The DOC agreed to work on interim solutions by sending a team to the office and forming an advisory committee composed of residents, city officials, and DOC representatives.

A concern for family safety brought community members together across divisions of ethnicity and race as well as between immigrants and U.S.-born residents. But the particular contributions of women to the community opposition complicate any simple, ungendered notion of family-based opposition. Women and men worked together, but their activities to relocate the parole office differed. The gendered division of work raises several questions. First, how did women's observations become "testimony" against the parole office? Second, how did women come to constitute the majority in a city-sanctioned advisory board that was chaired by two men? Third, how did women perceive the gendered division of tasks? The answers to these questions illustrate the significance of gender identity in community activism.

Women's Observations as "Testimony"

After the Concerned Parents and Residents group distributed a thousand flyers in the Highlands area, hundreds of people attended subsequent city council meetings as well as two meetings that were held at the Highlands Elementary School. While both women and men attended the meetings and spoke about disturbing events in the neighborhood, more women spoke than men. As mothers, women are typically responsible for the household shopping and for transporting children to school and to extracurricular activities. While not all women activists in Monterey Park were currently raising children, they still performed most of the household-related activities even if they worked outside the home, as is typical for women throughout the nation.[4] Where there is a threat of violence, their responsibility for children sensitizes them to observe their surroundings carefully and monitor the neighborhood closely. Their perceptions about who does not "belong" arise from a class and community identity. Throughout the three-year campaign against the parole office, local newspaper accounts identified women as the unofficial anti-parole office community organizers.[5]

DOC representatives adamantly denied any connection with crime in the neighborhood and asserted that parolees were unlikely to commit crimes in the vicinity of a parole office. But residents began socially constructing the way the parole office negatively affected the community, and the arguments relied heavily on women's observations.

Most of the specific references to "strange people" or unusual occurrences in the Highlands neighborhood, later attributed to the parole-office clientele, originated either from a woman's observations or a woman's experience. Sandra Aguirre, a Mexican American who lives about a block from the parole office, nodded vigorously as she described "strange people" hanging around the neighborhood market: "All of a sudden at the Hi-Ho Market, I go there a lot, I began to see [she hesitates as she searches for the correct words] . . . oh, men who, you know . . . without their shirts on, tattoos on their arms. They just looked rougher. And, I thought, where are these people coming from? They don't look like they could afford it here."

Sandra Aguirre's description omitted the ethnicity of the men. Her description focused instead on personal appearances that conveyed to her that they were not middle class. Since homes in the Highlands sell for over three hundred thousand dollars, she concluded that they were not residents and did not belong. She expressed her own middle-class community identity by designating the tattooed men who congregated at the market as outsiders.[6]

Sandra's awareness of people who seemed not to belong was supported by another woman, who noted "well-dressed black men" in the market: "You know there are very few blacks in Monterey Park, or otherwise it wouldn't stand out. Two well-dressed black men were in the market, and I asked [one], 'Where do you work?' He said, 'Right across the street.' I asked him what it was, and he told me: a parole office!" This woman immediately called city hall and the police department demanding to know what was going on. Her inquiries were sparked by her perception of the men as unlikely residents, given her image of the community's identity and its ethnic and racial composition. Then, noting the men's attire— suits and ties—she assumed they must be working in some nearby offices.

At public meetings women and men reported undesirable activities they believed were related to the men seeking parole services. For the first time since she lived in the area, Cindy Yee found broken beer bottles in the unfenced Highlands school yard, which serves as a park for adults after school hours. Peggy Moody, a parole advisory board representative from Alhambra, discovered sleeping bags hidden under some bushes near her home. Vince Ramírez told about how a parolee had approached his teenage daughter, who was waiting for a schoolbus, and insisted that she accept a ride from him. The girl refused.

A Concerned Parents and Residents Committee, composed primarily of residents from the Highlands area of Monterey Park, formed a few days after the assault. Media coverage about the campaign credits Annie Rodríguez, Kate Kariya, and Rosemary López for doing the most to mobilize the Monterey Highlands community. These women drew on their ties to existing community networks, including Neighborhood Watch groups, family networks, the PTA, and Girl and Boy Scouts. Rosemary López, co-chair of the PTA, referred to "branches in the community": "Annie would be at the top. Then you have your branches. Annie has her community connections with Alhambra, I have my connection to the PTA, and Cindy Yee knows about the PTA and the way City Hall works."

The Significance of Language

Language barriers were the main obstacle to community mobilization confronted by the multi-ethnic, U.S.-born group of women. Using various strategies, they were able to communicate the undesirability of the office to at least some new Chinese immigrants. The experiences of the women differed but illustrate how they worked to overcome communication problems and how their door-to-door work led to a different perception of the new immigrant participation than that held by men who helped in other ways but did not do most of the face-to-face work. Women's perceptions are significant in showing that mobilization is possible even in a community with substantial numbers of new immigrants.

Women's perceptions of the participation of new Chinese immigrants differed according to the success of their various outreach strategies. An Anglo woman who gathered many signatures on petitions opposing the parole office had difficulty communicating with new Chinese immigrants:

> Well, if it were a second- or third-generation [person], the reaction was very favorable. But I was able to tell, just by going door to door, where the newer immigrants lived just from the shoes outside the door. Then there was the language problem. I couldn't get through to them. So if I would come to a house and I would see the shoes outside the door, I wouldn't bother to ask them to sign because I know that they are very reluctant to sign anything.

I also walked door to door in Monterey Park one afternoon to distribute invitations to a Neighborhood Watch meeting. Predictably, shoes outside the door—sometimes as many as five pairs ranging from children's to adult sizes—indicated a Chinese speaking family. Since I was walking with a bilingual Chinese graduate student, without exception we were warmly received and invited inside the homes to discuss the purpose of the meeting. Had I not been with someone fluently bilingual, I too would have been apprehensive about approaching the homes with shoes on the porch.

Dorothy Donath and Peggy Moody, Anglo women, walked door-to-door to collect signatures on petitions and invite people to meetings in their homes. Knowing that some of her neighbors were new Chinese immigrants, Peggy asked her son to work up a flyer. He entered a newspaper article on his computer, then added a small graphic of a gun with a dotted line representing a bullet moving toward a man standing in its path, arms outstretched over his head as if being robbed. The intent was to suggest that the parole office would bring violent people into the neighborhood. She described how they approached these neighbors:

> First, we would go to the door, and when they didn't speak English right away, we would ask does anybody speak English here? Then we would show them the flyers and point to the little man with the gun and say this could happen to you! We would use sign language too. They all signed the petition. But they don't come to our meetings.

The two women attest that the flyer "did the trick"; only two people refused to sign the petition. The failure to get Chinese residents to attend a meeting in a private home was solved by the women in Monterey Park. They held meetings at the Highlands Elementary School.

The women from Monterey Park Highlands carried a petition translated into Chinese. When they encountered someone who seemed to be Chinese speaking, they produced the Chinese version of the petition, which the person usually signed. I asked Annie if immigrants had responded to her efforts to mobilize. She answered, "In the Neighborhood Watch meetings at the school, they were cautious but they did come to the meetings. They asked a lot of questions. They wanted to know who the people were who were going to the parole office. We did have about a third new immigrants at our meeting at the school. Of course, we handed out a thousand flyers."

Using the elementary school as a base, Concerned Parents and Residents launched a letter-writing campaign among the elementary school children. The co-chair of the PTA, Rosemary López, explained that the letters were a strategy to get attention from officials in Sacamento. They would underscore the proximity of the parole office to the elementary school and reinforce that the opposition was based on concern for children's safety:

We felt that we needed some visibility and impact. The parents that I spoke with thought it was a good idea to get the children involved. So, I contacted the principal of the school and the board members and sent out a newsletter to all the parents to see if they wanted their children to be involved in the letter-writing campaign after school. It was pretty successful. I would say about 120 kids showed up.

We communicated with some new immigrants because we had about ten percent who were kids who seemed to be immigrant. Usually, you can tell because the child does not speak that well. And we had to help them a lot with the letters.

Two months after the community mobilized, through announcements in the local newspapers, city representatives invited residents to call the city manager if they were interested in participating on the official Citizens Advisory Board. The cities appointed a thirteen-member advisory board, later expanded, after considering those who applied and by inviting the captains of Neighborhood Watch groups in the affected communities of Monterey Park and Alhambra.[7] I asked Marijune Wissman, a core activist from Alhambra, how the Alhambra representatives happened to be all women. She explained, "The women from Alhambra are mostly retired. The Monterey Park representatives are younger, but they weren't working then. Now, some of them that no longer attend went back to work . . . and they have kids." Marijune went on to add that it seemed more women had continued attending the meetings than men:

> At the first meetings that we had in Monterey Park, it seemed that there were more men. But since then, it seems there are more women. Now, most of the Alhambra block captains are women. And, I think that they were active from the PTA days. I think as time went on, the women took over. When school started, I think the PTA in the Highlands jumped in and helped, and it seemed more women were involved.

These observations show the interconnections of women's responsibilities as mothers, the lasting networks they establish through the routine work of mothering, and how the networks may be activated when needed. Women's participation in wage labor also shapes how they pursue the work of community activism.

Men perceived immigrants as less responsive to the community effort against the parole office than did women. The principal of Highlands Elementary School, Pat Carroll, perceived Asian immigrant participation as minimal:

> New immigrants were not really very involved in this. This is a middle-class community. Of course some of the residents are from Hong Kong and Taiwan, but many of the Asians who live here are second and third generation.

For example, Cindy Yee and Ron Hirosawa were very in-volved. I am not saying that new immigrants were not in-terested, but maybe the language barrier precluded their involvement.

He went on to say he felt the new immigrants were just begin-ning to get involved. A man who went to the initial Concerned Parents and Residents meetings also felt the Chinese immi-grants showed little support for the community efforts.

"Women Do the Detail Work"

The gender balance of residents attending parole advisory board meetings was about two women for every man. Never-theless, the group selected a Japanese American man to chair the board. One woman felt "we needed a figurehead," and a man explained, "it was either Ron Hirosawa or me because we had the most experience with this kind of thing" (chairing meetings).

Marijune Wissmann felt Ron was the best choice because of the way the women tended to digress from the issue: "It was kind of unanimous [choosing Ron as chair]. We just sort of ap-pointed him. He is a teacher at a school in L.A., and he is very bright and vocal and he kind of pulls us together. We get to talking and gossiping and we kind of get off the subject, and he pulls us back on the subject. You know how women are . . . we can go in all directions" (laughing softly). From her per-spective, the women needed someone to manage and direct them. Rosemary López agreed with this perception. However, she added that women seemed to have a different style of do-ing community work: "The women have the patience. And generally that is what it takes to sit down, take your time, and go more into detail work like calling, doing the footwork, writing down everything and following up. It's time consuming and I think it takes patience." She compared the ways women and men contributed to the work of the advisory board:

Men would rather just go there and make their statements. And that's why we have Ron there [as chair]. Because we need somebody to make our statements who will be heard. And of course he is vocal. So we are happy that he is our spokesman, and he's involved enough to be there. His role is figurehead, and he also steers the group when he sees us going off track. A lot of times I guess women try to get picky, and so you have to have that combination of the two.

There is a perception that men and women approach their work differently as well as take on different kinds of work. As the women see it, men come to make their statements and be heard. Women care take of the "detail" work that requires patience and sustained attention. They discuss these differences, but they make no reference to any hierarchal relationship between them. It is stated matter of factly that this is how things are.

Not so surprisingly, the gendered division of labor in the Monterey Park community mobilization effort reflects the participants' segregation in the workforce. Although there has been change, women continue to be concentrated in sex-segregated fields. The women who mobilized were white-collar workers. Marijune Wissmann, a retired legal secretary, recorded, transcribed, and distributed the proceedings of the parole advisory board's monthly meetings. She did so with meticulous care, providing a well-documented record of the conflict. Ron Hirosawa, a school principal, and later, Vince Ramírez, an engineer, chaired the meetings. Vince also developed a poster-size map to show city council members the proximity of the parole office to the Highlands neighborhood and the elementary school. Samuel Kiang, an engineer and lawyer and immigrant from Hong Kong, gained experience and recognition for his participation in the parole office conflict. He went on to win election to the city council in 1990. None of the women expressed an interest in seeking a position in city government.

Following the formation of the Citizens Advisory Board, some of the women stopped attending meetings, but they continued to participate in the neighborhood, waiting to activate letter-writing campaigns when the Concerned Parents and Residents committee decided to do so. Their continuing involvement preserved the group's base of neighborhood support and kept it from becoming the project of a few representatives of institutions such as the school, police department, and the DOC.

Multi-Cultural Consensus: "Enough Is Enough in East L.A."

In the multi-ethnic context of Monterey Park, with a large new Chinese immigrant population, of what significance is ethnic identity in mobilizing at the grassroots? Throughout the discussions, hearings, meetings, and one small demonstration of about forty residents, I never saw any display of ethnicity.

On one occasion, ethnic and inner-city childhood connections surfaced. A realtor hired by the cities of Monterey Park and Alhambra to search for an alternative site suggested the office be moved to East Los Angeles. Several members of the group who grew up in East L.A. objected, asserting that the Eastside had enough negative projects.

Annie Rodríguez told how members of the advisory group were split on the possibility of an East Los Angeles location:

> We told them not to ever do that again because it was a waste of time. Ron Hirosawa, Vince Ramírez, and Deborah Marshall and I all grew up in East L.A. Even in those years, you know the police were more abusive to Hispanics. We didn't have much say-so in the schools either. So we said, 'Enough is enough in East L.A.!'

Monterey Park residents indeed were defending their idea of a middle-class suburban quality of life. To that end, they worked with the city council to get the parole office moved out of their area. They did, however, have a sense of equity in the distribution of parole offices, contrary to the NIMBY argument. They objected to the parole office being moved to the Eastside, which already had several. Ten percent of the parolees resided in Monterey Park while most lived in Pasadena where there was no parole office.

A small demonstration outside the parole office also illustrated how the group chose not to assert an ethnic entity in their public statements. About forty-five people participated in the demonstration. All carried signs written in English and expressing concerns for family safety. Vince Ramírez carried a sign that read, "My daughter almost!" (The statement referred to several times when parolees insisted that his daughter accept a ride from them rather than take the bus.) A woman's sign read "Protect our children." Only one woman brought her children along. Councilwoman Judy Chu marched along with the city manager and the city treasurer. About four police officers stood outside the parole office observing the demonstrators while parole office representatives offered them a tray of donuts.

Class and Community Identity and Strategies

In 1990, almost two years after the DOC agreed to relocate the parole office, several of the activists who served on the parole advisory board began to feel that the DOC was not taking their concerns seriously. They discussed the non-disruptive tactics they had used and expressed a wish to "go all out and picket," but they felt constrained from doing so because their membership on the parole advisory board. The board included representatives from the parole office, the city manager, and usually two city council members, who generally discouraged any public demonstration of opposition and attempted to steer expressions of dissent toward nonconfrontational forms.

The disappointment expressed by the citizens who had worked diligently since September 1988 reflects their perception that "we did as we were told—we formed a Citizens Advisory Board and kept a low profile with the news media and didn't demonstrate or give interviews."[8] Now they faced frustration at the continued presence of the parole office and felt betrayed by the DOC. Having trusted the political system to be equitable, they also believed "following the rules" would allow them to convince the DOC that the parole office had been inappropriately placed too near a school and residential area and posed a danger to children and adults. Now, looking back on their strategies, they thought a more aggressive and less compliant response may have been a better choice.

Since a good number of the women who mobilized are the first generation to move into a suburban setting, they have few ties to what one Asian American man calls "high-powered people." They are middle-class people who moved from a working-class neighborhood into a suburban setting and carefully avoided "making waves," as one Mexican American woman put it.

In the early weeks of community mobilization, when they asserted public opposition, DOC representatives made public statements warning that the tactics could backfire. Jerry DiMaggio, the DOC regional administrator, frowned on the children's letter-writing campaign and was quoted in the *Los Angeles Times* as saying, "This was a low point when the PTA decided they would have kids draw pictures of people being strangled and stuff, with little notations saying 'Don't let this happen to me,' and mailed the whole package off to the governor." There was a polite debate among parole advisory group members over the kind of strategies to be utilized—confrontational and militant, or cooperative and civil. Two women felt that the composition of the advisory board, which met with representatives from the DOC, the police department, and other authority figures, constrained the use of the more militant strategies that might work better than the "conciliatory" approaches they pursued. "In the beginning," one woman said, "we wanted to picket and make a big deal out of it. The parole office people told us to keep it cool so we didn't stir up the people in Pasadena. We didn't, and they found out on their own [about a proposal to relocate the parole office to their community]. We listened to them and on hindsight, we should have stuck to our gut feeling, I mean go all the way."

The Alhambra City Council as well as the Department of Corrections representatives successfully convinced the group to be conciliatory. The Parole Advisory Board meetings were held at the Monterey Park city hall. Board members sat around a table, and the city always provided coffee, punch, and a plate of cookies at the back of the room. Meetings followed a regular format that included reports on the search for an alternative site and on crime statistics in the neighborhood. Once community members agreed to this strategy, they felt they confronted an impasse.

New Activities in the Public Sphere

As was the case for women in East Los Angeles, women in Monterey Park have extended themselves into the public sphere and in that sense redefined the boundaries of gender identity. While their household responsibilities have remained constant, they have become public figures in the community. After media coverage in the local newspapers, city council members and others in the community identify the core of women as "contact persons" in the Highlands neighborhood.

Only a few of the women's husbands regularly attended the parole advisory board meetings after the initial community-wide hearings. I asked one woman how her husband responded to her involvement. While he disapproved of the conciliatory tactics, he also objected when her involvement disrupted family time: "He would just listen and give his advice to do it with a bit of splash. But when they had meetings on Sunday evening, he would give me some negative feedback and say that's when we watch *Sixty Minutes*, and he saw it was interfering with family togetherness." She managed to get her children to help her fold flyers and pass them out, making it a kind of family activity, and she says her activism did not interfere with her household responsibilities. However, she no longer attended meetings, partly because of her husband's objections but mainly because she returned to working full-time.

After the Concerned Parents and Residents successfully ousted the parole office, the group dissolved. In 1993 another controversial proposal developed—a large card club that would promote gambling. The club was proposed for a working-class corner in Monterey Park, bordering East Los Angeles. Hundreds of people packed the Monterey Park city hall, overwhelmingly opposed to gambling (Horton 1995, 174–82). People held orange and black placards reading, "SAVE OUR NEIGHBORHOOD" (Ibid, 181). Representatives from East Los Angeles's United Neighborhood Organization (UNO) also adamantly opposed the card club. Several women distributed petitions through block committees that had been formed during the fight against the parole office. The women reactivated their neighborhood networks and gathered over a thousand signatures in a single week and defeated the project. And so the pattern of activating the networks resurfaced again in 1994 in an anti-billboard campaign (see Chapter Nine). Even though the women and men activists chose not to establish a formal community organization, they monitor issues and keep informed, reemerging under new names that target the concern.

The Monterey Park residents' struggle over the parole office shows how a perceived threat to family safety drew together a group of residents differing in ethnicity, race, and immigration status, but sharing a middle-class identity. Mexican Americans and Asian Americans expressed no specific ethnic identity in the mobilization process.

Once the undesirability of the parole office was established, largely through women's testimony, women mobilized by crossing ethnic boundaries. However, the strategies some of the women reluctantly accepted reflect the social history and political organization of the community. In the context of a middle-class, multi-ethnic community with a small and accessible city council, residents worked closely with local officials. They accepted the Citizens Advisory Board's definition of an appropriate strategy, tailored to avoid interfering with parole office activities. They heeded a warning to keep quiet, believing that enlarging the controversy would only hurt their chances of ousting the parole office. The strategy proved successful and confirmed the residents' confidence in their ability to control neighborhood conditions.

Becoming an Activist: Comparative Contexts

In Monterey Park and in Eastside Los Angeles, gender identity—women's social obligations to their families and community—prompts women to take a leading part in grassroots mobilization. They framed or legitimized their activism in terms of family interests; rather than challenge the social division of labor in the household, they added social activism to their own responsibilities.

In both communities women employed gender identity to legitimate their community involvement. The fact that they used a traditional private role such as motherhood to frame new activity that is public and political deserves scrutiny. They validated their community activism by making it an extension of the traditional work they already do. This allowed them to become involved without jeopardizing traditional domestic arrangements.

In general, some of the obstacles activists faced in the two communities and the strategies they used are similar. In both, women bridged gaps between established residents and immigrants. On the Eastside, however, this required bilingual and bicultural women of Mexican origin to engage with recently arrived Spanish-dominant Latino immigrants. In Monterey Park, a multi-ethnic group of U.S-born women found ways to overcome language differences to communicate with Chinese immigrants.

How do the strategies used by the two communities differ? In Eastside Los Angeles, there were countless collective actions and mass demonstrations. In Monterey Park residents met monthly with city officials and representatives from the DOC, an approach that they finally lost patience with. Then they chose to mobilize a "small demonstration to get their point across." As with the women in Eastside Los Angeles, they found it an exhilarating experience.

What were the differences between women's and men's work in the two groups? There was a gender division of labor in both communities. In Boyle Heights, the women readily credit a Catholic priest and a male urban planner for inspiring, forming, and guiding their eight-year resistance to the proposed state prison. In Monterey Park, women did the work of mobilizing, calling people to remind them of meetings, getting all to sign in at meetings, and transcribing the minutes from tape-recorded meetings. The chairs, however, were male, and the women perceived the men as "keeping them focused." One woman said this arrangement worked because women are competent at attending to the "detail work" of day-to-day communications and record keeping, which they carried out when the parole office was first becoming a contested issue. In the Concerned Parents and Residents Group as in Mothers of East Los Angeles, women participated in greater numbers than did men.

Women retained responsibility for the domestic sphere and did not directly challenge husbands to assume this work once they became active politically. However, they engaged their husbands and family in their activism and in essence co-opted them into the political enterprise, thereby avoiding conflict in domestic relations.

Even though men assumed the position of leadership at meetings, the work women did greatly determined the success or failure of community action. Women in each group speak of the knowledge they gained by mobilizing around a contested neighborhood issue that caused them to question and confront official decisions. Their observations led them into political involvements that revealed the shortcomings of government bureaucracies and the need for citizens to monitor them. They also saw the importance of their activism in forcing the state to respond to their sense of equity and justice. All have made momentous steps toward a sophisticated and multi-dimensional understanding of political mechanisms. They have become "public persons" and as such a new community resource.

In the low-income neighborhoods, women creatively transformed family networks, ethnic identity, and the shared history of an oppressed community into political resources. In the suburbs, where women's lives become more private and less explicitly "ethnic," women let go of some community conventions. Though less dramatic than the Eastside case, the Monterey Park controversy also made women aware of the power of their community networks.

SEVEN

Creating Community in Eastside Los Angeles
"We Have to Do It!"

The everyday work that women must do to care for their families ultimately helps create community—the "conditions necessary for life."[1] For many women, the community is both a living space and a work site. While most women desire congenial surroundings in which to meet their responsibilities, those who are core activists have developed successful strategies for shaping their environment.

How do they build the social resources for influencing the conditions in their community living space? What is the process by which they draw their neighbors into the enterprise and link family concerns to a wider network of resources? Their work influences conditions in their neighborhoods, but how does it affect household arrangements? Do husbands offer support, object to their wives' outside involvements, or join them in community work? For each family, the answers vary and are not predetermined. The outcomes depend in part on the ways women negotiate between two sets of social relations often perceived as separate.

As individual cases, the women's stories describe movement from household to neighborhood institutions, which continues for a few into electoral politics and public positions. Several women cite family responsibilities ("doing it for the kids") as the basis for their activism. In abstract terms, the types of work women do in the community are often conceptualized as an outcome: the reproduction of family. The theme "outcome" is useful for sorting out the women's work as a process crossing into different sets of social relations. What do their very daily activities mean in terms of social relations *beyond* family? Women's work often bridged distances between newcomers and established residents and between state resources and needs in community infrastructure.

Neighborhood Work: New Immigrants and Established Residents

Superficial consideration of the Latino origins of most Eastside Los Angeles residents (94 percent) might mistakenly lead one to expect homogeneity and a rapid integration of new immigrants. As Chapter Two discusses, however, Eastside Angelenos vary widely in a number of respects, among them length of residence in the United States, language use, occupation, home ownership, and income. One of the few community studies of social interactions between recent immigrants and U.S.-born Mexican Americans suggests that the two groups hold critical perceptions of each other.[2] The study found no automatic incorporation of new immigrants into the Chicano community; instead it noted an absence of regular interaction between the two groups.

Schools provide a setting where immigrants and U.S.-born

residents may come in daily contact with one another, if not interact directly. At Roosevelt High School, located in Boyle Heights, cliques of students habitually "hang around" particular pockets of the campus. English-speaking and immigrant Spanish-speaking students gather at opposite ends of the school grounds. The new immigrant students complain that the Mexican Americans call them pejorative names such as "wetbacks, *mojados*, T.J.'s, and *ranchos*."[3]

Do similar interactions occur among the adults of Eastside Los Angeles? The period between 1965 and 1980 marked one of the largest influxes of new Latino immigrants into Los Angeles County. Attitudes toward immigrants influence how women mobilize given that almost half of the over eight hundred thousand Latino residents in the city of Los Angeles were not citizens, according to the 1980 Census. Furthermore, immigrants who arrived after 1965 are also more likely to reside next to earlier (pre-1965) immigrants than to U.S.-born residents (García 1985).

Women who are active in the neighborhood react in different ways to the immigrants. They evince a sense of empathy but are also aware of difference. The newcomers are at once "the other" and the "self" as a faded reflection of the second generation's immigrant history. Mexicans call the second generation *pochos*. The term *pocho* literally means "faded" and is used colloquially to refer to U.S.-born Mexican Americans who are assimilated and therefore "faded" Mexicans.

"Here, There Is Something Happening All the Time!"

Rosa Villaseñor, a fifty-one-year-old woman of Cuban and Puerto Rican descent, rents a spacious three-bedroom apartment in a densely populated, privately owned 1950s-era housing tract called Wyvernwood.[4] A forty-year resident of East-side Los Angeles, she has spent twenty years living in Wy-vernwood. She has seen the renters in the housing complex change from a mix of ethnicities to become predominantly im-migrant Latinos.

The coping strategies used by these immigrants often vio-late what established residents see as the neighborhood norm. As a result of Rosa's concern for these transgressions, she has become acquainted with many new immigrants. They refer to her as "Doña Rosa," indicating respect for her as an influential person in the complex.[5]

Rosa, who is frank and outspoken, is recognized in the neigh-borhood. She sternly scolds those who offend neighborhood norms—adults who litter, youth who write graffiti on walls, and young men who race their cars through the small winding streets. Not one to mince her words, she says she thinks the new arrivals must be from the "ranches"—something akin to calling them "hicks"—and she admonishes them until they stop the disruptive behavior.[6] She recites her usual lecture to the unruly neighbors:

When they race through here I tell them, "A car is not a horse and it is not a mule. Someday you are going to kill somebody, so you better stop." They say "Ay, Doña, don't talk to us that way!" But they stop. I also threatened to make a citizen's arrest if I saw them in the street littering or doing worse things. But you know, I would never re-ally have the heart to call the cops on them. But I tell them "really mean" so they think I am serious!

She balances the harshness of her scolding by sharing informa-tion on health clinics and "help hotlines" that offer rape and drug information. When the neighbors need to know something, they call her. Rosa reflects rather philosophically about the activity just outside her doorway: "See, in this community, you go out the door and you see everybody. Even if they are no good, they are out there! [Laughing.] I think I would miss that. Here there is something happening all the time—it keeps me going!" Her husband, Frank, agrees about the problems of Wyvernwood and notes that Rosa's activism had helped improve conditions a bit. Then he adds that he had "not taken the opportunity to move in 1970 when he could afford it." Now, in his late fifties, he carefully considers the burden of a mortgage, a substantial financial obligation at his age. To compensate for the declining quality of life in the apartment complex, Rosa and an established immigrant woman from El Salvador worked together on neighborhood concerns. Sergeant Frank Hurtado, Neighborhood Watch liaison for the Eastside's Hollenbeck police station, calls them "his best activists."[7]

Rosa knows all her immediate neighbors and many other people throughout the complex, which houses more than a hundred residents. She has gone door-to-door to get signatures on a petition asking for police foot patrols. She acted immediately after the murder of a young boy by rival gang members.[8] Although the complex has become increasingly overcrowded within the last decade, it had a reputation for being relatively free of gang violence. She explains how she responded to the shock of the boy's murder: "I never felt the need to get involved in this neighborhood because it was so peaceful. But after the shooting, I said I have to do something. So every night at six o'clock after I made dinner, I would go from apartment to apartment to get people to sign the petitions." As Susser (1988) noted, working-class women take on activism as an "extra job." Rosa usually went out to gather signatures after she prepared dinner for her husband.[9]

She describes the strategies she used to convince the largely immigrant residents, many without citizenship documents, to sign a petition to bring in police foot patrols. Her bilingual fluency was crucial to her success in obtaining two hundred signatures. As she explained,

> It would take me about half an hour just to explain to the people. First, I would ask if they would want me to speak Spanish or English. They were scared of the gangs, of the police, or maybe, I thought, because they were doing something wrong. So a lot didn't want to sign. If they didn't sign I would go back the next day and tell them, "Si firma esta nota, no va a pasar nada." [Nothing will happen if you sign.] I would tell them, "La persona que no firma, es porque tiene miedo, como [que] está haciendo algo malo." [The person who does not sign must be afraid because he is doing something wrong.] Pero él que no está haciendo nada malo no tiene miedo!" [But if he isn't doing anything wrong, he won't be afraid.] [Rosa laughs at her high-pressure tactics.] See? And they would sign!

Rosa obtained the signatures by presenting arguments in a sequence that illustrates her perceptions of material conditions and social relations in the housing complex. She understands immigrants have many fears: fear of deportation, fear of becoming crime victims, and fear of family members committing crimes.

She addresses those fears by arguing that collective action will help. She has observed and confronted the teenage sons of some residents in the act of removing parts from stolen cars and selling them to other residents. Using this information, she reasoned with residents whose sons may have engaged in the activity that signing the petition would bring less "trouble" or "implication of wrong-doing" than refusing to sign.

Rosa's method represents one approach to managing acts of violence and crime in the immediate neighborhood.[10]

Rosa notes how crowded the complex has become and acknowledges that, given the cost of living, she understands why families "double and triple up." She knows of a case where three Latino families—six adults and five children—share the $650 monthly rent for one two-bedroom unit. While she speaks with empathy about their plight, she sees it as "no excuse" not to maintain the gardens and the apartments. She remarks that they make frequent trips across the border for weddings, baptisms, birthdays, and other family-related events. The frequent absences necessitated by what some have called binational families often lead to poor upkeep.

"¡Tantos Gatos! ¡Tantos Perros!–Like My Old Neighborhood!"

The neighborhood across Olympic Boulevard and one block north of the Wyvernwood housing complex differs in the dwelling styles, upkeep, and density. It is more typical of Boyle Heights. Small, neat, wood-framed, single-family homes line the street. Newer immigrants and established residents live side by side, but the residential density is lower than that in the Wyvernwood complex. The practices of some of the new Latino immigrants also invoke negative reactions among the longer-established women. With some exasperation in her voice, one woman complained, "Some of these [new immigrants] think they are living on a ranch over here. Sometimes all of a sudden in the morning when you are asleep, you hear roosters crowing, and then the roosters are always walking around the street."

But not everyone shares this woman's annoyance. I asked others how they felt about the roosters that are, in fact, often to be found walking casually down the middle of the asphalt street. Angie Flores answered by recalling the Mexican American and African American neighborhood of her youth:

> Well, some people say [about the new immigrants], "tantos perros, tantos gatos!" [Too many dogs, too many cats!] The roosters walk around here all the time. But I remember on Forty-first and Long Beach [in Southeast Los Angeles]—"El Hoyo," where I lived in the forties—they had roosters too. So I am used to that. As for the dogs, I don't need to have one because I can hear the neighbors' dogs barking at each house as someone walks down the street.

Angie switched from English to Spanish to convey other people's complaints about the new immigrants. Like many other second-generation Mexican American women living in Eastside Los Angeles, she sometimes mixes Spanish and English in a single sentence. Unlike some of her neighbors, she saw the barking dogs as an asset because they alerted her to the exact location of strangers walking down the block.

She emphasized that she had never seen "so much poverty" (before the late 1980s). Moved by what she saw, for a full year she assisted her parish priest's efforts to counsel undocumented workers regarding the Immigration Reform and Control Act of 1986 (IRCA). The sponsors of IRCA called it an amnesty law. Designed to gain control of U.S. borders, it legalized millions of undocumented workers who came to the United States before the cutoff date of January 1, 1982, and imposed harsh sanctions on employers who knowingly hire undocumented immigrants. The cutoff date was particularly punitive for the majority of Central American refugees, whose numbers increased sharply beginning in 1982.[11]

Angie tells of her work with immigrants:

> We started helping the people fill out forms. First it was
> only on Wednesdays from eight until twelve; then it was
> two days a week for about four months because people
> would keep coming and coming. We would take their
> names, addresses, whether they were married, and how
> many children. My *comadre* [godmother] lives across the
> street from the church, so she would keep the files in her
> house. In case someone gets picked up [by the Immigra-
> tion and Naturalization Service], he [the priest] would
> call my *comadre* and she could look up the card and
> vouch for them. Her husband just passed away, so she
> wants to keep active. Some would have only a place to
> pick up mail, and I thought maybe they didn't have
> homes. They were so afraid their families would be sepa-
> rated because some children were born here and some
> [were] born over there [Mexico]. I felt so sorry for them
> that I wanted to do what I could for the "illegals" and for
> the community.

Angie's account illustrates a view of recent immigrants as the
pobrecitos [poor ones], suggesting that she empathizes with the
problems of the undocumented immigrants. While she does
not lay blame on immigrants, she observed that the decline in
public services, such as the loss of the local post office, and the
declining quality of private businesses, such as supermarkets,[12] corresponded to the influx of new Mexican immigrants
and the exit of Jewish residents.

In communities where immigrants compose a large portion
of the population, successful grassroots mobilization must
overcome communication obstacles. In some instances, U.S.-

born Latinas or others who have resided on the Eastside for many decades share practical information about community resources and impart to immigrants the standards of community life in the neighborhood. Mexican American women working in the community use bilingual skills daily and say it enhances their Spanish fluency.

Community Needs and Community Resources

Women activists bridged the gap between perceived community needs and existing resources in two ways. First, their collective work helped provide books and equipment needed by the parochial schools their children attended. Second, women identified and communicated community needs to public officials responsible for allocating resources. In one case, achieving their goal required community mobilization. In another case persistent requests and some volunteer effort succeeded in attracting new city funds to a local recreation center, resulting in improved services to the neighborhood.

In Boyle Heights, the parish boundaries demarcate one space where community identity develops and associations flourish. Two general observations about the relationship between the Catholic Church and the Mexican American community are appropriate at this point. First, each parish pastor has a certain degree of latitude in determining the nature of his community involvement. Second, a distinction exists between the Catholic Church as a formal institution and the parish as the neighborhood base for many families. The parish church may be the site of schooling and family counseling and a link with other institutions.[13] Most of the core activists in Mothers of East Los Angeles volunteered over many years for parish fund-raising. Sometimes their work benefited the local parish, such as fund-raising for church facilities. Other volunteer work directly benefited the children, such as fund-raising to provide textbooks.

"Pillars of the Church"

Angie Flores also speaks of her forty years of volunteer work for the church: "We helped for forty years to get the funds to build the church. Jamaica after jamaica [charity bazaar] . . . not just one jamaica, not two jamaicas, it was about three or four per year." Angie's husband, Robert, who worked in construction, also donated his weekends to helping build a garage and driveway for the church. "My husband has been opening the church for twenty years. He also made the garage for the school and the driveway. He got all these construction guys to go work there. After it was done, the father [parish priest] asked how much is it going to be. My husband told him, You don't owe anything. Everybody donated their work."

She commented that the priest calls her husband and her the "pillars of the church" because of all the work they have done. However, she says now they need to cut back somewhat. Her husband suffers from arthritis and walks with the aid of a cane. Angie thinks the arthritis resulted from working in wet cement during his thirty years in construction work. Their son, who moved a few doors away, now assumes some of their former responsibilities at the church.

Their children's educational needs led almost all the women into volunteer community work. A mother's traditional responsibilities include overseeing her child's progress in school, interacting with school staff, and supporting school activities. In these processes, women meet other mothers and begin developing a network of acquaintances and friends based on mutual concern for the welfare of their children. All the activists I interviewed had sent their children to parochial school.[14] Thus their community activism was closely linked with the parish and often began with the entry of their children into school.

During the 1950s, the Catholic Church began building parochial schools attached to the parishes in East Los Angeles. Pastors observed that some first-generation residents were slow to join the parish organizations, until their children began attending Catholic school. Priests called the parochial schools a drawing card via the Mothers' Club, later renamed the Parents Guild.[15] Erlinda Robles, a Mexican American woman who until the 1990s lived on the street where she was born and raised, participated in the Talpa Parish "Mother's Club" throughout the 1960s. She describes her volunteer work and the tensions that existed among parents, priests, and nuns:

I wanted my kids to go to Catholic school, and from the time my oldest one went there, I was there every day. I used to take my two little ones with me, and I helped one way or another. I used to question things they did. And the other mothers would just watch me. Later they would ask me, "Why do you do that? They are going to take it out on your kids." I'd say, "They better not." And before you knew it, we had a big group of mothers that were very involved.

My husband used to call us the "Tamaleras de Talpa," and the women would laugh. He called us that because once a week we would have a sale. Every Sunday we used to have a breakfast fund-raiser with eggs, burritos, and tamales. We used to start about Wednesday making tamales. Some would clean beans, others would clean the *ojas* [dried corn husks used to wrap *masa*—corn meal dough—for tamales]. We had enough women doing it so it worked out OK.

Tamaleras, literally translated, is a plural feminine noun that means "tamale makers." In Mexico women who earn a living making tamales occupy a low position in the national occupational hierarchy, and they eke out a subsistence wage. When Valentín Robles labeled the women's work group *tamaleras*, he reflected the irony of continuity and change as Mexican American women in the United States labor to produce tamales, not for individual or family subsistence but to create community resources.[16]

As Erlinda described the traditional Mexican food women prepared for the fund-raisers, I asked how they had decided what items to offer. She said ethnic food sold the best. After mass in the morning, people wanted "their Mexican food." When women tried selling "Anglo food" such as hot dogs or ham and eggs, sales decreased and people complained. This preference continues into the 1990s; another woman confirmed that parishioners have said that they can easily make ham and eggs at home and prefer to purchase Mexican food.

Food choices express more than habit; they also provide a way to bind an individual to a group. As in other cities and ethnic communities, second-generation community members may purchase ethnic food for special occasions and avoid time-consuming preparation.[17] The point is that the preference and preparation of Mexican food makes an identity statement about the common origins of immigrants and U.S.-born Mexican Americans.

I commented that the food sales entailed a lot of work and a very long day spent in preparation. My observation came from the perspective of someone who has prepared tamales on rare occasions, and then only reluctantly. But as she reflected on the meaning of the collective activity, beyond the prospect of material benefit for the school, Erlinda stressed something besides hard work:

> It was a lot of fun, now that I think about it. I made good friends—some of us are still friends to this day. The priest would give us the money to get the ingredients. Then we would cook all the potatoes. The men would come at night and help us grate all the potatoes [prepared as a side dish for eggs]. On Sunday morning, someone would go at five o'clock and start heating the tamales, so by the end of seven o'clock mass, the food would be warm. We would stay there until after twelve o'clock mass. Then we would stay until two-thirty and clean the kitchen.

The church kitchen became a place where Erlinda's husband, Valentín, then enlisted in the navy and often away, could be sure to find her if she was not at home. Thirty years later, Erlinda still speaks of the other mothers whom she knew from the "Mothers Club." Their participation in collective work to create resources was the "glue" that helped build a sense of community. Women worked for the betterment of their immediate families and for the working class Latino community of Eastside Los Angeles.

When Erlinda Robles volunteered for the Mothers' Club in the 1960s, women's participation was not yet required. Erlinda recalls that a relatively small group of women usually carried out many hours of work that benefited many. By the late 1970s even fewer parents participated, and the financial needs of the parochial school had increased. The church began to mandate parent participation in fund-raisers. By this time the church had renamed the Mothers' Club the Parents Guild. The decreased participation of women may indicate their reduced availability for intensive volunteer work as increasing numbers of Mexican American women sought wage labor after 1970. Although friendships continued to be established, Rosa Villaseñor, the Parents Guild president, had increasing difficulty rounding up the volunteers needed to put on the weekly breakfasts. She explained how she had to demand participation of one single mother:

> She said she could not afford to pay or participate because she was a single parent going to night school and working. I told her that it was not fair for her to get away with having all the other mothers doing her work. She was doing things to better herself, and that was fine for her. I told her either she paid [her child's full tuition fees] or she should come on Sunday mornings at least for the *desayunos* [breakfasts]. I couldn't let her get away with it because then the other women would say, Well, why should I do it? She wasn't too happy about it, but she started helping on Sunday mornings.

I reacted with sympathy to the story of a single working mother pursuing an education. From an individualistic point of view, she could have used the free time to study. But from Rosa's position of responsibility for the group, excusing the woman from collective efforts would work toward her individual advancement and to the detriment of a system of volunteer labor. It would sabotage group cohesiveness and commitment.

Gendered Relations: "We Did All the Work and We Had a Say-So!"

The social division of labor in the parochial schools was quite sharply defined in the 1960s. Nuns assumed the role of teachers and counselors, and the priests assumed the administrative positions. Until the 1970s nuns formed the teaching staff for parochial schools. They were paid literally in room and board, which made the cost of schooling accessible to the poor. But as fewer women became nuns, teaching staffs became predominantly composed of laypersons, thus increasing the costs and the tuition. These divisions eventually led women parishioners to question what was just and then to request the participation of nuns in the Parents Guild so they could help decide the use of funds produced through women's volunteer efforts.

In one case some women thought nuns should be entitled to more authority in the Parents Guild. The women decided to negotiate directly with the priest in charge of the school. Erlinda Robles speaks of her experiences working closely with a parochial school during the early 1960s:

> They [the priests] would invite the nuns who were the teachers only to the first [parents'] meetings. So the nuns didn't know anything about the mothers. They were left in the dark. Then we started insisting that the nuns start attending the meetings. They were so happy, you should have seen their faces. Then we wanted the fathers to attend too. That way they could feel they were part of it. So

then they changed the name to the Parents Guild. After the nuns started attending, the priests knew when they were outnumbered. We had nuns who were ahead of their time. The nuns lived in the convent next to the school, and a lot of mothers would go to them for counseling. There were always kids and mothers going to the place they lived. The priests didn't like everyone going to see the nuns. But I told one priest, They are always available to the people; you are not. From noon until two o'clock you take a nap and are not to be disturbed! The nuns don't do that.[18]

They [the nuns] used to drive a lot of mothers and kids around, and they had an old station wagon. So we told the priests, "We think the nuns deserve to get a new station wagon, and we will do the food sales to earn the money." The nuns didn't want the priests to think they put us up to the idea, so they tried to say no, they didn't need a new station wagon. But we insisted. And they got it after all.

Erlinda's description captures a complex set of social relations in the parish. The patriarchal character of the Catholic Church, reflected in the division of labor between priests and nuns and the decision making process in the Parents Guild, created situations that women questioned. Guided by their own observations and perceptions of equity and their practical concerns, the women carefully challenged existing decision-making practices that excluded nuns. The women considered the nuns' direct, day-to-day work with their children and wanted them present at Parents Guild meetings. Similarly, the women used their volunteer work to enhance the effectiveness of the nun's activities, for example, by purchasing a new station wagon.

Erlinda Robles also spoke of strategies they used to draw fathers and husbands into the enterprise: "At the beginning, the priests used to say who the president of the Mothers Guild would be; they used to pick them. But we wanted elections, so we got elections. Then we wanted the fathers to be involved, and the nuns suggested that a father should be president and a mother would be secretary or be involved there [at the school site]." Of course, this comment piqued my curiosity because it seemed contradictory that women should want a man for president when women ran the guild. I asked why the mothers accepted the nuns' suggestion; the answer was simple and instructive:

At the time we thought it was a "natural" way to get the fathers involved because they weren't involved; it was just the mothers. Everybody [the women] agreed on them [the fathers] being president of the Parents Guild because they worked all day and they couldn't be involved in a lot of daily activities like food sales and whatever. A mother was vice-president and took care of all the food sales. The president presided over all the meetings. During the week a steering committee for fund raising used to make all the plans for the group and then meet with the president and let him know. One time the president did make a decision on his own to have a fundraiser that required the group to cook on Mother's Day. At the general meeting the group opposed him . . . because he didn't have the right to decide that. Nobody showed up that day to cook except him, his kids, and his wife. So he learned he wasn't going to get away with that. But now that I think about it, a woman could have been president and done the job just as well!

The group demonstrated dissatisfaction by boycotting the event and effectively conveyed the message that decisions needed collective approval. The 1990s gave Erlinda a new perspective on her 1960s perception of what was "natural" for men and women.

Women brought men into the group by giving them managerial functions. Nevertheless, the men were not making day-to-day decisions or dictating the direction of the group. This should alert researchers against measuring power and influence solely by looking at who holds titles.

Juana Gutiérrez, a core activist who worked with an adjacent parish school, complements Erlinda's accounts of the mothers' work to support the quality of their children's education:

I worked at Santa Isabel. The first year when I was the vice-president I did all the work for the president too because he was a man and he worked [had paid employment]. I moved the people to make breakfasts every Sunday. At the end of the year, I gave the father [priest] seven thousand dollars. He was very happy. The school needed a new refrigerator and air conditioning, so they were able to get them.

Every weekend I got three or four different mothers from the school. I was there every weekend. I would go buy everything—the sisters would give me a blank check, and my husband would help a lot. After I bought the food, I gave the sister the receipts and after the sale, we would figure the profits. We would make about four to five hundred dollars' profit!

Parish and parochial-school activities accounted for a significant portion, but not all, of the women's community activities. The core activists also shaped the conditions in their communities by making use of public resources to help meet the needs in their communities. As the following discussion illustrates, women state the work they do is to better the community in general.

Collective Action and State Resources

Bridging the gap between the community's needs and the community's resources may call for different actions. When women wanted drivers' training classes, community mobilization was necessary. When women sought the renovation of a recretion center, a small group of neighbors persistently communicated needs to a city commission. After volunteering time to keep a recreational area open, they successfully gained city resources to renovate the center, to develop recreational services, and to staff it.

Making Driver's Training Available

In 1966, when Erlinda Robles chaired the parents' steering committee for the Evergreen Recreation Center, located in Boyle Heights, she worked to obtain an adult driver's training program. The center offered programs such as weight-control groups, cake decorating classes, and teen activities. But a group of women decided they wanted to learn how to drive. The issue of driver's training may sound insignificant in the context of the 1990s. In the 1990s, however, the community was described as highly transit dependent because of its high proportion of young people (40 percent of the population was under twenty years if age), and its low income (the median family income was 40 percent below the citywide average). More than one-third of the families did not own autos, and 42 percent owned just one (Escobedo 1979). Erlinda described the situation:

> I would take my kids to the Evergreen Recreation Center, and a temporary director, a Russian man who had grown up in this neighborhood, asked the ladies who went there what kind of programs they would like. One lady from [Our Lady of Talpa Church] said, "Driving. I want to learn how to drive." But as hard as he tried, he couldn't get the classes for us. Then one day there was a representative from the Urban Affairs office [for the city of Los Angeles], and he told me, "Don't start at the bottom; start at the top." So we got about 150 women together and went to the Board of Education and made our request for driver's training class.

The strategy of using mass numbers—150 people taking buses to the Board of Education—to emphasize a "request" fits in the context of 1960s protest tactics, but for most women in the group this was a novel experience. Their presentations to the board, letter writing, and phone calls finally led to a partial success. Erlinda continued:

> They finally said we could have a pilot program for driver's training. We got about 150 women and two men to sign up for the course, but they wouldn't give us behind-the-wheel training. We never had a formal group. We just went and met with a few other women and Henry Ron-

quillo, community liaison for the Office of Urban Affairs.
I remember my phone would be ringing constantly.
Sometimes I would just start crying, and my husband
would say you better quit. Especially when the California
Driving School started attacking us on the news and saying bad things against the program, like "a little knowledge is dangerous." If kids could get behind the wheel,
why couldn't we? The California Driving School said
they were going to put a bunch of women behind the
wheel and let them free. We chartered two buses two
times and got the women enrolled in the course to go before the Board of Education and ask for the [behind-the
wheel training] program.

Erlinda recognized the driving school's tactics to degrade the
women and allege they were incompetent, dangerous, and
less responsible than teens. The driving school objected to a
school-based program that would provide for free a service
that they offered commercially. Attacking the program as inadequate was a way to undermine it. The women argued their
adult status should at least be commensurate with that of
youth.

Erlinda, who never liked speaking in front of large groups,
nevertheless enjoyed being involved in community issues. Because she was one of the key organizers of the community request for a drivers' training program, a community liaison
with the Office of Urban Affairs pushed her to make a presentation before the Board of Education:

He [the community liaison] would make me speak. I
think when I get mad things come out of me. I spoke in
front of the Board of Education and told them we wanted
this program for the last ten years and that we were lim-

ited in our school and community volunteer activities because we didn't know how to drive. We could not afford
to enroll in a private driving school; at that time they
charged between nine and twelve dollars per hour.

Erlinda argued that the ability to drive would contribute to the
women's effectiveness as volunteers and also allow some to
seek work outside the home:

A lot of those ladies wanted to work but the work was
too far by a bus. A lot of ladies got jobs after they got their
licenses. The women really needed to drive, and the
recreation director backed us up because they needed
more people to be able to drive the kids to field trips. The
mothers wanted to learn for the kids, for jobs, and to help
around the community. Everything we said was true—a
lot of those women began driving other kids around too.
It was not a luxury; it was a necessity.

Here the participation of women as mothers and unwaged
community workers became a way to gain community resources that would give them options to enter the labor force
and meet the needs of their children and of their community.

After an eleven-week battle, the parents' group won a victory over a group of determined private driving school owners. The driving schools blasted the program "as big government again throttling private enterprise."[19] Nevertheless, in a
unanimous decision, the Los Angeles Board of Education
authorized pilot programs at two adult schools and driver's
training programs were added to the regular adult classroom
instruction. Later Erlinda found out that the program was incorporated into a work incentive and training program for
women on welfare. They actually brought the driver's educa-

tion instructor who taught the Evergreen pilot program out of retirement so he could develop the program.

Erlinda Robles, along with several other women, completed the driver's training courses and decided to celebrate their success by holding a potluck and inviting the instructors and other community members. For the main course they planned to make tamales for everyone. The priest hesitated at their request to use church kitchen facilities. There were similarities in the way the women pursued the purchase of a station wagon for the nuns and the way they obtained access to church kitchen facilities to prepare food for an event that was not church related. Erlinda explains how they used their extensive volunteer work for the church as leverage:

> The majority of the ladies who worked on getting driver's training classes were the ones who always did all the cooking for the church fund-raisers at Talpa Church. Since the church had a large kitchen available, we asked the priest for permission to use it, but he said no at first. But we reminded him that we used to cook in the church about once month, and if he didn't let us he wouldn't see us around anymore. So he changed his mind.

The collective work of women in the parish and their efforts in local political arenas merged. They combined the two spheres of activity in their demand to use the church's kitchen facilities to prepare food for an event that would be held elsewhere (an event that was not directly parish based).

Boyle Heights Recreation Center

Juana Gutiérrez lives across the street from a park and recreation center that is exactly one block square. In the early 1980s, conditions in the neglected park across the narrow street from her home began to worsen. The way she acted on her concerns about the park illustrates another way women mobilize to attract state resources. Juana described the situation:

We had a lot of problems with drug dealers in the park across the street. I didn't want my kids or my neighbors' kids involved in drugs. I made Neighborhood Watch meetings with the police and city commissioners. At this time Councilman Snyder was in office. He answered when we called. We told him about the problems in the park. He could not *believe* it because he had never been to the park.

I told him to go right down there and see the burned car that is parked in the middle of the park. When [the burning of the car] happened, we called the police and nothing happened.

Juana's efforts gained small concessions from the Parks and Recreation Department while the Parks and Recreation commissioner relied on her volunteer labor and that of her husband. Juana continued:

So the park commissioner finally ordered lights for the park. Then he came and talked to me. He said, "Mrs. Gutiérrez, I know because of the budget we don't have anyone to turn on the lights at night or open the restrooms. Would you like to have the keys and do it?" I said, "I will do it, not for pay, but as a volunteer. I will open the restrooms every morning and close them at night." Someone else would come and clean them. Sometimes my husband or my kids would turn on the lights at night.

I suggested this must have been a tiresome job for her. She answered, "Yes, but for my community and my kids, I did it. You know some nights, I would say, I am not going to turn on the lights; I am tired. Then the phone would ring and the neighbors would tell me, 'Mrs. Gutiérrez, no va a poner las luces?' [You aren't going to turn on the lights?] For five years I did it."

To me the sacrifice seemed quite substantial, but Juana did not stress this aspect. She continued the account to explain how her diligence won stable staffing for the park. She learned from Assemblywoman Lucille Roybal-Allard that some monies were available for hiring recreation directors in the local parks. She explained how she involved some of her neighbors to begin pressuring for a recreation director for the Boyle Heights Recreation Center:

> When I heard the city had the money for other parks, I called to see if we could get some for our park. They told me they didn't have the money for Boyle Heights. I got the people together and went to talk to the commissioners. For two years, about eight neighbors and I tried to get the position for a recreation director for the park. We called the office, we sent letters, and we went to the Office of Parks and Recreation [of Los Angeles]. Finally we got a position. Now the kids get trips to the beach and other places.

When Juana Gutiérrez took me on a walking tour of the park, at least sixty kids and some adults were using it well before four in the afternoon. As we walked around, Juana recalled how brown and barren the untended hillsides were before they hired a gardener. Without her explanation, I am sure I would have taken for granted the green grass and newly planted shrubs. Quite fittingly, the young Latina gardener planted cuttings from Juana's rose bushes, and they now grow in the park. She commented on how well the park is doing, satisfied that her job is complete: "Now we have a director and four or five helpers, and thank goodness I don't have to do anything over there."

These two accounts—of how driver's training became available for community members and a park was rehabilitated—demonstrate that women's community activism extended beyond the simply defensive or reactive. They illustrate the women's conscious use of power to be proactive and to secure additional resources and services sorely needed in their immediate neighborhoods. In the case of the driver's training classes and the subsequent celebration at the church, the women combined access to resources from their voluntary secular and religious activities. Furthermore, the two accounts clarified how family units may often form a network in blue-collar neighborhoods and reach out for public resources.

Managing Households and Husbands: "As Long As His Meals Are Ready"

Approximately half of the core activists in Mothers of East Los Angeles worked for wages only during brief periods of time. Among the married women I interviewed who were over fifty years old, none currently worked for wages. A few had worked intermittently when their children's school tuition increased beyond the capacity of their husbands' earnings. Most women stated they preferred to care for their children themselves, rather than work for wages and have to send them to day care. Since their husbands had stable employment and salaries sufficient to support the family, they chose to stay home after they married.

The women's husbands worked in a variety of predominantly unionized blue-collar jobs—a bakery, construction, a large machine manufacturing plant, the armed services and then plant maintenance. Not one woman stated that her husband refused to allow her to work.[20] The women, several now of retirement age, often referred to the decision not to work in relation to the types of jobs for which their educations prepared them. They regretted being counseled into the home economics classes rather than being encouraged to gain marketable skills. Angie Flores, mother of three sons and now sixty-five years old, speaks of her experiences at Roosevelt High School in 1941:

> In my senior year [of high school], I had to go to Roosevelt, but they didn't have room in "commercial" [the clerical track]. They wanted me to take home economics. I said, Well, in that case, I wanted to quit school because I already know how to cook and sew. Then the war [World War II] broke out, and we moved and later in my senior year I lacked the money for graduation clothes and I quit high school.

She worked for a short time in a spinach-packing house next door to her home, then quit work when she married. When I asked if her husband preferred that she not work, she recalled his words: "Well, Angie, if you want to go on working, go ahead; but I married you so I could support you." According to Angie, she quit work because he earned good wages as a construction worker.

Another core activist, who chose not to marry and or to

have children, attended community college and worked as a secretary all her life. Able to convince the high school counselor to allow her into the business track, she developed accounting and secretarial skills. As she recalled,

> They [the high school counselors] tried to get me to take home economics by saying it would lead to a glamorous job in the entertainment industry—making costumes. Or in millinery, making hats. Can you imagine? Where would I be now? Nobody wears hats today. But I hated cooking and sewing. So I asked for bookkeeping. They tried to deter me, but my dad told me I had the right to take whatever I wanted. So they finally gave me the classes. There were so few of us minorities at Garfield then—so few Mexicans made it to high school. I graduated and then took classes in business school. When the war broke out I got a secretarial job in a defense plant.

While she was employed full time, she says, she never had time for becoming involved in political activities other than simply voting. For single women without children and without the attendant responsibilities that lead them to form social networks, life's passages are often what lead to community involvement. This woman had attended mass regularly, but she became more active in church activities shortly after the passing of her father. When she expressed her sense of great loss to the priest, he suggested she might ease her grief through volunteer work with the youth. She followed his advice, and her activism in the church involved her in community social life for many years. However, single and self-supporting, she terminated regular volunteer work with the church when the work there conflicted with her job responsibilities:

In 1959 I started volunteering as a counselor for the Resurrection Church youth group—the "Queen's Teens." Father García [one of the few Mexican American priests]
had these kids coming to meetings and would take them
[the youth] to movies in Hollywood, sometimes at Grau-
man's Chinese Theater. He wanted to introduce them to
other things, a better way of life. They went on trips to
the beach, the mountains. Then I taught catechism for ten
years. Everyone knew Father García because he was
raised in the community on Sixth Street. When he needed
something done or something built, he would call the
men and work with them hammering and sawing side by
side.

I also belonged to the "Guadalupanas." They held that in
Spanish. They had a group for the men, another for the
women, and one for the children. The Guadalupanas are
a group that work for the procession of Our Lady of
Guadalupe.[21] They do the fund-raisers for the procession
at East L.A. College on October twelfth.

After a while it got to be too much when I was working.
See, I had to walk home at night because they [the other
parishioners] would get in little groups and "chit chat."
Then it would be so late by the time they could give me a
ride home. I had to get up at five-thirty to go to work at
six o'clock, so I stopped going. But I knew many of the
ladies from the women's council for years.

Employed full time, she chose not to continue the intense
church involvement pursued by the women who had children
attending parochial school. She maintained close ties with
the church and participated in special events throughout the

years. When she retired, she resumed a closer working relationship with the church and began keeping the accounts for the large week-long fiesta held in the summer.[22] She voted regularly, but until her retirement and the prison issue came along, she had never been involved in a community controversy.

The married women who worked for wages were a bit younger than the other women—just turning forty. Given increasing inflation, the choice to remain home and raise children was not an option for the younger women in the group. For these women, the current cost of living required two salaries. Other married women entered the labor force only at points in family life when the financial need was great—particularly when their children entered high school and tuition escalated beyond what one wage could cover. As soon as the child graduated the women left work. One woman worked so her son, attending college out of state, could afford the trips back home. Women who took an active part in their communities saw their first responsibility in the household, but completed that to have the right to contribute outside the home. Most of the husbands of the active women worked at blue-collar jobs that often demanded rising before dawn. For example, Angie Flores's husband, Robert, worked laying cement. I asked Angie how he felt about her extensive volunteer work and how she balanced it with her household responsibilities. As she tells it, her mother lived with her at the time and handed down her view of how to treat a husband:

> My mother used to live here with me, and she used to help take care of the kids. She would say, "Just have his [Angie's husband's] food already set up so he can serve himself when he comes home at night. And he wouldn't say anything as long as he didn't have to change diapers.

. . . We [Angie and her mother] used to take the kids with us when we went shopping or to the movies in the evening.

Angie's husband did not dictate the conditions under which she could go out on evening entertainment excursions, and she felt they had worked out a mutual agreement about family responsibilities. The agreement allowed her flexibility even during the time he was at home. She recognized and respected "changing diapers" as his outer limit. He accepted a self-serve dinner waiting for him on top of the stove rather than demanding that she be home to serve him.

Rosa Villaseñor, who is fifty-one years old, describes similar household arrangements. She has two daughters in their early twenties who are attending college and living at home. She describes her husband as very dedicated to their daughters; just in case anything happens, he stays home when she goes to meetings:

My husband used to work two jobs—sixteen hours a day for about five years. Poor thing. Now he gets up at four A.M., and like most of these guys [in East Los Angeles] he doesn't have an easy job. When they come home, they take a shower and want to relax. The men you find at meetings are retired or they don't even work. He never objected to me doing anything as long as I feed him and do his clothes. I had to take care of that if I wanted to do what I wanted to do!

This passage illustrates how the women did community work while keeping up the private household work of mothers and wives. Furthermore, the women recognized that preserving household stability made it possible for them to work in the community. They negotiated rather than simply complied with their husbands in order to engage in community activity.

The organization of households tells much about the flexibility of women's time and their assertiveness in defining the boundaries of their work. The intensity of volunteer community work and activism ebbed and flowed in relation to the time they spent working for wages. However, even when free time was available, husbands had to believe in the benefit of their wives' community activities. Some community members explain (and in essence trivialize) women's volunteer work by saying, "They do it because they have the time."[23]

This simplistic explanation devalues women's work and misses the fact that they could engage in other activities. All men and women who are not in the workforce and maintain a home and family do not become community activists, although for at least some it is an option. For one woman, retirement provided the opportunity to become a self-described "community activist." For women without children, life's passages paved the way to community activism. For some, changes in the organization of family life corresponded to entry into community activism.

Discussion

Everyday life and organized politics overlap in Boyle Heights. The women expressed a sense of belonging to the community and to their families; conversely, they perceive their families and their communities as belonging to them. Their activities and their life stories support a strong notion of integration and membership in the larger community.

The neighborhood is the immediate physical and social space for the family, and with limited resources women devise ways to influence its formation. In some instances, they do not identify their community work as political. For them it holds a kind of middle ground between home and electoral politics and reveals that the "social" and "political" are hardly separate categories. Feminists recognized the merging of the two conceptually differentiated spheres when they coined the slogan "the personal is political." Thus, the argument that the work of women in the interests of family is based on gender rather than class misses the complexity and meaning of women's work under particular economic circumstances and in particular community contexts (di Leonardo 1987).

The core activists in Boyle Heights all had well-developed associations in the community before joining the Coalition against the Prison and MELA. Their volunteer work in local parishes and in the neighborhood demonstrated a civic consciousness intertwined with family responsibilities but not solely defined by those responsibilities. In practical everyday life, women who are mothers do carry out responsibilities that are gender specific. But this is only part of the story, not the entire story.

The church, priests, and nuns were all significant resources in the community. The women negotiated with priests to have input into the expenditure of resources, the use of space, and the administrative procedures that affected their children's educations. The women worked to involve the nuns and secure the resources to purchase what the nuns needed—for example, the station wagon.

Ethnic, class, and community identity gave meaning to their activism beyond an expression of gender identity. When they spent endless hours preparing the Mexican food preferred for parish fund-raisers, they did so as women who were members of a Mexican community. Symbols of Mexican culture and origin "color" the community and social relations. Food and bilingual communication are obvious expressions of Mexican American culture; volunteer work for immigrant rights signifies an empathy for new Latino immigrants derived from common immigration histories. Even though interaction between immigrants and long-established residents was not without tension, they used language and social skills to bridge social distance.

In everyday associations, women gained significant experience raising funds, working in groups, negotiating with (usually male) authority figures—priests, husbands, city officials—and managing their households and families. The women implicitly expressed their conception of civic membership as they bridged the spaces between their homes and the community. Bridging the distance between the two means different kinds of work: negotiating between the schools and their children's needs, assisting new immigrants to secure citizenship, "keeping an eye on the neighborhood," and bringing in state resources to maintain public places. Women expressed a consciousness rooted in collective goals and work. The emphasis was not on individual advancement but on pressure to maintain the system of volunteer labor necessary to enhance collective resources.

EIGHT

Creating Community in Monterey Park

"Keeping an Eye on the Block"

The types of work women do in the suburbs mirror those of women in the inner city: "keeping an eye on the block" and serving in child-related organizations such as parents' clubs or PTAs. Unlike the large governmental structure of Eastside Los Angeles, however, Monterey Park's small city government provided opportunities for middle-class residents to influence elected officials and serve on city commissions, such as those pertaining to parks and recreation, arts and culture, and human relations. Many women did so. They also served on committees charged with organizing city-funded community festivals. Most of their activities entail weekly meetings and work at small fund-raising events. This kind of access is not so readily available through the massive units of the city and county of Los Angeles.

Neighborhood Work

In Monterey Park the differences among residents have to do not only with ethnic and racial origins but also with length of residency in the United States and foreign-born or native-born status. In their stories about carrying out daily community work, women speak about these differences as obstacles and limitations. They also tell about the strategies they use to diminish the social distances.

In the interests of their children, women interact with other parents and begin bridging the social distances between their own families and those of different ethnic and racial origins. Elementary school children may be aware of ethnic differences but have not yet settled into ethnic cliques. They may form cross-cultural friendships in school that spill into after-school activities. Or they may unintentionally cross boundaries into a neighbor's space. Such actions open communication between adults of different ethnic or racial origins. The examples discussed below illustrate the ways children serve as links between neighbors. They also reveal the limitations of child-based adult interaction. The first instance considers the ways children serve as links between women and families. The second case illustrates how children serve as the impetus for mothers to persist in the face of bureaucratic obstacles and successfully bring outside resources into the community.

Mothering and Crossing Ethnic Boundaries

Some Monterey Park residents commonly charge new immigrants with not "getting involved" in community activities. Rosemary López, who has chaired the PTA for two years, makes significant observations about Chinese immigrant mothers that qualify this assertion. For example, she has seen significant numbers of immigrant parents go on field trips with their children. However, she notes that language difficulties present an obstacle to their full participation: "Maybe they don't stay for the parties because they don't speak English that well. But they do give something for their kids to take to the parties. Their tendency is to stay back. And we try to talk to them and make them feel more welcome. But it [distance] is breaking down."

The "breaking down" means crossing boundaries in the face of language differences and communication difficulties. Through organized school projects, according to Rosemary, women are drawn into community tasks. However, it is a process fraught with frustrations:

There are some ladies that get involved, but it is really hard to understand them because they have a thick accent. Some have been here for years, too. One lady who is in charge of our membership wants to help, but I have to ask another lady to help me understand what she is saying. I am trying to explain to her and I say, OK? And she is going "yes, yes, yes" and nodding her head, but I don't know if she really understands.

These kinds of interactions emerge from organized school activities. As children make friends in school, they begin socializing outside of school. This leads to parental interaction in informal settings. Sandra Aguirre, a Mexican American woman with an elementary-age son, speaks of how children bring together families of different ethnic and racial backgrounds. However, her perceptions of cultural differences present obstacles to close relationships:

When Ricky was in kindergarten, a Japanese American woman and I started getting to know each other because the little boy [her son] and Ricky were very good friends.

You know the Japanese here are very cliquish; actually, so are the Hispanics. And their group of friends started to get together a Boy Scouts troop and she invited Ricky to join. There were two Hispanics out of ten and four Chinese. What I am saying is that I got to know the parents.

While she attributes a "cliquishness" to the Japanese Americans, she indicates that she entered the clique through her child's friendships and did become acquainted with parents of different ethnic origins and immigrant status. She discusses the variations she observes among the "others" in relation to her own sense of ethnic identity. She adjusts her social interactions according to these understandings. Sandra describes an illustrative incident:

The Japanese have been here a long time—like about third generation. The Chinese are new. There is one Chinese woman from Australia, and she is very "anglicized." Her husband is more traditional. But she is moving back to Australia, and she gave me three dresses that she never used, and I wanted to hug her but I backed off. [Instead] I said, "Oh, Pam [exclaiming happiness about the gifts]!" I wanted to hug her, but she kind of backed off . . . so I just said, "Thank you."

In the ways just described, mothering draws women of different ethnic, racial, and immigrant status together. Women who are established residents interact with and start "breaking down" the distance between the new immigrants of Chinese origin. But for women without school-age children, occasions for social interaction may be more limited.

"Monitoring" the Neighborhood
and Crossing Ethnic Boundaries

Three Anglo women who are retired and active in the parole-office controversy describe their interactions with immigrant neighbors. Marijune Wissman, who raised two sons and has lived with her husband in the area for twenty-five years, laughingly told me that her son calls her a "window monitor." This refers to her habit of sitting at the dining room table, observing the people who walk past her home, and commenting on their status in the neighborhood. What her son calls "window monitoring" is not exclusively a woman's activity, but it is commonly carried out by women concerned about what occurs in the immediate vicinity of their homes.

Deborah Marshall, an Anglo mother of a grown son, takes window monitoring to the next step. She admits candidly, "When people don't look like they belong in the neighborhood, I go right up and ask them what they are doing here!" When I asked how she knew when someone did not belong, she explained that she has belonged to a homeowners' association for many years and knows her neighbors. At times differences in ethnicity may prompt her to confront someone, as when she saw three Mexican-origin men walking toward a neighbor's house; they turned out to be doing yard work.

Children often violate the social conventions observed by adults. Getting acquainted with neighbors sometimes occurred when children violated conventions by playing in a neighbor's yard or even speaking to a neighbor. Roberta Randall, who has worked with Deborah on neighborhood issues including the parole office, is another long-time resident of the community. She began a lasting friendship with one of the first Chinese families to move into her neighborhood when a child traversed the great social distance into Roberta's yard. Her account reveals much about the way she generally views Chinese immigrants as neighbors, the neighborhood norms of conduct, and the strategies she used to bring the two into some accordance.

Just as many other established Anglo residents can do, Roberta cites a litany of annoying behaviors she sees as common to new immigrants. These include failing to maintain the appearance of their homes, such as by neglecting to water the lawns, or having extended family members living in a single-family residence, which compounds the shortage of parking space in the neighborhood. Space for cars, of course, holds special significance in Los Angeles, home of the automobile culture.

She tells how she communicated to one family what she perceived as neighborhood norms:

> The little boy, little Eddie, was about ten years old then. He used to come over and talk to me and my husband. I said to Eddie, "Who are all those people living in your house?" He told me they were his cousins. I said, "You can't have all that many cousins." He says, "They are my momma's friends, and we call everybody our cousin." I told him, "Well, you better tell your momma, this is an R1 [residential, single family] zone, and the police will come and cause her trouble if she has more than one family living in the home!" After that they [all but the original family] were all gone.

Sharing housing is a strategy commonly used by recent immigrants to deal with economic constraints, housing shortages, and limited social networks. Roberta's remarks aimed at

socializing her neighbors to neighborhood norms and bringing them into middle-class Anglo conformity.[1]

Roberta tells how she became friends with the family after
the boy expressed an interest in going fishing with her husband and her. She went to talk to Eddie's mother and got permission to take him along on a fishing trip. The families became such good friends that the Randalls served as sponsors
when the Chinese family applied for citizenship. As she recalled, "When little Eddie's parents started going to school to
learn English, I stood up for them when they went for their citizenship papers. Now Eddie is a CPA—he is thirty-two years
old—and he still comes to see us. He calls us his second parents. They are wonderful people. Couldn't ask for better
neighbors."

The good relationship Roberta established with the Chinese
family relied in part on the family's compliance with what she
perceived as proper neighborhood protocol. Her efforts at socializing these Chinese immigrant neighbors were informal
but nonetheless effective. She says her newest immediate neighbors, Chinese immigrants who moved in about four years ago,
are also good neighbors. She has taken on a socializing role
with the Chinese woman, who often seeks her assistance when
she needs to call city representatives or the police.

The magnitude of the recent Chinese immigration has
meant a dramatic change in the community, and the efforts of
established residents to socialize new immigrants have become increasingly difficult. Another resident speaks wistfully
of the community that she feels is slipping away. To her, the
support of neighbors during stressful family times distin-
guishes her twenty-five years of living in Monterey Park:

We have a strong sense of community in this area because we socialize a lot. We have cocktail parties. And we

have our own little support group because we are all getting to the age now where a lot of us are retired. If somebody's husband is sick and has to go to the hospital, we
help out. We have about ten of the original families right
in this area. All of the women participated in the PTA
when our children were small. But every house that goes
up for sale, an Asian person moves in.

Language, age differences, and the growing Asian immigrant
population make social interactions between retired Anglos
and young Asian families increasingly difficult. In addition to
daily neighborhood interactions, community members have
planned events to promote cross-cultural ties.

Community Work: The Cinco de Mayo Festival
at Barnes Park

Barnes Park, adjacent to Monterey Park City Hall, is a large,
green public facility that is well equipped with a stage and
concert shell, swimming pool, baseball field, tennis courts, and
a recreation center. Observing a typical day there reveals how
residents segregate themselves by ethnic and racial origin and
immigrant status. On the day I visited, several groups used the
common space at Barnes Park in different ways and at different times. At seven in the morning about forty Chinese immigrants, middle-aged and older, practice the very graceful tai
chi. Walkers moving briskly around the park, mostly elderly
Asians and Anglos, also use the public space during early day-
light hours. At midday a few young and middle-aged Asian
American and Anglo women supervise their preschool children on the swings and slides. By dusk young Mexican American men play on organized baseball teams while Asian men

and women play tennis on the adjacent courts. In the recreation hall, a male Chinese immigrant instructor teaches "American" ballroom dances to predominantly Chinese immigrant adults. (His teaching method differs from any other dance class that I have observed. Using a long, slender stick, he sharply taps out the musical beat and vigorously blows a coach's whistle to reinforce the rhythm. The couples diligently pound out the cha-cha-cha steps.) I observed little, if any, interaction among the different groups of people at the park.

Community festivals celebrated in public spaces offer an opportunity for different ethnic, social, and age groups to bridge their differences.[2] It is a time when groups who typically use the same public space at differing times and in different ways can come together and share a cross-cultural experience. The Cinco de Mayo (Fifth of May) celebration of 1989 illustrates how women worked to bridge ethnic and racial groups in a public way while expressing their own cultural identities.[3]

The Cinco de Mayo celebration in Monterey Park, much like any celebration, embodied varied meanings at different times—different for those who planned it and those who simply attended it.[4] The earliest Cinco de Mayo celebrations, in the early 1980s, focused on expressions of Mexican ethnicity. Following the first Cinco de Mayo celebration in about 1983, Anglo Americans revived Fourth of July festivities in the same park; until then the Fourth of July had not been observed in several years. The growing Asian immigrant population and the celebration of another ethnic/racial group in public space prompted renewed interest in celebrating the Fourth. The revival was especially promoted by Barry Hatch, a councilman who staunchly supported English as the official language and often spoke of illegal aliens taking over the city and country. (For example, Horton [1995, 97] quotes him as saying, "Congress has blinders on [regarding immigration] and people are coming in at will. I mean there's no stopping the Asians, for one. There's no stopping the Latinos for another. Now, who's next?") The 1989 Cinco de Mayo celebration aimed not only at asserting Mexican American identity but also promoting community harmony, specifically with respect to the Chinese immigrants.

On the heels of expressions of ethnic antagonism in the community, the Cinco de Mayo committee, chaired by José Calderón, invited Chinese immigrants, along with everyone else in Monterey Park, to participate in planning and carrying out the 1989 festival. The theme "Somos una Familia" (We are a family), proposed by the Mexican American members, was intended as a message of "unity, peace, and harmony." Once the organizing committee selected the festival theme, they faced the challenge of expressing the abstraction of ethnic identity through material symbols and performances. The groups agreed to include three Chinese performances in the program. Lucia Su, a long-time resident, volunteered to ask Chinese merchants to donate raffle prizes. When I asked if she had a business herself, she said, "No, but it would be easy for me to get the donations because it would mean free publicity for the merchants." Two Chinese businessmen, who did not attend meetings, raised a thousand dollars for the Chinese Lion's dance, which is traditionally performed from the second to the fifth day of the new year to scare away evil spirits and bring good wishes. They also publicized the event in the Chinese-language news media. The specific contributions of Chinese immigrants reflected their economic status and business activity in the community.

Second- or third-generation Mexican American women in suburban Monterey Park chose to express their ethnicity in ways that reflect the ways traditions change in new settings. Not surprisingly, food figured into the symbolic ethnic expression, and women took responsibility for planning the types of food to be offered. However, in contrast to the extensive cooking carried out by women in East Los Angeles, the Mexican American women on the committee did not engage in large-scale, elaborate Mexican cooking. Instead, they invited one of the few Mexican restaurants in Monterey Park to prepare *carne asada* (large, paper-thin slices of grilled beef) and sell a Mexican dinner of meat, beans, and rice. A Mexican American woman, the mother of two boys under twelve and a full-time wage earner, suggested that we sell nachos and cheese dip. She explained, "Oh, it's really easy! You just buy commercial-size canned cheese dip at the discount food center and bags of nachos, and then we sell them for a dollar per serving!" In the end, the Mexican immigrant mother-in-law of one of the male Anglo committee members made *agua de jamaica* (a tartly sweet, raspberry-colored iced tea made from hibiscus flowers) and brought homemade tamales. Both items received rave reviews from customers. The nachos and canned cheese dip also sold well, mostly to children accustomed to this commercialized version of Mexican food commonly sold in theaters and fast-food chains.

A husband and wife team decorated the stage with explicitly Mexican items. Suspended from the roof of the bandstand shell were two large, star-shaped piñatas, one multicolored and the other covered in green, red, and white crepe paper—the colors of the Mexican flag. A large painting of the head of a male Aztec warrior in a bright-turquoise, full plumed headdress transformed a beige stucco side wall into a colorful mural. Several large clusters of red and green balloons adorned both sides of the stage. Two national flags, Mexican on the right side and American on the left, sent a bicultural message. However, no representations of Chinese culture decorated the stage.

The entertainment included Mexican, Mexican American or Chicano, and Chinese cultural performances. The Mexican-origin performances illustrated cultural change over time and geographical place. A mariachi group (representing Mexican national culture), Aztec dancers (pre-Cuauhtemoc indigenous culture), folkloric dancers (Mexican folk culture), the "Latins Anonymous" theater group (contemporary Chicano cultural-political commentary),[5] and the "Aliens" band (contemporary Chicano rock, blues, and Latin rhythms) represented diverse expressions of Latino culture. Three presentations represented Chinese culture: the Lion's Dance, a young male Asian American group demonstrating martial arts, and an all-female group performing indigenous Taiwanese dances and wearing costumes strikingly similar to those of the Aztec dancers.[6]

At noon people began arriving in family and ethnic groups. Chinese immigrants speaking Chinese, Mexican Americans speaking English, a few Anglo families, and Anglo senior citizens set up picnic areas on the lawn. The families and older people stayed until about six o'clock. People watched politely and appeared attentive to the performances. As I took photographs, I noticed five elementary-school girls—two Asian, two African American, and one Mexican American—sitting next to me, their attention diverted from the stage to watch another girl holding a rabbit on her lap. They said they all attended a local elementary school, and the event brought them to the park to enjoy each other's company. By the time the rock group performed, the audience was largely Mexican American and young to middle aged.

The 1989 Cinco de Mayo celebration in suburban, multi-ethnic Monterey Park illustrates how public cultural events are used to create, and simultaneously to cross, group boundaries through food choices and entertainment. Food need not be authentic, however, to make a statement about ethnic identity.[7] The second generation of any ethnic group simplifies food preparation, and this may be interpreted as declining authenticity and assimilation, or as persistence and change of ethnic practices as they are expressed in the United States. Recognizing the persistence and change in ethnic traditions emphasizes the complexity and questions unilinear conceptions of ethnic identity (Barth 1969; Brown and Mussell 1984). Seemingly simple ethnic symbols such as piñatas and Mexican flags accomplish the work of communicating difference, unity, and organization.

The Cinco de Mayo organizing activities conveyed information about the social relations and social positions of men, women, and ethnic groups in the community. Mexican American women took on the job of organizing the food to be provided, but did so in such a way as to require relatively little work from themselves. Full-time wage earners with children seldom have the time or inclination to prepare complex ethnic dishes. One Chinese immigrant woman had ties in the Chinese business community and worked on this portion of her social networks to bring in raffle prizes. Women organizers outnumbered men, working together to carry off the event.

Bridging Community Needs and Public Resources

Women also bridge gaps between state resources and attract state funds for reinforcing communitarian infrastructure. The two examples discussed below show how women as mothers and women as professionals may act in different ways to accomplish this task.

Cindy Yee, the mother of three children of elementary school age, moved to Monterey Park fifteen years ago. Attracted by the multi-ethnic character of the area, she regretted not closely investigating the quality of schools, which she subsequently found to be inadequate.

Cindy has been active in the PTA since her children started attending school. Largely through dogged persistence, she and other parents prompted local elected officials to seek funds to renovate and expand the elementary school, a project that cost $1.7 million. She recalls one of her first approaches to the local school board concerning the issue, in 1982:

> The conditions were just deplorable. The kids' lunches were bussed in, and they had to eat out in the cold on that windy hill. There was no cafeteria, auditorium, office facilities, or library. So a little group of us went and asked the school board to buy two [prefabricated] bungalows [to be moved onto the school grounds and used as classrooms]. See, we had a lot of property on our school, but they wanted to force us into double sessions because the buildings would not accommodate the students. The board said they couldn't buy them.

Cindy recalls that this issue was debated for over a year, with the school board stubbornly repeating that it lacked funds to meet the parents' request. Frustrated, she eventually called her local councilwoman, who wrote a letter of support. Then she took a group of parents to talk to a staff member in the state assembly office. Cindy incredulously described what happened next as a lesson about the intractable, inefficient school board: "[City Councilwoman] Lilly Chen wrote a letter to Sacramento and then [state assemblyman Charles] Calderón's aide went to the State Allocation Board meeting with my list of the school's needs. [The board allocates funds for school needs.] He just brought it before them, and we got $1.7 million! That tells me the school board was just not doing their job!"

The school board had ignored her initial requests for better school facilities on the grounds that no money was available. When the ground-breaking ceremony took place, the superintendent didn't invite her to be present, but the assembly office did.

In keeping with her notion of what "good mothering" included, Cindy Yee worked to improve the facilities at the school, which now attracts many teacher applicants; she says the teachers call it "the Beverly Hills of the area." The issue required her to mobilize a small group of friends, neighbors; she also became acquainted with local representatives.

The Child Care Task Force is another successful example of women's work to garner California state funds for the community. In one way, it is similar to the other cases in that the interests of children were expressed as the link between different community institutions. This case differs because all but one of women in the multi-ethnic group worked in child-centered professions, among them a librarian, a child-care center owner, and a child-care center director.[8] In the case of the librarian, the community's lack of child-care facilities complicated her working conditions, so that provision of proper child care was forced onto her agenda.

Local media exposed how parents were using the community library as an "unofficial child care center." The librarian had noticed larger and larger numbers of children arriving directly after school and staying until seven in the evening. The librarian felt the practice was "getting out of control." She summarized what was occurring: "The library is used as a day care. I even have 'Saturday drop-offs' [i.e., children] that stay all day and often come in with a sack lunch!" Interviewed in the *West San Gabriel Valley News Digest* (June 7, 1989), she revealed that as many as fifty to sixty children were routinely using the library as an after-school facility. Although the librarian never specified the ethnicity of the children, over 80 percent of them were Asian American, corresponding to the city's changing demographics.

Elva Martínez, who owns and operates a day-care center in Monterey Park, discovered the state of California was accepting proposals for publicly subsidized child-care centers. She knew that the need for child care in Monterey Park exceeded the capacity of existing private facilities. Pressed by short notice, she went before the city council for approval to submit a proposal for a child-care center sponsored by the city. At the meeting, several Anglo senior citizens expressed disapproval. One man declared, "I see three women on the city council, and I know they raised their children without community assistance. I paid for [the care of] my own children, and I know [in Monterey Park] when there are two incomes in the family the second income goes to put a Mercedes Benz in the garage!" The speaker addressed his comments to the women on the council, and he received some applause from two small groups of elderly Anglos in the audience.

The expressions of opposition revealed much about the different historical and economic era in which they raised their own children. They also indicated the antagonism that characterized the politics of Monterey Park in the decade of the 1980s. Lower-middle-class Anglos resented not only the "foreign takeover" of the community but also the greater affluence of the new Chinese immigrants. The city council turned down her appeal on the grounds of short notice, lack of information, and possible cost to the city.[9]

Later, Elva Martínez and a Chinese American city council member, Judy Chu, called together a Child Care Task Force and planned a strategy. Meetings were announced in the local newspaper. Parents attended the first meetings, but the women with professional expertise turned from women's experiential discussion of community child-care needs to the issue of structured work around proposal writing. The task force decided to write a proposal and lobby one of the city councilwomen who voted against the proposal. The strategy seemed practical and efficient, but working class women were excluded from the process, which drew on the skills of the professional women.

Monthly meetings of the Child Care Task Force focused on the process of preparing the proposal. Task force members were contacted only when a "community presence" was required at a city council meeting. Elva explained, "I concentrated on discussing the pros and cons with the two women [council members]—both raised children in Monterey Park and they were open to the issue. I didn't really bother with the two councilmen, who were both bachelors without children. I knew I needed three votes, and I got them."

Briefly, this case illustrates how professionals used technical expertise to get at outside resources for the community. At the same time they unintentionally stymied parental participation. But children were again the vehicles for adult connections. The child-care center developed into one of the few city programs that sustains itself by charging parents according to their income.

Managing Households and Husbands:
"There Is Still That Tug of War"

How does women's community involvement affect relations within their homes? Do Monterey Park women perceive their husbands as supportive or equals in their community activities? How does "doing for the kids" as an explanation for community work pertain to involvements not so directly linked to child-related concerns? The answers show a pattern of negotiation between husbands and wives and the boundaries of women's activism in relation to the "needs of children."[10]

The multi-ethnic women actively opposing the parole office in the Highlands area worked for wages during a substantial period of their lives. Their jobs took up time they might otherwise have spent doing volunteer work in the community. They all graduated from high school and had specialized training in "white collar" occupations: two had positions as legal secretaries; the others worked in computer data processing, practical nursing, and bank loan processing. All earned well above the legal minimum wage. During the times they were out of the workforce, they became more involved in groups such as the PTA. At all times they took responsibility for the bulk of household duties.

Their husbands, some of whom had completed college, worked in white-collar jobs or semiprofessional positions: among them were a police officer, computer programmers, an electrician for the city, and a small-business owner. The women see their husbands as supportive of their community work as long as it does not interfere with family and household responsibilities. A few husbands attended meetings regularly.

Other women who were active in Monterey Park were involved in community issues in more formal and structured ways. Three general types emerge: the neighborhood activist who is not officially tied to any city-sanctioned group, the participant in city commissions (via an unpaid advisory position), and the representative elected to the local school board. Some women have begun with grassroots and neighborhood activism and moved into city electoral politics. Between 1988 and 1994, women held three seats on the five-member city council. Louise Davis's election to city council in 1976 marked a significant break in the "old boys' network." She attributes her victory to her involvement in the PTA (Horton 1995, 72–73). The first group doesn't even entertain the notion of making activism official.

When I asked a Mexican American community activist in her late thirties if she ever considered running for office, she spoke of the obstacles she saw for wives and mothers:

I have tried to stay involved where my children were concerned. We did this involvement as a family. We were up there [at school] at night and on weekends. My husband would help put up booths et cetera. The kids were receiving direct benefits from it. I think women get involved at those levels because their children are involved. I noticed that women are a little hampered by home responsibilities.

Even if you have your husband's support, there is still that "tug of war." I don't have time yet; maybe when I am fifty. No matter how supportive their husband is, women still cook the meals and keep the household together. Sure, they may do a little wash or mop the floor. But I think women are a little less free to get into the political arena.

She discusses the level of her activism in proportion to the demands of her household responsibilities and her husband's support. He encourages her activism because he feels it is important for the children, but he dislikes "that kind of thing" himself and prefers that she be the one to "go up and do the talking, be on the boards."

Rosemary López, another second-generation Mexican American woman, mentioned that her husband gave her a "little negative feedback when the Sunday meetings interfered with weekend family time." She stated, "It'd be different if the meeting's during the week when everybody [kids and husband] is taken care of, doing their homework, and I just go. But when it starts to intrude on the family's togetherness, there's a little resentment."

If we draw together what women in Monterey Park say about the relationship between their community activism and household responsibilities, it differs only slightly among the women. For the most part, women maintain the responsibility for domestic work and community work. They do not challenge the traditional arrangement in the household. Instead, they work within the defined boundaries; at times they stretch and push the boundaries further out into the community.

Marijune Wissmann's husband, a retired police officer, supports her volunteer work and sometimes attends meetings with her. She explains his role:

> He doesn't like to get out there after being on the police department. He says now that he is retired, he will help all he can. He knows all the laws involved, so sometimes he gives me questions to ask at meetings. He is sort of a silent advisor. He said he is the chauffeur, and he doesn't object to my activities. He has been out there for so many years he is sort of taking a vacation.

Cindy Yee said her husband, also a second-generation Chinese American, tolerated her community activism. She sums up his attitude as, "Okay, fine. It is for the kids." During a period when she says she "became obsessed with trying to get a high school built in Monterey Park," she tells how hectic things became in their household: "You know, he would be coming in and I would be going out. I was going to meetings, and he had to watch the kids. Dinner was on the table already, but the house was a mess. I was also supposed to be making plans because we had our house added on to. But I just dropped everything." I asked her if he picked up any of the slack on the household duties. She laughed wryly and simply said, "No." She explained that he has a difficult job and when he comes home he just wants to relax. He says that she does enough [community work] for both of them. People have suggested that her community experience would make her a great candidate for city council, but her family responsibilities are her priority.

Becoming a Public Person: "Political Careers"

Although the household division of labor may not change much, women who are active do change in the sense of becoming "public" persons. What women make of their community activism varies. Some speak of personal empowerment, a few go on to political careers and participation in the conventional political structure, and others prefer the "gadfly" role. One example is Cindy Yee, a long-time resident in Monterey Park, who recalls an early experience regarding the controversial spraying of pesticides on residential neighborhoods. She says her old friends cannot believe how she has changed: they recall how shy and quiet she was in high school.

The controversy began with the discovery of the Mediterranean fruit fly, which threatened California's multimillion-dollar agribusiness and prompted the state to mandate aerial spraying throughout urban and some suburban Los Angeles neighborhoods. The spraying angered many residents, who reported respiratory illness after repeated applications of malathion, a potent pesticide. Citizens mounted opposition during the spring and summer of 1989, to no avail. They were told that aerial spraying of malathion was not harmful to human beings, even though the chemical has been banned in Japan for over ten years and residents were advised to cover their cars in order to protect the paint. Cindy describes the after-effects of the first malathion spraying in her neighborhood and how she began speaking out:

> Right after the first spraying my friend's daughter had an asthma attack and was hospitalized. A lot of people got sick with diarrhea. It would only happen during the spraying, and they sprayed once a week. So I called our mayor and said this spraying stuff doesn't sound too healthy for us, and so she set up a community meeting for residents to ask questions to this panel that included one of the doctors from County Health Service.

Cindy described this experience as marking the start of her long history of community activism: "I was not an activist. I didn't like speaking in front of people. Now I don't mind it." (In fact, I have seen her speak up at numerous Monterey Park city council meetings, and she expresses herself with confidence and focus.) She continued, "At that community meeting I raised my hand to ask a question and got picked to come before the podium first, and I was really scared. Then, to make it even worse, all of a sudden a news camera from Channel 7 news was pointed at me. Man, I was sicker than a dog [i.e., nervous]! I took a deep breath and thought I've got to do it, and ever since then it just kind of took the fear out of me."

Alice Ballesteros speaks of how her community activism drew her into city commissions. However, like Cindy, she limits her activity in deference to family needs. She is a married white-collar worker who is the mother of three. A second-generation Mexican American, monolingual (English), she began community volunteer work through the city's sports groups. Just as the other women activists do, she links her motivation for community activism to "good mothering":

> I started out being involved in the sports group when my daughter was eight years old—Monterey Park Sports Club. They have a membership of about eight hundred families. They play baseball, soccer, and basketball. I was a team parent; then I joined the board. I would attend all the meetings. When one of the officers resigned, someone appointed me to the board. After that I became president.

She speaks of this upward mobility to elected positions as happenstance and not something she particularly pursued. Her career in parent-teacher groups followed the educational progress of her children from elementary to high school:

> Then I became involved in the PTA at the elementary level. I have three kids, so I also joined the Booster Club at the high school. I was involved in all three schools! A few years ago, I finished my involvement with the sports club. Then about six years ago, I got appointed to the Parks and Recreation Commission in Monterey Park. And again, there was an interest in recreation and sports, so that was a natural place for me to put my time.

Alice also managed the campaign for a Mexican American man who successfully ran for city clerk. She initiated the campaign by sending campaign literature to the sports club families. Other community activists say Alice could easily win a spot on city council.

Dora Padilla, a high school–educated Mexican American woman married to a high school teacher, has been a member of the Alhambra District School Board for fifteen years. Her case illustrates how some women may seek elected positions as a result of their grassroots community activism. She explains how she unexpectedly won the school board seat in 1976:

> I was staying at home. Then when my child started elementary school, I began attending PTA meetings. They said they could use volunteers in the classroom, so I started going a few times a week to help out. Then what I saw was that the Spanish-speaking children were being left out. There was no one there to translate for them, and they were very lost. Also at PTA meetings when a Mexican, Spanish-speaking parent would come, they were also very uncomfortable because there was no one there to help them.

> Dora Padilla's case reinforces the pattern: "My husband is a high school teacher, and he always thought it was great that I was involved. I never had any conflict with the time away from home because I did all my household work when my husband was at work. I didn't have a job, so my job was 'mom' and community involvement!"

> Dora explained how her volunteer work in PTA and other children-centered groups created a firm foundation from which to launch a grassroots campaign that won her a seat on the school board. Her work, as she proudly

states, centered on gender-specific responsibilities and community. The ability to carry out the expected house-hold work during her husband's work hours meant the traditional domestic arrangement remained virtually unchanged.

Some stress they would never consider running for office because they would lose the ability to criticize from the out-side. Deborah Marshall sums up the sentiment, "They told me once you are in there you are seen as having a self-interest, so I decided never to run."

Creating Community: Comparative Contexts

Like the activists of Eastside Los Angeles, women in Monterey Park are involved in school activities, and children link com-munity members. While the welfare of children is the typical entrée into community work, in neither community do *all* ac-tivists have children. A simplistic assumption that biological motherhood spurs women's activism misses the full picture. Life cycles, work histories, and familial commitments shape women's activism.

Women's voluntary work and the associations and net-works derived from that work predated issue-oriented ac-tivism in both communities. Women played a key role in shap-ing the social relations in each community. The process of becoming an activist unfolds through the stories women tell about their first community volunteer work.

Most volunteer work took place in small social groups working cooperatively toward modest goals that would bet-ter the immediate community—a refrigerator for the parish,

books for the elementary school students. This work solidi-
fied community friendships and networks. Some efforts
brought in resources from outside public sources, resulting in
improved recreational facilities and staffing and better school
facilities. Efforts that led women to seek resources outside the
neighborhood compelled them to find their way around bureaucratic obstacles, and they gained insights into city power
relations.

Superficially, the difference between the inner-city and suburban women originates in the absence of the parish-based activities that I learned about from the women in Eastside Los
Angeles. Laughingly described as *tamaleras* because of all the
tamales they made and sold, the Eastside women contributed
long hours and hard labor to make possible the purchase of
school necessities. More significant, the women established
long-lasting friendships with other residents. In contrast, several of the women in Monterey Park attended church regularly,
but their community volunteer work is focused elsewhere

The women in Mothers of East Los Angeles also live in a
community that is 95 percent Latino (according to the 1990
Census), while Monterey Park women live and work in ethnically diverse settings. The suburban women participated in
the community through the school PTA groups, but their work
and strategies differed from those of women in East Los Angeles. Women in Monterey Park did not have to become a volunteer workforce to supplement community resources. When the
Department of Corrections violated their sense of community
standards, they activated their networks. Similar to the
women in Boyle Heights, the Monterey Park women mobilized collective action, albeit in smaller numbers, around issues of community safety. Even though they have more income, they perform most of the daily work necessary for the

maintenance of children. They continue to socialize new residents to community norms.

The community context, whether Latino barrio or ethnically diverse suburb, represents far more than a setting for women's activism. The position of the community in the socioeconomic hierarchy influences where and how women invest their involvement. Community concerns hinge on the community's position in the larger social and political picture. In Eastside Los Angeles, where more community involvement is needed to create safe conditions for families and to generate social mobility than is generally necessary in a suburban setting, the women have had a long and rich history of routine struggle on a daily basis.

The socioeconomic class of the community determines women's public resources and the issues that they pursue. For example, in Boyle Heights women organized to refurbish an abandoned city recreation center and purchase books for the parochial school. In Eastside Los Angeles, where the density is greater (89,000 residents within approximately a six-mile radius) and people have low incomes, public spaces get heavier use than in Monterey Park (65,000 residents within a six-mile radius) where most neighborhoods are insulated and uses of public space are designated and controlled. Though the provision of recreation services is a significant issue for both communities, the Eastside centers are more heavily utilized.

In Boyle Heights women had long histories in the community: all but one was born and raised there; one lived there for over thirty years. Several of the suburban activists had grown up in East Los Angeles but are now considered well-established residents in Monterey Park. Women in the two communities diverged in other ways, including age, work histories, and marital status. For example, all but one of the women from Boyle Heights are married and have children; one is single and never had children. While all are between forty and sixty-five years old, more of the Monterey Park women fall into the younger end of the age range and have worked for wages either full- or part-time over the last twenty years. The women from Monterey Park also show greater differences in work and family organization: two are divorced and have children; the others are married and have children.

Women's associations in both communities predated their contemporary activism. In the context of everyday neighborhood associations and activities, women learned valuable skills and devised strategies useful in later political situations. Women also played a key role in shaping community social relations; much of their work bridges gaps between community groups and may lead to new possibilities for political participation. They also bridge gaps between immigrants and U.S.-born community members and between community needs and state resources. The church as the center for community life and the expression of ethnic identity is most apparent in Boyle Heights. Ethnicity may be expressed in different ways in multi-ethnic settings; in Monterey Park residents sought to create interethnic bridges between Latinos and new Asian immigrants. These bridges may eventually lead to political cooperation.

Community activism on the Eastside retains a grassroots character, and grassroots activists seldom if ever move into elected positions. In Monterey Park there is a greater range of activist "careers." Some women who were once community activists now serve on the school board. Once elected they continue to interact with grassroots groups, but women activists in both communities observe that holding an official position constrains one's ability to be critical.

N I N E

Women Transforming the "Political"
"Traditions Are Not So Traditional"

Nine years have passed since I first sat in Juana Gutiérrez's living room. Covering her walls today are plaques, awards, and photos of her being honored by public officials. One award bears the presidential seal and congratulations from President Clinton. Before we eat lunch, she clears a thick day calendar and stacks of letters, flyers, and invitations from her dining room table. Just as it was nine years ago, her home is a busy workspace; the telephone rings, there are messages about meetings and events. Community and home and family still merge together. Juana's daughter Elsa, now the mother of a fourteen-year-old boy, is managing the community water-conservation project that MELA-SI has developed over the last five years. The neighborhood-based group has gained much attention as the first Los Angeles community partnership focused on water conservation. The small nonprofit group generates jobs and reinvests in the community.

Elsa and Juana share amazing news: in August Elsa and her son will travel to South Africa at the invitation of officials in Johannesburg who wish to begin a community partnership built around water conservation. They have asked Elsa to share her expertise. Juana explains that she cannot go because she has too much to do at "home," meaning both community and family. Elsa knows the logistics of the operation, and she will represent Madres del Este de Los Angeles (MELA-SI).[1]

In May of 1997, I returned to visit Annie Rodríguez and Cindy Yee, core activists in the Monterey Highlands. Annie and Cindy express a sigh of relief and tell me about their latest successful grassroots political experience—stopping billboards from invading the community! In Monterey Park a large advertising agency had attempted to reverse the city's ban on billboards.[2] The city council, with the exception of Councilwoman Judy Chu, seemed to favor the billboard companies. Vince Ramírez, Lucia Su, and Marcia Spira cochaired the Residents against Billboards Committee, themselves reflecting the multiethnic character of Monterey Park. The same residents who ousted the parole office joined in a citywide informational campaign and placed an initiative on the city elections ballot. The initiative put the power to control billboards in the hands of residents rather than the city council members. The ballot, translated into Chinese, Spanish, Japanese, and Tagalog, gained overwhelming support. Meanwhile, the billboard company sued the cochairs and the residents' group for failing to comply with an election code provision requiring public notification.[3] Vince Ramírez's daughter, now a lawyer, joined Lucia Su's son, who is also a lawyer, to defend the group. They won.

At first glance, maintaining a moratorium on billboards seems a rather mild concern. But for Monterey Park residents, and those in other communities, a barrage of billboards opens the door for degradation of the community—selling out to commercial interests instead of maintaining the beauty of the landscape for residents.[4] Furthermore, residents objected to the products and images displayed on numerous billboards.

Alcoholic beverage manufacturers are a close second behind the tobacco industry for investing in billboard advertising, and they have saturated low-income neighborhoods, particularly in Latino and African American communities. In Eastside neighborhoods, billboards clutter neighborhoods and typically feature scantily-clad women and other culturally offensive images to promote their products.[5]

Later, Annie and her husband, Nick, invite me to have dinner in a nearby Chinese restaurant. They comment on the fact that the Chinese-language newspapers provided extensive coverage of the billboard initiative, and the overwhelming resident approval of it suggests the political participation of immigrants. As we enjoyed dinner in the small, busy restaurant near their home, Annie commented that last year, when they first started eating there, the owners could barely speak English; now they converse with us regarding items on the menu. Annie and Nick say they sometimes miss the old restaurants that served coffee and pancakes, but they have learned to enjoy and take pride in Monterey Park's popular Chinese restaurants. The rapid influx of Chinese immigrants, which generated so much animosity a decade ago, has subsided as residents go about their daily lives. In both Monterey Park and Eastside Los Angeles, women conclude that only a watchful community, not regulatory agencies or elected officials, can maintain the quality of life in the places where we live.

In both communities, women's activism originated in family concerns and community networks, then generated broader political involvements. This pattern is similar to that found in other studies of women's activism. Within the circumstances of their lives, they use existing gender, ethnic, and community identities to accomplish larger political tasks. These stories demand that we rethink the usual definitions of tradition and social identity as unchanging.[6]

Family and Community Activism

The idea that politics is a "public" activity separate from the domestic or "private" sphere is a male-biased viewpoint. As we have seen, the routine work women do in the community is as significant as their more formal "political work." Political participation not only crosses boundaries between the public and private spheres but also relies on the relationship between the two. Women link work in the home, their identification as wives and mothers, and their activism. They are rooted in traditional social identities, then "loosened" from them. In some cases women transformed their identities as they moved beyond the neighborhood boundaries into new public, political arenas. Individual women may be empowered, and public recognition may draw them beyond single issues. It may also be that oppositional activism becomes conventional and constrained within existing city-sanctioned groups. In either case, women's activism is loosened from its roots and enriched by visions of change.

Eastside Los Angeles

In this working-class inner-city Latino community, activists connected environmentalism and racism and called attention to the environmental racism threatening their community. (Environmental racism refers to the practice of siting hazardous, pollutant-producing projects and industries in low-income minority communities.) Besides broadening their own understanding of the political world, the Eastside women's opposition to the construction of the first toxic-waste incinerator in the center of the city heightened the larger Los Angeles community's awareness of ethnic and racial community struggles around environmental issues. The activists demanded recognition that the health risks to inner-city residents were as important as those posed to wildlife. Their contributions and concerns about the quality of community life moved from the confines of family and neighborhood and into more public, dispersed, citywide arenas.

The women based their theories about grassroots activism in everyday life and in their work as wives and mothers. Rather than allow themselves to be constricted by them, they used traditional and social identities in community action. In some instances their activism became something new, extending beyond the traditional household sphere and beyond a single neighborhood issue.

These women's routine community work had political implications. It preceded their activism in the conflict over the prison and the toxic-waste incinerator. In Eastside Los Angeles, the extensive collective efforts of women in the parish setting required ongoing negotiations among priests, nuns, and nonactivist women. The women were firmly committed to the parish church, which represents a strategic place to do collective work. As women created extra resources for the education of their children, they expressed gender, ethnic, and class identity.

Labor-intensive food preparation and fund-raisers would seem to be quite traditional women's work. But women's voluntary efforts also made it possible for them to challenge traditional practices within the church. Their needed contributions gave them authority to enter into a dialogue with the priests about school administrative practices and how the funds they earned would be spent. For example, they requested that the nuns who taught their children and worked most directly with parents and children be included in parent-school meetings. Later, they were able to secure the use of church facilities for community events that were not church related. It is important to note that they did not abandon the church when disagreements arose; instead, they negotiated with the priests and persuaded them to meet their needs. Their lives were intimately connected to sustaining the home, the church, and the neighborhood.

The style and strategy of these women's activism followed a pattern congruent with their family and community relations. As they became more active in community issues, they continued to meet their family and household responsibilities. Particularly significant is the way they negotiated to be activists. For the most part, their husbands supported them. As one husband saw it, "The women are carrying the flag for the family." Perceiving the women's activism in this manner extends family boundaries beyond the household and the neighborhood. Conversely, women always acknowledged their husbands' support, which the men demonstrated by their verbal affirmations, attendance at demonstrations, and material support of the household. The strategy maintained one realm of traditional social relations and reversed the usual gendered pattern of political participation, where men are the key actors and women support them. Although some change has occurred on the U.S. political scene in the last thirty years, the general division of labor in local politics continues, and significantly fewer women than men serve in elected offices (Flammang 1997, 138).[7]

Thus, what is new is not a redivision of household work between husbands and wives. The transformation occurred as women and men redefined women's "natural" work to include community activism. This may be viewed as taking on an extra job. The fact that men supported their wives' work reversed the traditional and expected participation patterns. Women worked in conjunction with local political representatives and with the parish priest and in the context of a community with a long history of grassroots activism and political vulnerability. Women within the traditional sphere were actors and negotiators rather than merely submissive followers. Maybe it is time to develop a less static and more historical and dynamic concept of tradition.

Earlier studies of Mexican American families wrongly looked at tradition, in the form of "familism" and "mother country attachment," as inhibiting political participation. Lacking in concern for context or social processes, the research methods and subsequent findings offered no clue to the conditions under which these traditions might become resources for political action. In Eastside Los Angeles, ethnic and gender-based traditions were refashioned into strategies for resistance. Thus, symbols of Mexican culture textured social relations and community. The sense of "being Mexican," ethnic solidarity, and communal responsibility characterized mobilization efforts. Emphasis on ethnic identity drew support from middle-class Mexican American political organizations.

The Eastside Los Angeles case is an instance of successful and dramatic community mobilization. There were unexpected offshoots from the activism of these inner-city working class women. As the group attained more public visibility, other political groups sought them out to request their support. This produced some tensions among the actors in the first two struggles—the parish priest, the Mexican American women elected to public office, and the women activists. The process of deciding which issues to pursue and what strategies to adopt became more complicated than it was when the group was fighting a single issue within parish boundaries.

Mothers of East Los Angeles emerged from being a single-issue group to achieve public recognition and legitimacy in the Eastside and other communities. At the point that a grassroots group gains recognition beyond a single issue, it may come in conflict with its roots. Once a collective is recognized by other people, it becomes qualitatively different. The possibility of broader political activism calls for a reassessment of the group's objectives, strategies, and organizational structure. In the Eastside case, women became spokespersons for the community alongside priests and male leaders. Several women split from the original group and started a new organization, MELA-SI. The two groups continue to work on other urban-land and quality-of-life issues. For example, they have participated in a citywide controversy over the renovation and reconceptualization of Olvera Street, a historical Mexican site, actively supported the United Farm Workers grape boycott by picketing local supermarkets, and contested the renewed attempt to construct an oil pipeline through urban Los Angeles neighborhoods. The point is that political participation may lead to new forms of consciousness and changed political strategies.

Monterey Park

Monterey Park's community infrastructure, far superior to the Eastside's, influenced family strategies. Most of the women I met placed their children in public school because the suburban schools were of a better quality than inner-city public schools. Therefore, the women in Monterey Park did less volunteer work in the schools than the women of Eastside Los Angeles with children in parochial schools, where parents were required to volunteer.

Surprisingly, household relations regarding the women's activism were similar in the two communities. Like their Eastside counterparts, Monterey Park men supported the women. But in most cases they were less involved in the women's activism than the men in the working-class community. In Monterey Park the formation of an advisory board meant that activities became largely confined to monthly meetings. Men occasionally attended meetings with their wives, but women took the lead in pursuing concerns that were raised at meetings.

Compared with the Eastside Los Angeles case, the social and political relations in Monterey Park led to less confrontational strategies. Department of Corrections (DOC) officials discouraged independent action on the part of the neighborhood group. In a stable and relatively privileged community not subject to the many negative projects suffered by the Eastside, there was no history of Alinsky-styled grassroots activism. Instead, the women agreed to a strategy that relied on the good faith of the Department of Corrections. Although in retrospect they questioned the wisdom of this approach, the strategy succeeded. As they became more involved in the political conflict, they began reformulating their conceptions of local politics and its relationship to state politics.

Women in the suburban setting had more variation in their activist careers than did women in the barrio. There was more diversity in the paths leading from grassroots activism toward more structured political positions. The middle-class status of the women and the fact that Monterey Park is incorporated and has a "small town" system of political representation provided a different structural context from that of Eastside Los Angeles. In the suburb, some women moved from volunteer positions into unpaid positions on city commissions. Others successfully ran for local school board. Those more critical of the elected representatives chose to remain "gadflies," eschewing any official position. In some cases, the middle-class activists opted to limit their political careers; the Eastside working class women did not enjoy such varied options.

For Mexican American women who moved from the Eastside to Monterey Park, suburban living meant enhanced city services and lower residential density, all of which contributed to an improved quality of life and reduced the need for grassroots activism. As one woman noted, "In Monterey Park people were not fighting for their daily bread." Another woman in Eastside Los Angeles concurred that suburban middle-class women do not need to do all the collective work that women on the Eastside do. Necessary services are publicly provided, or families with adequate incomes may purchase them.

When activism was called for, however, it was complicated by the need to mobilize across ethnic boundaries. Monterey Park women had to break communication barriers and find symbols and strategies that would impel others to join them. This meant transforming everyday lived experiences and traditional family concerns into oppositional symbols and strategies. Ethnic solidarity did not become a basis for mobilization and the pursuit of political objectives. Women activated networks they had established through their responsibilities as mothers, touching on church networks but not making them the center of organizing activity, as they were on the Eastside.

As some studies predict, suburbanization of Mexican Americans does change the way they express ethnic identity. But the change suggests more than simply a decline in ethnicity and an increase in assimilation. There were no new Mexican immigrants to sustain and reinforce cultural patterns and practices. Collective expressions of ethnic identity took place in planned, structured community festivals. Women arranged celebrations to express cultural identity in more private ways. Some continued their kin and friendship networks in Eastside Los Angeles. Others regularly held birthday parties, wedding showers, and other celebrations at a particular Eastside restaurant that caters to middle-class Mexican American professionals. They traveled back and forth across the Eastside and Monterey Park boundaries much like Mexican immigrants travel across the Mexican-U.S. border.

Women's Activism and Private-Public Dichotomies

Ethnic, racial, and class contexts shape the conditions within which women work. It is from these conditions that women's social constructions of community, gender, ethnic, and class identity led to community activism. Women translated personal experiences and observations into collective interests and into solutions to common problems. They used social identity as a political strategy to legitimate their activities to their families, to local elected officials, and to the media. Social identity and material conditions are thus connected in a dynamic relationship. Women's grassroots participation is active, critical citizenship.

Feminist analyses of the interrelations between work and family also pertain to male-centered conceptions of political participation. Feldberg and Nakano Glenn (1984) assess the different conceptual models used in the sociology of work, noting that they vary according to who is being studied. A gender model, linking work and family, is used for studying working women. A job model, making no link to family, is used for studying working men. Similarly, for studying political participation, a gender model is used by social scientists studying women who enter community politics. Their activism is not interpreted as active citizenship but rather as an extension of household work. No gender model is used to study men who enter politics. Their status as men within families seldom enters the analysis. The findings of such studies are thus incomplete. The bias begins at the point of conception, that is, when the research questions are formulated and conceptual frameworks are constructed. Using a gender model to analyze men and women's grassroots leadership may reveal previously neglected dynamics and avoid essentializing their behavior.

Eisenstein (1983) analyzed how nineteenth-century women were able to reconcile the era's image of the ideal woman (the cult of true womanhood) with labor-force participation. Perhaps contemporary Mexican American women do something similar when they involve themselves in grassroots political activism. Eisenstein's richly complex and persuasive argument challenges a functionalist analysis that focuses on women as wives and mothers and sees these identities as persisting because of the coherence of the dominant value system. She recognized that women did not alter or challenge their domestic obligations; their "defining" social roles centered on their families and home, to which they retained a strong commitment. "They did not defend their mode of living on its own terms, but assimilated as much as possible to the traditional one." Women activists in Eastside Los Angeles and Monterey Park also negotiated to maintain harmony in the household while they became increasingly politically active.

Women throughout the world have cogently demonstrated how symbols of women's traditional roles may express political opposition. In South Africa women used symbols of mourning, wearing black clothes or black sashes when the government banned protests against apartheid. During the 1980s, Chilean women demonstrated, banging on pots and pans, in opposition to the presidential nomination of a military general responsible for massive brutality (West and Blumberg 1990,

27). Motherhood and family may also become metaphors for community concerns and resistance. In other circumstances, family metaphors may be used in a less liberating way. But the point is that women in traditional spheres can use tradition in multiple ways to accomplish larger political work. Prevailing interpretations see women as becoming political participants *in spite of* their responsibilities as mothers and members of families. In fact, women may be powerful *because* they have responsibilities, social networks, and daily routines separate from men (Suad 1983, Feijoo 1984, Yudelman 1987, March and Taqqu 1986).[8]

Conceptualizing Political Activation

Women's community involvement is seldom perceived as political, and scholarly conceptual frameworks and definitions reinforce the perception that it is not. Dominant political science and sociological conceptions of the political exclude not only women but also ethnic, racial, and working-class groups. The long history of women's work in communities in particular is often subsumed under their role as mothers and wives. It is "naturalized" as women's work and depoliticized. In a related way, those who express ethnic and racial concerns are tagged as pursuing narrow special interests. Minority working-class women are the ultimate "others" in terms of postmodern ethnographic conceptions. Implicitly, white middle- and upper-class men are the norm, and an unstated gender model casts what all "others" do outside the political realm.

Sociologists have incorrectly predicted that the gender gap in electoral politics would disappear as women became more like men—that is, as they entered the labor force. The prediction ignores the fact that occupational segregation by gender and household division of labor persist. During the last twenty-five years, unprecedented numbers of women entered the paid labor force, married as well as single women. In 1990 more than two-thirds of all employed women worked in services and retail trade. Close to half of all women workers were employed in relatively low-paying service administrative support occupations such as secretaries, waitresses, and health aides, and African American women were more likely than white women to work in these occupations (Ries and Stone 1992, 306–7). Sex segregation, together with economic growth in service industries, contrives to reinforce instead of ameliorate sex inequality in the workplace (McFadden 1997, 269). Whether or not women work for wages, they continue to assume responsibility for 80 percent of household duties (McFadden 1997, 436; Pesquera 1993). Similarly, de facto segregation and discrimination contribute to the persistence of ethnic and racial identities.

When conceptual frames and definitions of the political exclude women who represent over 50 percent of the population, political studies miss the dynamic of social change. As Bayes observes, the "others"—those subordinated—are strategically positioned to make innovative, insightful critiques of the contradictions in the dominant political system. Inner-city residents live the discrepancies between the political system's credo of equality and the declining quality of life in large metropolitan centers.

Working class women of color, sometimes called "three times oppressed," are certainly among those most subordinated. When women of color transform their personal experiences into political action, gender, class, ethnicity, race, and community identity condition their activism. Their practices and strategies demonstrate the inadequacy of examining political participation apart from class context and social identities. People do not become blank slates—"generic citizens"—and lose their identities when they enter politics; rather, their social identities become a frame of reference. However, these social identities are not static; they may change in the process of political action.

Studies of political participation based on a conceptual design devoid of context will exclude much of women's political participation. Mishler succinctly and simply described the paradox in social science methods:

> One side of the paradox is that we all know that human action and experience are context dependent and can only be understood within their contexts . . . the other side of the paradox is that this ordinary and common sense understanding of meaning as context dependent has been excluded from the main tradition of theory and research in the social and psychological sciences. (1979, 2)

I have emphasized practices, processes, and context rather than women's individual characteristics divorced from social networks. This meant putting women at the center, following their social relations within contemporary conflicts and back into their preexisting community networks.

Women's interpretations of their communities, their gender, and their ethnicity affect the style and intensity of their activism. Their social identities are based on their position in their families, their ethnicity, and their communities. Rather than a set of hindrances to political activism, those social identities may be interpreted as facilitating political activism. In short, political participation grounded in the politics of urban settings is structured by people who are gendered, ethnic and racial beings living in communities of particular class and ethnic compositions.

Implications for Future Study

Contextualizing studies at the community level is requisite to understanding how women, members of the working class, and ethnic and racial minorities become politically active. The changing socioeconomic context of urban communities and the particularities of the women at the core of the book provide two benchmarks for future studies.

First, given the urbanization of suburbs in major metropolitan areas, middle-class communities are no longer guaranteed the isolation from urban social problems they enjoyed in the past. Women's activism may become more central to local politics as quality of life is threatened. Women in both working class and middle-class communities often maintain order, socialize new residents, and "keep an eye" on the quality of community life. The growing "internationalization" of major cities presents a different set of obstacles to community activists, requiring them to cross boundaries marked by differences of ethnicity, race, and immigrant status. Family networks and concerns for children's safety—matters central to women's reproductive, unwaged work—may offer bridges across these and other differences.

Second, the women in this study were of a particular generation and age group. Many, nearing retirement age, had husbands who held stable employment at wage levels that could meet family expenses and allow them to purchase homes. In the working-class community, most women focused their energies on unwaged work. If real wages continue to fall, however, it is likely that fewer and fewer families will follow the household strategies of the working-class Eastside community.

Greater job insecurity, stagnant wages, and a growing gap between the upper- and lower-income sectors suggest that economic conditions no longer allow most women to focus a large portion of their energies on unwaged community work. The women of this study represent a particular era and place in U.S. social and economic history. The most significant occupational developments in the post–World War II period have been the growth of middle- and working-class families dependent on two full-time incomes and poor working-class families dependent on the income of a single woman (Berensen 1984). But Ferree (1984) argues, given gender segregation in the workplace, that working-class women and some middle-class ones continue to maintain a strong social identity with family instead of work. This means they will still find ways to meet the work of that particular social identification.

If gender is to be fully addressed as a dimension of political activism, future studies will need to explore similar themes from the perspectives of women and men of the same class and ethnic and racial groups, or compare perceptions of women and men across ethnic and racial groups. In that way, one could begin to understand how women and men interpret political empowerment along lines of different ethnic and racial identities. As studies of women and minority and working class people suggest, a subordinate position has the potential to provide alternatives to the mainstream view. Alternative views can be the departure point for resistance to domination and challenges to the state's definition of social justice.

Conceptual and Methodological Reflections

Chicana and Chicano studies and critical feminist studies begin with a critique of the male Eurocentric bias in social science.[9] From this position, all research is ideological; that is, it has a vision of what our social relations ought to be. Unlike mainstream scholars, critical scholars speak from the margins to challenge research that claims objectivity and detachment from a political agenda. These critiques of mainstream scholarship strive to develop alternative histories and theories that do more than "set the record straight." Ideas may be used as political tools to dismantle sexism, racism, and class bias and better the conditions that people confront in their everyday lives. Building on a rich history of critical scholarship, this book documents the process by which Mexican American women in a barrio and in a suburban Los Angeles setting became grassroots activists.

I am indeed fortunate to be writing in the late 1990s, when critical scholarship is representing more and more previously excluded voices. The 1990s also mark a particularly exciting moment to enrich the relatively new field of Chicana and Chicano studies, which is beginning to integrate feminist perspectives.[10] Regardless of the marginal position it holds in relation to mainstream social science, critical scholarship is always a source of new ideas and paradigms—precisely because it rejects dominant views that often erase, minimize, or misrepresent the significance of gender, ethnicity and race, class, and struggles against inequity. Critical scholarship also converses with mainstream scholarship so that it may influence how others think, see, and produce knowledge.

Critical feminist, ethnic, and sociological studies inform this book. Feminist studies expand the definition of leadership as the work of those who mobilize others rather than simply those who hold official positions in organizations.[11] Chicana and Chicano studies affirm ethnic identity as a potential resource for political resistance. Interpreting Mexican American women's political activism from a critical-studies perspective challenges and transforms social science concepts, assumptions, and methods that have ignored our experiences.

Women Disappear in the Sociology of Urban Politics

Women of all colors curiously disappear in the sociology of urban politics. I call it a curious disappearance because our self-perceptions as women or men organize our lives in very specific ways. However, when social science studies refer to individual citizens, the focus is on men's activities. Theories that explain how individual identities are transformed into collective identities and action omit gender as a necessary category of analysis. If I had attempted to begin my study within the existing conceptual frameworks, I would not have been able to investigate the complexities of Mexican American women's activities. The details of women's lives would not fit discrete categories; therefore I question the mainstream conceptual frameworks rather than attempt to make my study fit into them. What mainstream social science says and what it fails to say can be instructive because it reveals *how* the marginalization of women takes place. All too often, gender disappears from accounts of the Chicana and Chicano experience in the United States, just as Chicanas and Chicanos disappear from the sociology of urban politics. How can this be explained?

One feminist critique calls the ways women are omitted from studies in political science the "tricks of the trade" (Theile 1986).[12] First, studies of politics or leadership will focus on arenas where women are not central to the action; they examine men's activities and assume that they represent the world of politics. All political activity is then universalized as what men do. Second, when women are politically active, their work is seen as "natural," "an extension of the family"— that is, an activity essential to being a woman but not *really* political or central to an understanding of politics. Third, and most often in sociological analysis, the activity is stripped of its context by lifting it out of its geographical place and historical time. The objects of study are ungendered social movements or mobilizations of preexisting networks where gender, race, and class are treated as unproblematic or unimportant. To varying degrees, sociological analysis pushes discrete categories and binary divisions to build theory; the more abstracted and sophisticated the theory, the more likely it is to exclude the experiences of women of color.

The dominant paradigms of urban politics and collective action—resource mobilization theory and new social movements theory, different in other ways not immediately relevant to this discussion—have converged on a central question: How are personal problems and individual identity transformed into collective identity and collective mobilization? The theories emphasize the social life and traditions of communities and their creative use in solving new problems, the mobilization of preexisting social networks often based in families and neighborhoods, and everyday neighborhood interaction as important dimensions of collective action.[13] When mentioned at all, women are casually referenced and gender is conceptually unimportant. The gendered character of community activism receives marginal attention, a comment buried within a descriptive account.

In resource-mobilization theories and social-movement theories, gender and ethnicity become visible only when the movement is a feminist or nationalist one; however, everyday family life and community networks are in fact gendered, as is ethnicity.[14] For example, studies of the American civil rights movement highlighted the previously neglected factors of African American identity and preexisting social networks based in black churches as important in creating political unity. African American women scholars explored the gendered nature of these preexisting networks and made visible African American women who helped to initiate and organize the Montgomery bus boycott and whose daily work helped to build and sustain black churches.[15]

Theories of urban politics would greatly benefit from reassessing the empirically rich and conceptually groundbreaking social history of women's collective activism. The social histories constructed through women's collective action, however, have not simply been overlooked. The omission of women and a gendered analysis inclusive of ethnicity and race represents more than simple oversight; rather, "it is a conceptual practice of power"(Smith 1990). Women perform the "detail work" in households, communities, and workplaces, and they do additional face-to-face emotional and interactional work that remains unrecognized, uncounted, and devalued. How can we understand the way sociological theory resists gendered analyses and thus causes women to "disappear" in analytical accounts of urban political participation? Sociologist Dorothy Smith (1977, 149) states, "The world as we know it 'sociologically' is largely organized by the articulation of the discourse to the ruling apparatus of which it is a part." She further explains how women are are forced to 'stuff' their experience into predefined categories *or the experience is ignored.*

Used uncritically, social science concepts can render invisible the lived realities in which these relations exist. Making the categories used in social science part of the problem to be explained also reveals how knowledge is constructed and how power is reinforced thereby. For example, Chicana sociology students grapple with locating a theory to explain experiences shaped by gender, ethnicity, and class. As students we learn that some topics are considered relevant and others are not.

The suppression of local and particular activities as sociologically less important than abstract grand theories and "master frames" perpetuates a male bias that excludes a unified approach to gender, ethnicity, race, and class (Smith 1990).[16] When social science erases gender, ethnicity, race, and class and in the process obscures more than it reveals about urban politics, we need to create new concepts of political participation and leadership.

"Decolonized" Feminist Insights for Social Science Blindspots

Just as feminist critiques have revealed male bias in research, women of color have revealed the way early feminist studies focused on the experiences of European American women. Theorizing solely on the experiences of one ethnic group shuts other women's struggles outside the conceptual framework (Collins 1991, hooks 1990, Lugones and Spelman 1983, Sandoval 1991). Third World women scholars have challenged feminists to "decolonize" their vision of social change and give up the search for the generic woman who has no particular racial, class, and ethnic identity. Decolonizing feminism means rethinking conceptual frameworks and political agendas and redefining and widening the analytical terrain to include other bases of oppression such as ethnicity and race, class, and imperialism (Spelman 1988, Johnson-Odim 1991).[17]

New Conceptual Frameworks: Affirming Women's Activism

Reconceiving leadership and political participation as the work that moves people to political action makes a space for looking at women's activities. Reconceiving social identities as strategies for solving problems affirms the varied ways that women of different ethnicities, races, and classes become grassroots activists.[18] Practices women use in particular circumstances and in particular times and places become the focus. The process of using social identity as a strategy is multidimensional. How one chooses to identify oneself or express ethnicity may change dependent on who is present. One's social identity is symbolic and dynamic. Likewise, thinking about social identity as a strategy avoids essentializing women's political activities as natural extensions of gender roles. Instead, ethnicity, race, class, and gender are intertwined social constructions.

People who assume leadership roles do not abandon their traditional identities but neither are they politically confined by them. They reweave their identities and culture. Conceiving identities as interpreted within particular places and historical times offers a middle ground between "agency," the freedom of an individual to do as she desires, and "determination," the rigid limitations on an individual's freedom.

Early feminist critiques of the family identified it as the ultimate site of oppression, but women may be subordinated in a family that provides benefits and resource networks not available elsewhere (Sen 1980). For many minority working-class women, the family can be a base for political resistance. Family has an emancipatory potential because it cultivates the dream of a better future for children (Marshall 1994). Women who participate in grassroots community activism often assert that their experiences as wives and mothers are intimately linked to their political activism (Cockburn 1977, Feijoo 1984, Kaplan 1981, and Flammang 1985). More than a simple expression of the traditional female role of wife and mother, women's community activism has the potential to transform that role. The relationship is not unidirectional.[19]

Political activism among Mexican American women and men may change family relationships. As a shared enterprise, it may promote family unity and enhance women's status in the family. When women gain access to new sources of information and social contacts, they may develop new self-confidence (Baca Zinn 1975). The history of Mexican American women's activism in labor organizing offers insights for understanding the complexities of their community activism and family relationships. Zavella's (1987) study of Chicana cannery workers found that husbands resisted supporting women's activism because they perceived it as intruding upon women's household obligations. Women active in the United Farm Workers (Rose 1990) often continued to meet household responsibilities and avoided conflict with husbands, while workers who organized the Farah garment workers' strike in Texas (Coyle 1980) developed critical consciousness about women's issues. Women's political participation may depend on their success in redefining household responsibilities and renegotiating the domestic division of labor. Disruption of domestic routines may bring about new activities for men and women. The new activities open up new possibilities for reconstructing gender categories (M. Rosaldo 1980, 417).[20]

Ethnic identity, conceived as a social relation rather than an isolable and singular trait or attribute, is specified by gender and by class; it is expressed in the context of other social relations. Studies of Chicanas and Mexican women's workplace activism illustrate how ethnic identity may emerge as a political resource. Mora (1980) followed the growing ethnic consciousness of Mexican women who went on strike in the Tolteca food-processing factory in northern California. According to Ruiz (1987), in the 1940s Chicana workers' collective identity developed in the context of the gender-segregated northern California food canneries. Interethnic networks also developed among Russian Jewish and Mexican American women who worked together. Union activism drew strength from these gendered networks.

While some inroads have been made, many communities and workplaces remain segregated. Ethnicity and class often converge with the stratification found in almost all major U.S. cities. Latino, African American, and Native American neighborhoods are more likely to be low income and therefore vulnerable to inadequate services and infrastructure. However, the ethnic or racial identity of a community may also help to unify residents. Neighborhoods not only reflect inequality; they help organize in response to it (J. Logan 1978).

African American women and Latinas who live in low-income neighborhoods segregated by race or ethnicity may find gender and ethnic identity a meaningful base of organization. In a study of black female community activists (Gilkes 1980, 1982), residential segregation, ethnic identification, age grouping, and gender roles were found to be critical dimensions for understanding their work. Racism had the collective effect of binding the black community together in spite of its diversity. The women saw the work they did as a response to the concerns and problems they faced as wives and mothers. They transformed personal problems into public ones and also converted gender networks into politicized networks as they became involved in grassroots mobilization.[21] They perceived the community as united by external threats and white racism as well as by its own inner resources.

Even though the cultural-deficiency perspective has been extensively critiqued for perceiving cultural attributes as static, negative, uncreative, and useless, it continues to guide survey research about political participation. National surveys have examined the low levels of political activism among the Latino population as a whole, and have found that middle-aged and college-educated persons tend to join more political organizations than do younger, less educated minority individuals. For Mexican Americans, the impediments to joining voluntary organizations listed by most studies include primary kinship systems, fatalism, religious traditionalism and traditional cultural values, and persistence of mother-country attachment. In most cases differences between men and women are not investigated (García and de la Garza 1985, 553).

From another perspective, low levels of political participation may be partly explained by discrimination on the basis of one's ethnicity, race, gender, or class. These subordinate statuses have been expressed as "twice a minority" (Melville 1980) and "triple oppression" (Mirande and Enriques 1979) in an effort to emphasize the structurally organized sources of inequality. Mexican American women's grassroots activism counters the simple assumption that familism, poverty, and ethnicity predict political passivity. The variables on the list of impediments to political participation are potential facilitators and resources. Spelman (1988) argues against conceptualizing oppression as additive and states that "identity may be a source of pride as well as the occasion for an oppressed situation." Asking how women may use ethnic, racial, gender, and class position and identity to resist structural sources of oppression challenges cultural-deficiency approaches; research on women and social change must recognize both the conditions of subordination and the possibilities for resistance.

Women's narratives bring to life concepts such as class, kinship, and ethnic and gender identity. Placed in the context of lived experiences in community settings, the variables may be understood as the social relations that they are intended to represent. Women's perceptions—that is, the meanings that they give to their lives and communities' events—are creative and interactive social constructions, reflections and interpretations of their histories and dialogues with members of their families, other communities, media representations, and policy makers. The re-creations and interpretation of these meanings can influence and shape what people actually do. The meanings people give to a situation guide the first step toward action. In African American and Latino communities, women express gender as well as ethnic identity as reasons for community activism.

There is no predetermined path to collective action; people interpret their material conditions in ways that may help reproduce practices that oppress or liberate. The way an individual understands her social relations influences what actions she will take, what will be seen as appropriate or inappropriate responses. One's interpretations determine what is inconsequential or offensive. If she is not offended by an event, a woman may disregard it; if she is offended but sees herself as powerless, she may not take action. But if she is offended and sees even a remote possibility of victory, she may transform the personal problem into a collective problem and seek a collective solution, thereby making social change as women activists in Eastside Los Angeles, Monterey Park, and throughout the world have done.

Appendix

Concepts and Terms

As I interviewed activists and observed and participated in hearings, meeting, demonstrations, and cultural events, I looked for expressions of social identity. Gender, ethnic, racial, class, and community identity are neither predetermined and static nor the result of some linear, unidirectional "socialization" process. Rather, social identity is a creative, interactive, and situated process. The key concepts are processual categories rather than lists of characteristics.

Social identity, as I define it, is expressed in social situations, often political ones, and is used as a way or as a **"strategy"** to accomplish an objective. Ethnic, racial, class, and gender identities are not isolable but may be emphasized or combined differently depending on who is present and how the actor assesses the situation. This definition does not question authenticity or suggest premeditated manipulation. Instead, it interprets expressions of social identity as creative, resourceful, and useful in accomplishing a political objective. Social identity can be used to promote group unity, legitimate moral authority, confront the opposition, and challenge and redefine the state's definition of the common good.

Gender identity is related but not restricted to instances when women express their community work as an extension of family roles, including as wives, mothers, sisters, and daughters. Other expressions of gender identity might be rooted in the differences women perceive between their own activities and those of men. The gender identity of Mexican American women in each community is not generic but is specified by class, community, ethnicity, and race. Similarly, rather than thinking of **ethnic and racial identity** only in relation to self-identification and decontextualized expressions such as food or language preferences, I observed how it was expressed in interactive situations.

Community identity, whether of the inner city or suburban areas, results from social processes and a "dialogue" with others—other communities, the media, and individuals. It is a socially constructed category but must correspond to a changing historical and material reality (Suttles 1972). The relationship between community identity and material reality is most emphatically exposed by the fact that suburban residents are no longer homogeneously white nor are they sheltered from the ills of the inner city—traffic congestion, growth, and pollution. The suburb of Monterey Park is undergoing great transition and reassessing its identity in terms of its class and ethnic/racial composition. These historical and contextual conditions are relevant to the way women carry out their community work.

For the purposes of this study, **community,** whether a territorial or a political space, is always an organization of social relationships. On some occasions, activists may refer to community as the entire city and at other times it may be the block or the neighborhood. In any case it is spatially defined and experienced through social interaction with other residents. Social interaction and social relationships occur through **communitarian work,** volunteerwork carried out in small groups. The work is aimed at reaching collective goals that build community resources. **Grassroots community activists** live and work within the community. Their work does not constitute an officially sanctioned "political career," being either appointed or elected, although some women activists have won electoral office.[1]

Social class can be conceived of in several ways. From a Marxist perspective, all workers who do not own the means of production belong to the working class. I make a distinction between the "middle stratum" or middle class and the blue-collar or working class, a distinction based partly on people's relation to work and partly on their own perceptions. In Los Angeles, moving to a suburb is seen as "moving up" the socioeconomic ladder. Although Mexican Americans are at the bottom of the socioeconomic hierarchy in the suburb I studied, they had more economic resources relative to the residents of Eastside Los Angeles—enough to move out of the barrio. In this study class refers to where people live as well as what they do for a livelihood.

Sacks (1989a) critically assesses theories that unify race, class, and gender. She suggests "a definition of the working class in which membership is not determinable on an individual basis, but rather as membership in a community that is dependent upon waged labor, but that is unable to subsist or reproduce by such labor alone. . . . It is rooted in the relations to the means of production that are collective and grounded in community rather than individual and restricted to the workplace." In suburbia, wage workers were in white-collar clerical positions, with little autonomy over the labor process. In the main, their husbands also worked in white-collar positions. However, most of the women in the suburban setting had approximately one additional year of schooling compared to that of the women in the inner city. There were significant differences between the median family incomes each community.

But most striking was the difference in the quality of the community infrastructure. Several studies of suburbanization in the United States document that the process "split the working class." Higher paid, more highly skilled workers took advantage of government-subsidized housing loans and moved out of the inner city, leaving the lower paid, less skilled workers behind (Katznelson 1981, Parson 1982). The point helps clarify why the individual characteristics of Mexican Americans in the inner city and those in the suburban setting seemed less different than the quality of infrastructure in their respective communities.

Notes

Chapter One. Introduction:
Putting Women at the Center of Politics

1. The terms "Eastside" Los Angeles and East Los Angeles both refer to the area east of the downtown Civic Center. The names are often used interchangeably to designate areas that are distinct but have similar demographic profiles; East Los Angeles proper is unincorporated; Eastside Los Angeles immediately east of the Los Angeles river is part of the city of Los Angeles and is represented by the same political structure. The neighborhoods immediately east of the river include Boyle Heights, Lincoln Heights, and El Sereno; the statistics used in this section are drawn from these three areas. According to Acuña (1984, ix), all have historically shared public services and territory. See Noriega (1988) for an analysis of cinematic representations of Eastside Los Angeles, and see Valdivia (1993) for a critique of print-media coverage of gangs. I capitalize "Eastside," as does the *Los Angeles Times.*

2. For analyses of the empirical shortcomings and political implications of the term "Hispanic," see Acuña (1996), and Hayes-Bautista and Chapa (1987, 61–68).

3. See Sacks (1988) for a definition that expands the dimensions of leadership to include women's and men's activities outside of official positions in organizations. See Pateman (1970) for an early critique of political science and see Christiansan-Ruffman (1995) and Sapiro (1995) for more recent feminist critiques that echo Pateman's concerns.

4. See Victor Carrillo (1996) for an insightful discussion of the politics of translation and the Latino community.

5. See Appendix A, "Concepts and Terms," for further discussion of social identities.

6. Oral history illustrates what is meant by the historical contingency of sociological generalizations (Thompson 1978, Roy 1984). The 1970s and 1980s marked a resurgence in concern for the lives of ordinary people as well as a significant turning point in the reevaluation of ethnographic research methods. Some refer to the reevaluation and emphasis on the "reflexive" nature of cultural accounts as the "new ethnography" (Clifford and Marcus 1986). I interviewed a total of forty Mexican-origin women, four Anglo women, four Chinese-origin women, and one Japanese American woman. I also interviewed men in each community—four Mexican American men, three Anglo men, and two Chinese immigrant men. See Becker (1978) and Geiger (1986) for the methodological rationale for using life histories.

7. "Simple" description is also complex, problematic, and analytical (Emerson 1983, 20).

8. See Katz (1983, 127–38) for a critical essay that addresses the "four R's that haunt participant observation" in sociology: representativeness, reactivity, reliability, and replicability.

9. See Hardy-Fanta (1993) for a fine study of Latinas and political participation in Boston. The book explores themes similar to those in this book, focusing primarily on Puerto Rican women and men in a Boston community.

10. Díaz (forthcoming) argues that in order for the environmental movement to achieve a long-range political agenda in Los Angeles, it must coalesce with minority groups and immigrants. See López-Garza and Díaz (forthcoming) for an outstanding collection of articles that address the role of immigrants not simply as victims but also as participants in the economic and political restructuring of Los Angeles.

11. Geoffrey Mohan, "Mothers Rally to Halt Gang Killings," *Los Angeles Times*, October 8, 1995, B1. A group of women in the Boyle Heights Pico-Aliso housing project did form the Comité Pro Paz en el Barrio (Committee for Peace in the Neighborhood) to stop violence among gang members. Father Greg Boyle, well known for his work with gangs, collaborated with the women's efforts. They held "love

marches" and barbecues to encourage peace between rival gangs, and accused the police of brutality. One woman commented, "As mothers we can cross into different neighborhoods."

12. Horton (1990, 1995). The five other cities were Miami, Philadelphia, Chicago, Houston, and Garden City, Kansas. The Monterey Park research focused on politics in sites that related directly and indirectly to city politics: the city council, neighborhood organizations, civic clubs and associations, and numerous public events and festivals. For related publications by team members, see the work of José Calderón (1991, 1992), who focused on Latinos and interethnic politics; Leland Saito (1993, and forthcoming), who investigated Chinese immigration as both a resource and a problem for Asian American politics; and Yen-Fen Tseng (1994), who studied Chinese immigrant entrepreneurs, their organizations, and economic impact on the San Gabriel Valley. Finally, seee John Horton (1995), the principal investigator, who focused on Anglo residents and integrated a wealth of ethnographic detail into a critical ethnography that examines the complexity of the political changes that occurred in Monterey Park.

13. José Calderón, a member of the research team and a community activist, generously shared a list of people who had worked in a group opposed to an "English as the official language" ordinance, and I began calling women on the list. There was no exclusively women's grassroots group in Monterey Park as I had found in Eastside Los Angeles.

14. Feminists modify ethnographic methods by politicizing and historicizing social construction approaches. This means situating collective behavior within power relations in concrete historical instances (Morgen 1995, 235).

Chapter Two. Community Contexts: The Barrio and the Suburb

1. Vital Statistics of California 1993, 9.

2. Ibid. In 1993 California's birthrate (18.4) declined, but it continued to exceed the U.S. birthrate (15.7) by about 17 percent. According to the 1990 U.S. Census, California has the greatest percentage of foreign-born residents (21.7 percent of 30 million), followed

by New York (15.9 percent of 18 million), and Florida (12.9 percent of 13 million).

3. Kevin Roderick, "Californians: 30 Million and Counting," *Los Angeles Times,* May 16, 1990, A1.

4. In 1986 the Los Angeles County U.S.-born Latino population numbered 840,496; foreign-born Latinos numbered 1,645,868. The U.S.-born Asian/Pacific Islander population numbered 113,171; foreign-born Asians numbered 461,499 (Heer and Herman 1990, 15). Ethnic population projections from 1990 to 2000 are as follows: Latino, from 25 percent to 30 percent; black, 7.1 percent to 6.7 percent; Asian, 7 percent to 13 percent; and Anglo, 57.8 percent to 51.0 percent (Roderick, "Californians: 30 Million and Counting," 15).

5. U.S. Bureau of the Census, 1990 Census of Population, Social and Economic Characteristics (Washington, D.C., November 1993), 150.

6. Referred to as the "internationalization" of Los Angeles and re-structuring of the economy in many urban analyses. See Soja, Morales and Wolff (1983) and Morales and Ong (1993, 55–84).

7. Jill Stewart, "Two-Tiered Economy Feared as Dead End of Un-skilled," *Los Angeles Times,* June 25, 1989, B1.

8. The Service Employees International Union Local 399 launched a nationwide "Justice for Janitors" campaign, which has unionized the janitorial crews in many downtown office. Union workers make $5.00 to $5.50 hourly and receive overtime and other benefits (Bob Baker, "Most Century City Janitors Decide to Walk Off the Job," *Los Angeles Times,* May 31, 1990, B3).

9. Since the 1960s, a growing number of Latino immigrants have moved into south central Los Angeles. Community services and in-frastructure have lagged behind the growing population, resulting in overcrowded schools and competition for housing (Oliver and John-son 1984).

10. See Parson (1982, 255) for an insightful history of subsidized housing in Los Angeles. Los Angeles expended only a small percent-age of the total federal monies allocated to the city for public hous-ing. Red baiting and forceful opposition from the building trades, real estate interests, and racial and ethnic hostilities halted the city's

use of the funds. A report by the U.S. Senate Office of Research states a burgeoning poor population combined with the failure of developers to build low-cost housing units produced a shortfall of over half a million low-income housing units in California. Contrast the inequity between the eighty-six dollars per capita subsidized through mortgage-interest deductions for middle-income homeowners, compared to the twenty-seven dollars per capita to renters (Jill Stewart, "125 Million Low-Cost Housing Plan Expected," *Los Angeles Times,* May 30, 1990, A1).

11. See UCLA Ethnic Studies Centers (1987).

12. Some accounts note conflict between the groups (cited in Acuña 1984). Also see Gluck (1987, 70–98).

13. See Alinsky (1946) for an overview of the organizing model. See Horowitt (1989) for a detailed account of Alinsky's life and work, which began with the working-class Polish and Irish in Chicago. His legacy extends into many major metropolitan neighborhoods. See Boyte's (1989, 180) discussion of Alinsky's influence on grassroots politics, and Miller's (1987) less sympathetic critique of Alinsky and populism.

14. Recognition of individual women's leadership and participation in the groups is available in histories of East Los Angeles (Acuña 1984, 1988). R. Romo (1983) notes that women played a "significant role in the institutional life of the barrio . . . and did much volunteer work." However, a comprehensive account of women's grassroots activism in East Los Angeles has not been the focus of any systematic study. See Orozco (1992) for one of the first historiographies on the participation of Mexican American women in voluntary organizations.

15. See Tirado (1970) for a brief, useful overview of the CSO and other Mexican American political organizations in California in the period 1900–1970.

16. Cited in Horowitt 1989, 225. See Boyte (1980, 49) for a discussion of Alinsky's perception of the church as the key to organizing in first-generation immigrant communities because the church was the center of people's lives.

17. Ortiz (1984, 564). See Dolan and Hinojosa (1994) for a historical overview of Mexican Americans and the Catholic Church and further

discussion of its significant role in the Eastside Los Angeles community. For a contemporary analysis of social changes taking place in the Catholic Church, see Cadena and Medina (1996), who focus on Latinos and liberation theology (the belief that religious teachings should be interpreted from the perpective of the poor and advocate social change) and provide examples of pastoral practices in Southern California.

18. See Morales (1972), who analyzes the history of conlict between the police and the Mexican American community and offers a case study of the violence that erupted during the 1970 Chicano Moratorium demonstration in Eastside Los Angeles. Escobar (1993) also analyzes police-community relations with a focus on police infiltration into the Chicano movement in the years 1968–71.

19. Vern Partlow, "Bypassed Islands of L.A. Experiencing Awakening," *Daily News* (Los Angeles), December 27, 1950, 3. The infamous Bloody Christmas case provided a dramatic introduction to the best-selling crime novel *L. A. Confidential* by James Elroy (1990). The book served as the story line for a movie released in 1997.

20. Partlow, "Bypassed Islands of L.A. Experiencing Awakening."

21. "Congressman Lauds CSO Service," *Eastside Journal* (Los Angeles), May 28, 1964, 1.

22. Ibid. See Apodaca (1995) and Rose (1994, 194–95) for a more detailed analysis of women's participation in the CSO.

23. Amy Pyle, "Book Shortage Plagues L. A. Unified," *Los Angeles Times,* July 28, 1997, A1. Textbook shortages are common across the nation—worse in urban than suburban communities, and worst of all in low-spending states like California, which ranks forty-seventh in the nation for textbook expenditures. Fifty-four percent of California teachers did not have enough books to send home with students. The Los Angeles Unified School District annually spends $26 per student for textbooks, well below the $33 statewide average and $42 national average.

24. Marin (1991, 108). See Marin for a detailed analysis of the Chicano movement and the Eastside community organizations that preceded it. Marin is one of the few sources in which one may read women's first-person accounts of their activism.

25. Rose (1994, 195). García (1986) provides three practical ways—as great women, as workers, and as women—to integrate Chicanas into Chicano studies. Also see García (1990) for a historical overview of the development of Chicana feminist consciousness and activism within the community and in academia.

26. Ortiz (1984). In 1970, according to Ortiz, another boost to parish-based activism was the replacement of Cardinal McIntyre by the more liberal Bishop Manning.

27. Sekul (1988) names four former presidents who were Mexican American women, but he makes no conceptual point about gender as a significant issue. Also see Skerry (1984, 21).

28. Scott Harris, "Community Crusaders: Three Groups Wage Hard-Nosed Struggle for Social Change," Los Angeles Times, November 29, 1987, II:1.

29. All the statistical information is derived from the 1980 U.S. Census and compiled in a study by the UCLA Ethnic Studies Centers (1987).

30. Jeff Gottlieb, "Temperatures Rising in Monterey Park's Melting Pot," Los Angeles Herald Examiner, June 24, 1987, A2.

31. See Calderón (1991, 139–40) for an analysis of Mexican Americans and Monterey Park politics. He provides unique and invaluable observations from the perspective of one who helped to organize a multi-ethnic coalition to oppose anti-immigrant sentiments in the community.

32. Ralph Frammolino, "Paroled Felons Returning in Large Numbers," Los Angeles Times, February 20, 1990, B1.

33. See Carl Ingram, "New Forecast Sees a Worse Jam in Prisons," Los Angeles Times, June 27, 1989, A1.

34. I have extended Blumberg and Gottlieb's analysis (1989, 184–85), which sees "the waste issue as a metaphor for the broader issues of daily life in our urbanized and industrial society." They argue that the solid waste crisis exemplifies how our system creates problems and then fails to solve them. See the entire book for an excellent comprehensive analysis of the politics of the environmental waste industry.

35. Rich Connell, "Downtown Prison Site Selected," Los Angeles Times, March 21, 1985, I:1.

36. In September 1985, the bill passed the Senate with no senator voting against it. Eastside State Senator Art Torres, who later opposed the prison, demanded numerous concessions, such as consultation with community leaders, development of a greenbelt, mitigation of traffic congestion, and employment of Latinos from the community. In March 1986 the Department of Corrections did open a job-recruitment office in Lincoln Heights, in part to engender community support for the prison.

37. After community pressure, the DOC agreed to conduct a partial EIR. Prison opponents later contested the credibility of the EIR. They based their opposition on the fact that half of the state's prisons were filled to more than the overcapacity estimate of 190 percent on which the partial environmental impact report was based.

38. Since April 1991, Gloria Molina has served as the first Mexican American and the first woman supervisor for Los Angeless County's First Supervisorial District, which was created as a result of court-ordered redistricting and special elections. In 1991 a state court cited Los Angeles County for racially guided gerrymandering and forced it to reapportion district boundaries.

39. According to Pitt and Pitt (1997, 406–7), Men's Central Jail houses twenty-two thousand inmates, the largest single jail facility in the Western world.

40. James Vigil, Jr., whose father, Diego Vigil, was active in the Chicano movement, served as Assemblywoman Molina's field representative from 1984 to 1986, when he was accepted into Harvard Law School. He remembers that public hearings had been demanded for more than year and a half, and defeat of the the prison hinged on a large community turnout.

41. *Belvedere Citizen* (Los Angeles). "Prison Battle is Uniting All Fronts." July 22, 1992. 1.

42. Mark Gladstone, "Latinos Press Wilson to Sign Bill to Kill L.A. Prison Plans." *Los Angeles Times*, February 9, 1992, B1.

43. Margo McCall, "Monterey Park Residents Find Parole Office in Neighborhood," *West San Gabriel Valley News Digest*, July 21, 1988, 1.

Chapter Three. The Politics of Community Identity in Eastside
Los Angeles: "We Got Everything Nobody Else Wanted"

1. The off-ramp also marks the nexus of three Los Angeles freeways; therefore, radio stations reporting traffic congestion have unof-
ficially dubbed it "the East L.A. interchange."

2. Freeway construction destroyed 29,000 homes and displaced
10,000 people (Escobedo 1979). City council District 14, which includes Boyle Heights, is one of three districts with the lowest new
residential or commercial construction in the city (Flores 1989).

3. Roxanne Arnold and Michael Seiler, "State Prison, A Birthday
Gift They'd Like to Pass," *Los Angeles Times*, February 17, 1984. Several other communities, including the Santa Clarita Valley, a suburban community at the extreme northern end of Los Angeles County,
and San Gabriel, a suburban community several miles northeast of
East Los Angeles, opposed the prison's placement within their
boundaries.

4. Kenneth Reich, "Deukmejian Assails Parochialism in L.A.," *Los
Angeles Times*, June 22, 1990, A27.

5. In the 1960s and 1970s, groups opposing nuclear power plants
were criticized as self-interested; in the 1980s and 1990s, groups contesting land-use issues are the new NIMBYs. See Blumberg and Gottlieb (1989, 73), who offer a comprehensive discussion of the "politics
of garbage disposal" as a national and, at times, an international issue. The siting of undesirable projects is predicated on the assumption that poor and working-class ethnic communities will be less
likely to mobilize meaningful opposition (Cerrell Associates, 1984).

6. According to a host of official "counts" and critical sources,
gang activity on the Eastside has always been confined to between 3
and 5 percent of the total population. This small proportion of gang-
affiliated youth can disrupt daily life, but their activity is typically lo-
calized to particular blocks and neighborhoods (Vigil 1983).

7. Jill Stewart, "East Side, West Side, The Tug of War between
L.A.'s Rival Realities is Polarizing the City," *Los Angeles Times Magazine*, January 23, 1994, A10. Also see Hayden (1995, 27–29) for a discussion from an urban-planning perspective regarding the way class,

266 ▪ N O T E S

age, ethnicity, and gender affect residents' perspectives of Los Angeles neighborhoods.

8. The movie *The Bonfire of the Vanities* depicts the northernmost section of the Bronx as a place of crime and murder (David J. Fox, "'Vanities' Starts a Bronx Bonfire," *Los Angeles Times,* May 1, 1990, F1).

9. Bill Boyarsky, "Taking Politics to the Streets," *Los Angeles Times,* February 21, 1990, B2.

10. Wong (1995) observes that the demeaning images of Chinatown as an unsanitary, sanctioned segregation of Chinese people reinforced anti-immigrant sentiments and stigmatized the entire community. Light (1974, 368) also states that "whether accurate or not, 19th century reports of Chinatown filth and depravity affected American opinion."

11. See Parson (1982) for an excellent analysis of the politics of urban renewal in Los Angeles. Also see Logan and Molotch (1987). The financial center created north of the Los Angeles civic center dismantled (and failed to replace) seven thousand housing units in a low-income Latino community. During the 1960s and 1970s, CRA critics half-jokingly referred to it as the "Chicano Removal Agency."

12. See Hamilton (1984), who explores the complexity of competing community images in a redeveloping Chicago community. She concludes that urban planners must carefully scrutinize the image-making process since perceptions affect policy decisions. Pursuing a similar theme, Salter (1984, 15) examines how in Los Angeles the "once tarnished image of Orientals (as opium dealers and coolie laborers) has been polished to one of Chinese prosperity and suburban assimilation." Capek (1993) deconstructs the common experiences of poor minority residents in environmentally contaminated communities, who are typically ignored and stigmatized until they make a claim and convince themselves and others of the injustice of the situation. The significant elements of collective action around environmental issues resonate with what occurred in the Eastside: the significance of naming the problem, of using symbols as resources, and of acquiring sponsors in the media.

13. As mentioned in Chapter Two, restrictive housing covenants based on ethnicity and race were outlawed in Los Angeles in 1948, but current ethnic and racial residential patterns persist as a result of economic inequality and unfair housing practices.

14. Vern Partlow, "Bypassed 'Islands' of L.A. Experience Awakening," *Daily News,* December 27, 1950, 1.

15. All the excerpts from the census are cited in Hayes-Bautista and Chapa (1987, 63–64). The article also examines the historical and political context for the debates over labels, arguing for "Latino" rather than "Hispanic" as the most appropriate umbrella term for persons of Latin American origins. Also see Oboler (1995) for a thorough discussion of the problems generated by using umbrella terms for groups with diverse historical experiences.

16. Root (1992, 7). See the entire anthology for a fascinating collection of essays that address the issue of multiracial identity and imposed labels. Root states, "the existence of racially mixed persons challenges long-held notions about the biological, moral, and social meaning of race" (3). Faye Fiore, "Multiple Race Choices to Be Allowed on 2000 Census," *Los Angeles Times,* October 30, 1997, 1.

Chapter Four. The Politics of Community Identity in Monterey Park: "Things Looked Better Over There"

1. The organization expanded and has offices in South Los Angeles, East Los Angeles, and Pomona. The group provides referrals for jobs and substance-abuse counseling (John H. Lee, "Parents Join Archbishop at Anti-Gang Service," *Los Angeles Times,* February 19, 1990, B1). In 1995 Attorney General Janet Reno invited Rita Figueroa to the White House to receive the crime victim's service award for her work with Concerned Parents (Ian James, "Recognition Comes for Her Work, But She Shuns It," *Los Angeles Times,* July 12, 1995, B4).

2. Others who work with gang members in Eastside Los Angeles refer to unsanctioned police practices aimed at harassing gang members (see Shorris 1989, 1).

3. Some male Latino gang members in Los Angeles wear a black hair net pulled down to the middle of their foreheads to train short-cropped hair to lie flat. The net's functional use gives way to symbolism signifying gang affiliation, inasmuch as no other Latino adolescents ever don hair nets.

4. Inner-city residents cite the desire for better city services as the motivation for moving to the suburbs (Press 1982, 19; McDougal and Bunce 1986); Clarence Page, "Nothing Golden About Ghetto Life." *Los Angeles Times*, April 5, 1990, B7.

5. See Louis Sahagun, "Boyle Heights: Problems, Pride and Promise," *Los Angeles Times*, July 31, 1983, I:11. In 1985, at Garfield High School in East Los Angeles, I observed cliques organized in similar ways. U.S.-born students referred to the foreign-born with degrading labels such as "T.J.'s," while U.S.-born Chicanos were referred to as *pochos* ("faded" or assimilated Mexicans). In August 1997 I conducted a focus group among seventeen students who had graduated from Los Angeles high schools in June 1997. All confirmed that U.S.-born and some immigrant students raised in the United States continue to use derogatory language in referring to recent immigrants. See *Chicana Falsa* (Serros 1993) for prose and poetry exploring the sentiments and identity conflicts of a young second-generation Mexican American woman who speaks little Spanish.

6. The primary responses to rapid development in American cities were the "no growth" position and the more moderate "controlled growth" position. However, some single-family homeowners surrounded by high rises ally with developers and argue that "downzoning" infringes on their property rights. In 1987 the U.S. Supreme Court ruled that property owners must be paid compensation if zoning boards restrict them from developing their land (David G. Savage, "Supreme Court Orders Payments If Owners Suffer Land-Use Curbs," *Los Angeles Times*, June 10, 1987, I:8).

7. The Brown Act governs open meetings for local government bodies, such as city councils and school boards. The act seeks to strike a balance between the public's right to know and the need for confidential debate. Citizens refer to it when they want to emphasize their right to public access.

8. The restaurant is owned and operated by The East Los Angeles Community Union (TELACU), an economic-development group founded in 1968 that has received federal monies since the days of the War on Poverty (Acuña 1988, 383).

Chapter Five: Becoming an Activist in Eastside Los Angeles:
"For My Kids, for My Community, for My 'Raza'"

1. "Dawdling on the Prison" (editorial), *Los Angeles Times*, January 27, 1986, II:3. "The Great Prison Holdup," *Los Angeles Times*, April 18, 1986, II:4. "Prison Urgency," *Los Angeles Times*, August 22, 1986, II:4. "A Fair Prison Compromise," *Los Angeles Times*, October 3, 1986. Also see Acuña (1996, 65–88), who discusses the larger context of Eastside politics.

2. Editorial, "Corrections v. Molina," KNX Radio, Los Angeles, March 15, 1986.

3. The *Los Angeles Herald Examiner* stopped publication in November 1989, and in August 1990 the *Los Angeles Times* purchased 50 percent ownership of *La Opinión*, a sixty-four-year-old, family-owned business.

4. Jane Clayton, "Molina Victory May Give Council More Tilt Toward Slow Growth," *Los Angeles Times*, February 5, 1987, II:1. Molina's decisive victory in winning the city council seat was partially attributed to her commitment to fighting the prison.

5. Douglas Shuit and Jerry Gillam, "Governor Meets Top Lawmakers on Prison Issue," *Los Angeles Times*, September 3, 1986, I:3.

6. Several Jewish businessmen who were born and raised on the Eastside participated in the group. They no longer lived in the area but maintained businesses there representing the remaining fragments of the Jewish community in East Los Angeles.

7. Carolina Serna, "Eastside Residents Oppose Prison," *La Gente*, October 1986, 5.

8. African American women also adopted a strong work ethic, and mothering responsibilities could include "other mothers" as well as "blood mothers" (Collins 1991, 119–23).

9. The Mothers of the Plaza de Mayo began wearing mantillas in 1977, a year after they began organizing. The practice grew out of their need to identify one another at an annual pilgrimage attended by thousands of people paying homage to the Virgin Mary. Noting people's curiosity about them, they decided to use the mantillas

every time they went to the Plaza de Mayo. Later they embroidered their children's names into the head coverings.

10. Harriet G. Rosenberg, "From Trash to Treasure: The Environmental Justice Movement and the Mobilization of Housewife Activists" (paper presented to the American Anthropological Association annual meetings, New Orleans, Louisiana, Nov. 28–Dec. 2, 1990, 9). For an excellent analysis of women and environmental activism, see Meg Luxton, Harriet Rosenberg, and Sedef Arat-Koc, *Through the Kitchen Window: The Politics of Home and Family* (Toronto: Garmond Press, 1990).

11. Tom Chorneau, "Can the Home Team Defeat Prison Plan?" *L.A. Downtown News,* January 12, 1987, 1.

12. "Mil manifestantes protestaron ayer en las escalinatas del Capitolio de California," *La Opinión,* July 7, 1986, 1.

13. Leo Wolinsky, "Senate Rejects L.A. Prison Site in a Blow to Governor," *Los Angeles Times,* August 15, 1986, I:1.

14. Linda Breakstone, "Foes of L.A. Prison Manage to Thwart Bill's Passage Again," *Los Angeles Herald Examiner,* August 14, 1986, A1.

15. Leo Wolinsky, "Prison Plan Loses a Third Time," *Los Angeles Times,* September 24, 1986, I:3. Richard C. Paddock, "Governor Risks Latinos' Support on Prison Issue," *Los Angeles Times,* September 14, 1986, I:3.

16. Leo Wolinsky and Jerry Gillam, "Compromise Offered in L.A. Prison Dispute," *Los Angeles Times,* January 1, 1987, I:3. Tupper Hull, "L.A. Prison Bill Wins Temporary Reprieve," *Los Angeles Herald Examiner,* June 30, 1987, A3.

17. See Sharon McDonald and Robert McGarvey, "The Most Beautiful Women in L.A.," *L. A. Style,* September 1988, 245; Dick Russell, "The Air We Breathe: Viva Las Madres!" *Parenting,* November 1989, 127; Louis Sahagun. "The Mothers of East L.A. Transorm Themselves and Their Community," *Los Angeles Times,* August 13, 1989, B1; Louis Sahagun, "Mothers of Conviction," *Los Angeles Times,* September 16, 1992, B1; Bouvard(1996).

18. Rene Romo, "Opponents Brace for Hearing on Plan for Toxic Waste Burner," *Los Angeles Times,* November 22, 1987, I:6. The company received a permit to build an incinerator that would burn waste

paint products, benzene, and degreasing sludge, in the process producing tons of highly toxic waste, which would then go into a landfill. The *Los Angeles Times* opposed the incinerator; see "Better Take Another Look" (editorial), *Los Angeles Times,* December 5, 1988, II:3. The UCLA Chicano student newspaper covered the incinerator issue on a regular basis. For detailed accounts, see José Mendivil, "Incinerator Proposed—Dumping One More Project on East Los Angeles," *La Gente de Aztlán,* March–April 1988, 1. Also see Ron López, "Environmental Impact Report Needed before Incinerator Can Be Built," *La Gente de Aztlán,* February 1989, 18. Maura Dolan. "Race, Poverty Issues Grow Among Environmentalists," *Los Angeles Times*, April 28, 1990, A1.

19. Maura Dolan, "Toxic Waste Incinerator Bid Abandoned," *Los Angeles Times,* May 24, 1991, A1.

20. See Acuña 1996, 71; he states the split resulted from clashes over control and personalities.

21. Juana Gutiérrez, letter to the editor, *Eastside Journal,* February 7, 1990, 1.

Chapter Six. Becoming an Activist in Monterey Park: "The Elementary School Kids Are Still Too Young to Defend Themselves"

1. Margo McCall, "Monterey Park Residents Find Parole Office in Neighborhood," *West San Gabriel Valley News Digest*, July 21, 1988, 1.

2. Ray Babcock and Holly S. Wagner, "Parole Office Summit," *Alhambra Post Advocate*, August 11, 1988, 1. Alhambra police reported a 75 percent increase in crime in July, and Monterey Park police reported a 37 percent increase during that month.

3. Holly J. Wagner, "Residents Angered by Office," *Monterey Park Progress*, July 21, 1988, 1.

4. According to McFadden (1997, 430), even when both spouses work an equal number of hours outside the home, women still do 80 percent of the housework. Also see Arlie Hochschild, "The Second Shift: Employed Women Are Putting In Another Day's Work at Home," in *Men's Lives,* ed. M. S. Kimmel and M. A. Messner (New York: Macmillan, 1992).

5. Holly J. Wagner, "Parole Office Liaison Panel Planned," *Monterey Park Progress,* August 25, 1988, 1; Siok-Hian Tay Kelley, "Alhambra Heeds Protest against Parole Office Site," *Los Angeles Times,* September 4, 1988, 11. In Monterey Park men and women are evenly represented in the position of block captain of Neighborhood Watch groups. According to Yvette Cordero of the Monterey Park Police Department's Community Relations Office, in 1989 well over 75 percent of those who attended meetings were women.

6. See Stone (1962) for a discussion of how identity is situated through appearance. Through choices regarding clothing and grooming styles, individuals make statements about their social identity, and observers acknowledge the statements. Simmel (1904) also argues that symbols of class status may be used to convey and determine social-class identity.

7. Minutes of July 1989 meeting of Citizens Advisory Board, Monterey Park.

8. Mike Ward, "Neighbors Resist Parole Office in Their Backyards," *Los Angeles Times,* April 20, 1989, II:1 (San Gabriel Valley ed.).

Chapter Seven. Creating Community in Eastside Los Angeles: "We Have to Do It!"

1. According to Aptheker (1989, 160–73), "Resistance strategies employed in everyday life inform women's participation in those struggles traditionally recognized as resistance movements. . . . it is about creating the conditions necessary for life and not intrinsically oppositional." Aptheker's quote encompasses the heart of women's work in communities and its relation to grassroots mobilization.

2. Rodríguez and Núñez (1986, 140–41) found mutually critical perceptions in Austin and San Antonio, Texas: Chicanos see undocumented Mexicans as rural and backward, "rate busters" who are afraid to "stand up for their rights"; Mexicanos perceived Chicanos as "not being hard workers who despite citizenship were not doing well materially and did not control their children properly." Differences in music preferences caused local dance halls to schedule musical groups from Mexico on Fridays and Chicano groups on Satur-

days. See H. Romo (1984) for differing perceptions of schooling. Achor's (1978) study of a Mexican community in Dallas, Texas, also refers to, but does not explore, the heterogeneity among the U.S.-born and foreign-born population.

3. Louis Sahagun, "Boyle Heights: Problems, Pride and Promise," *Los Angeles Times,* July 31, 1983, I:1. The Spanish word for "wetbacks" is *mojados;* "T.J.'s" is a reference to Tijuana, the Mexican border town near San Diego. *Ranchos* suggests the new immigrants come from rural areas and connotes that they are country bumpkins.

4. The Wyvernwood complex includes 130 two-story buildings comprising eleven hundred units with spacious rooms. The management discriminated against Latinos until the mid-1960s.

5. Of the possible alternatives in Spanish for prefacing a woman's name, "Doña" denotes someone of important social status, which may rest on moral authority rather than wealth.

6. See Rodríguez and Núñez (1986) for a discussion of how asserting that someone is from the *rancho* or *ranchito* suggests that the person has not adjusted to the sophisticated metropolitan lifestyle. Established Mexican Americans attribute behaviors of new immigrants to their rural origins rather than to their Mexican or Central American nationalities. Alternatively, the terms could be used to chastise a Latino, regardless of his or her birthplace, who breeches etiquette.

7. Sergeant Hurtado of the Hollenbeck station, Los Angeles Police Department (LAPD), stated that women outnumbered men in Neighborhood Watch groups about five to one. I went with Neighborhood Watch members to visit the LAPD dispatch center, where dispatchers explained how incoming calls are handled. Three men and fifteen women went on the visit.

8. George Stein, "Surge of Violence Breaks Calm at Housing Project," *Los Angeles Times,* May 24, 1989, 3.

9. Rosa also scheduled our interview appointment and other visits I made to Wyvernwood "at about 7:00 P.M. after everybody is taken care of," as she put it.

10. In a Mexican American community in Chicago, Horowitz

(1987) found community residents coexisted with gang youth by avoiding contact with them.

11. Fuentes, Annette. 1987. "Immigration 'Reform': Heaviest Burden on Women." *Listen Real Loud*. Philadelphia: Nationwide Women's Program of the American Friends Service Committee. Vol. 8, no. 2 (Fall).

12. Scott Harris, "Community Crusaders: Three Groups Wage Hard-Nosed Struggle for Social Change," *Los Angeles Times*, November 29, 1987, II:1.

13. Moore (1966) noted that approximately 10 percent of Mexican American children in the Southwest were attending parochial schools in the 1960s.

14. The older women spoke of the fact that the increasing tuition meant that fewer families could afford to send their children to parochial school. A few of the younger women agreed. This has implications for community cohesiveness. Recently, the Los Angeles Archdiocese acknowledged that school tuition is beyond the reach for most Latino families, and it established a new tuition fund for the 1990–91 school year (John Dart, "Outreach Plan for Catholic Latinos Has Mixed Success," *Los Angeles Times*, June 5, 1990, A3).

15. See McNamara (1957), who interviewed pastors from parishes in Boyle Heights and adjacent communities in an effort to assess the degree of integration and acculturation of Mexican families.

16. See Williams (1984) for a description of the labor-intensive work of making tamales—buying, cleaning, cooking, stuffing, wrapping, and steaming. She discusses how Mexican American migrant women workers in Texas and Illinois blur the boundaries between family and public affairs by preparing and distributing tamales in the interest of promoting cohesiveness among kin and establishing channels of reciprocity among nonfamily members.

17. In an article that draws together secondary sources in support of the thesis that foodways operate as symbols and as the performance of ethnic identity, Kalcik (1984) mentions a scene quite similar to that in East Los Angeles. In front of a church in Youngstown, Ohio, a sign announces "Pierogi, This Friday"; they are sold by Slovak women who gather early Friday morning to begin preparation.

18. Spanish priests from the Claretian order have come to Los Angeles since the early 1900s. Many of them served at several churches in East Los Angeles, including Our Lady of Talpa (Grebler et al. 1970, 451).

19. Richard Kaywood, "Los Angeles Board Authorizes Driver Training," *CALDEA Calendar* (California Drivers Education Association), January 1967, 4.

20. Prior to 1980, many sociological studies attributed the lower labor force participation rates of Mexican American women to their jealous husbands. In their study of Chicano workers, Briggs, Fogel, and Schmidt comment that increasing participation of Chicanas in the labor force indicates a "diminishing of cultural influences that once deterred Chicanas from seeking employment" (1977, 32). Sowell (1981, 264) states "machismo concepts give the family a male-dominated flavor, make protection of women's chastity a preoccupation, and inhibit their employment." The accounts of the women I interviewed contradict the notion that they were under the "control of husbands." See López-Garza (1986) for a conceptual discussion of how much of women's labor remains officially invisible.

21. In full, the name Our Lady of Guadalupe, La Reina de las Américas [Queen of the Americas], which is another name for the blessed Virgin Mary and is the object of devotion among some Latinos in the Southwest. Devotions to the Blessed Virgin are practiced especially during the months of May and October. Other names used to refer to the Virgin of Guadalupe are La Guadalupanas or La Morenita, "the small dark one" referring to her Indian features and complexion.

22. Keeping the accounts is no small task; the fiesta at Resurrection Parish is a huge Eastside event, spanning several days and requiring a small street to be blocked off at both ends.

23. See Dabrowski's study (1983, 430) of working-class white women and civic action. She documents the contribution of the civic activities and presence of women and then attributes them to the "personal lifestyles of women which are conducive to community work."

Chapter Eight. Creating Community in Monterey Park: "Keeping an Eye on the Block"

1. Williams (1988) discusses a parallel situation in Washington, D.C., where long-established African American residents resent the doubling and tripling up of Central American immigrants. Saito (forthcoming) uses ethnographic methods to explore the concept of the "good immigrant" (meaning Anglo conformity) through the eyes of Japanese Americans in Monterey Park.

2. Even though the intent of multicultural events is to promote intercultural interaction and understanding, as Williams (1988, 129) suggests, "cultural festivals are experienced differently by different class and ethnic groups and promoting cultural understanding is an abstract and elusive goal."

3. A young Mexican American man chaired the Cinco de Mayo committee, but at all the meetings women outnumbered men, often by a three-to-one ratio. In terms of ethnicity, regular members—in addition to Mexican Americans—included one Armenian American woman and one Chinese immigrant woman, both established residents, and one Anglo man married to a Mexican immigrant woman. Over a period of three months of planning, attendance ranged from ten to twenty people and averaged about a dozen.

4. Historically, the Cinco de Mayo commemorates the battle of Puebla, where the French were defeated in 1862. In Mexico the day's significance pales next to that of the "Sixteenth of September" celebration of Mexican independence from Spain. In the United States, observance of the Cinco de Mayo varies enormously. Some localities treat it as a simple and culturally specific "May day"; elsewhere it takes on aspects of a political statement in which parallels are made between Mexican resistance to colonization and Mexican Americans' resistance to oppression in the United States. Some celebrations feature Chicano rock concerts that are commercially sponsored by beer companies; they attract thousands of youth, and some criticize them as occasions to promote alcohol consumption. See Maxwell and Jacobson (1989) for a brief, insightful analysis of how

the tobacco and alcohol industries have targeted the Latino community by sponsoring cultural events and offering free samples.

5. The theater group focused on assimilation as a problem among young Mexican Americans. While their skits were amusing to Mexican Americans and Anglos, I suspect they would be difficult for Chinese immigrants to appreciate. In one, a Mexican American woman suffering from assimilation—represented by "bleached hair and an overdose of white bread and Twinkies"—is saved by a paramedic-like team called the Mayan Patrol. They feed her tortillas and restore her Mexican American identity.

6. The seven young Chinese women wore red cloth headbands wound around their foreheads and tied at the sides, V-neck blouses edged in a black-and-white geometric motif with red capped sleeves, straight black knee-length skirts also edged in the geometric motif, and black cloth anklets. Their shoulder-length hair was worn flat and straight. They performed in bare feet. Yen Fen Tseng, an assistant on the Ford Foundation research team, informed me that the indigenous dance represented a very poor "tribe" in Taiwan, and given the people's poverty, it was highly unlikely the dancers themselves were of that indigenous group.

7. Kalcik (1984, 56). The entire collection of essays is a fascinating, rich, and grounded analysis of the changing content and persistent power of "foodways" as means to convey ethnic identity.

8. The Child Care Task Force was made up of eight women (not counting the Parks and Recreation Department coordinator): two Asian American women, both married, one without children; one divorced Mexican American woman with no children; two African American women who did not have children; three Anglo women, all with children.

9. Members of the Child Care Task Force perceived the city council vote against granting approval to seek funds as a "slap in the face" and "especially troubling" because at the same meeting the council declared 1989 the "Year of the Family." However, Councilman Hatch, who voted against the proposal, said he was "opposed to the government taking control of raising America's children" (Berkley Hudson,

278 • N O T E S

"Monterey Park Irks Some by Passing Up Child Care Grant," *Los Angeles Times,* February 5, 1989, B1).

10. Pesquera's (1993) study of Chicano families also found minimal change in the division of household labor.

Chapter Nine. Women Transforming the "Political": "Traditions Are Not So Traditional"

1. During her nineteen-day trip, Elsa López shared her community experiences with the MELA-SI water conservation project with women and men in South Africa. In one township named Hermanus, women were so impressed with Elsa's emphasis on the importance of women's activism that they named their own group Mothers of Hermanus.

2. Richard Winton, "Firm Offers Money to 2 Groups If City Reverses Billboard Ban," *Los Angeles Times* (San Gabriel edition), November 10, 1994. Regency Outdoor Advertising offered $70,000 a year for three years to the Monterey Park Chamber of Commerce and offered $45,000 a year thereafter; the donation would have no end dates. Councilwoman Judy Chu charged that this was an attempt to influence council members with close ties to the Chamber of Commerce. The company also ofered $10,000 a year to the Boys and Girls Club if the city council ended the city's ban on billboards.

3. Regency Advertising charged that those who circulated the petition to put the initiative on the ballot failed to comply with the election code requiring public notification of intent in a newspaper adjudicated to be of general circulation before any voter signatures were solicited. The lawsuit contended that the only public announcement appeared in an unadjudicated paper, thus making the billboard initiative legally defective. The Superior Court of California ruled that the elections code had been substantially complied with (Residents against Billboards Committee, press release, February 19, 1997).

4. The 1965 Highway Beautification Act was supposed to end the proliferation of billboards along highways, but environmentalists say there are still too many of them—nearly one for every mile of highway in California. Others argue that billboards are an established

part of the urban scene. Billboards are banned from highways in Hawaii, Alaska, Maine, and Vermont. Richard Simon, "It's a Billboard Jungle along L.A. Freeways," *Los Angeles Times,* October 22, 1995, A1. In Monterey Park one city council member argued that since the land along the freeways was already "blighted," it made sense to garner money by allowing billboards.

5. Maxwell and Jacobson (1989, 32) provide a concise analysis of the way the tobacco and alcohol industries manipulate cultural and sexual images to sell their products. They also present numerous examples of how advertising companies have effectively targeted the growing Latino population by contributing to Latino organizations and sponsoring events. The authors contend that the advertising compounds poor health practices in low-income communities. A city councilman from the neighboring city of Montebello complained about a racist billboard for a radio station featuring two disc jockeys sitting on a toilet, eating pizza, with their trousers around their ankles. The caption reads "Two Fat Mexicans" (Kim Hanrahan and Bill Rams, "Montebello Joins Debate over Proposed Billboards," *Alhambra Post Advocate,* November 10, 1994, 1).

6. In a brief overview of world systems analysis, Immanuel Wallerstein discusses how capitalism enters into so-called traditional settings and manages to set up profitable production using existing social relations. The quote reads, "If we are to understand the cultural forms these struggles take, we cannot afford to take 'traditions' at their face value. . . . We cannot afford to assume that traditions are in fact traditional" (1983, 76). See Curry-Rodríguez (1988) for a study of Mexican women who migrate to the United States, thereby breaking selected family traditions in order to pursue their own vision of the "traditional family," and Hondagneu-Sotelo's (1994) study of how traditional household duties and work relationships are transformed by the immigration process.

7. In 1992, the Year of the Woman, women held 17 percent of the seats in the state legislature and the House of Representatives (Flammang 1997, 232).

8. See Minault (1981), Bonder (1989), Chuchryk (1989) for cases illustrating the notion of motherhood as a metaphor for community

concerns. See Caufield (1974) for an essay conceptualizing the importance of ethnic and racial family networks as "cultures of resistance." Swerdlow's (1993, 234) study of women peace activists who organized during the 1960s illustrates how women politicized maternal interests at the level of national politics. She states that they were self-identified as "concerned housewives who celebrated domesticity and motherhood to challenge militaristic definitions of national interest."

9. Chicano scholars Vaca (1970), Romano (1970), and Rocco (1970) provided sharp critiques of the ethnocentrism prevalent in social science. Latino families, in comparison to other ethnic groups, were portrayed as having pathologically rigid gender roles characterized by abusive male dominance. In a different way, the "problems" of African American families are often linked to the dominance of the African American woman—that is, the "black matriarchy thesis" (Jones 1985, 7–10; Dill 1987, 103). For a feminist critique of social science and a discussion of the political implications of knowledge, see Stanley and Wise (1993) and see Collins (1991) for a black feminist perspective.

10. See Acuña (1996, i–xx) for a contemporary Chicano studies perspective on how power relations affect the dominant interpretation of reality. Acuña offers one of the few historical overviews of Los Angeles by a Chicano social scientist that includes a chapter on women.

11. Sacks (1988, 77) argues that "centerwomen" who sustain and mobilize social networks and "spokesmen" are equally important leadership roles. neither role is necessarily gender based.

12. See Randall (1982), Epstein (1981), and Sapiro (1995) for thorough summaries of how the assumptions of mainstream political science exclude and distort women's political participation. To understand community activism, we need to know how women and men perceive their circumstances and legitimize and redefine issues as they get involved (Susser 1988).

13. Social scientists theorizing about urban social movements place themselves in different conceptual "camps." See Melucci (1989), Darnovsky, Epstein and Flacks (1995), and Morris and Mueller (1992)

for reassessments of resource mobilization theory and new social movements theory. Morris and Mueller (1992, 351–73) acknowledge the insights of the black feminist perspective, but do not include any black feminist writers in the anthology. Sturgeon (1995) is one of the few theorists who suggest new social movements theory would add specificity to the framework by including an analysis of gender relations. Rather than fully examine these perspectives, I assert that the terms refer to gendered realities and then erase women. Rocco (1990, 4) observes a somewhat similar occurrence when postmodern accounts of the new political economy in Los Angeles erase the Latino workers who make the city run: "they are an integral part of the theorists' everyday life, serving their food, driving their cars, cleaning their homes or offices." See Castells (1983), a major Marxist theorist in urban sociology, whose edited volume includes empirical studies of grassroots activism. The accounts refer to the significance of women in urban social movements and then omit them from analytical discussions. For a critique of Castells from a socialist-feminist perspective, see Brownill (1984). Also see Lofland (1975), who notes the "thereness" of women as "scenery" rather than as actors in urban sociology.

14. See Larana, Johnston, and Gusfield (1994, 30–35) for an overview of new social movements in contrast to other theories of collective action.

15. See Barnett (1995) for a rich, full account of black women's work and leadership in the civil rights movement.

16. Smith fails to differentiate women by ethnicity or race. See Soldatenko (1992) for an excellent discussion of women of color and Smith's critique of sociology, and Soldatenko (1991) for an equally insightful account of organizing in the Los Angeles garment industry.

17. See also Romero's (1992) study of Chicana domestic workers for a critical discussion of class differences and the way feminists in the 1970s defined household labor as central to women's oppression.

18. DeLauretis (1986) states that "social identity is a strategy." Black feminists Dill, Collins, and Rollins also question the separation and ranking of subordinated social identities of gender, ethnicity, race, and class.

19. See Lawson (1980) for a study of women who mobilized around tenants' rights.

20. See Mackenzie (1987) for a discussion of women and urban restructuring.

21. Age and the generation to which women belong will influence how they enter into grassroots community activism. Each historical period provides a different set of ideologies and events, so the decade in which a woman comes of age may be significant (Morgen 1988). Older women do significant work to maintain the social networks that sustain community action (Gilkes 1982, 292). In some instances, African American women's social construction of community expressed emotional attachment to the neighborhood and a positive identification with place dependent on their past memories and visions of the neighborhood (Schoenberg 1980, S263; Saegert 1989). Also see J. Brown (1985), who notes that as women age, they gain new freedoms.

Appendix. Concepts and Terms

1. Hunter (1953) divides leaders into several categories: social, economic, religious, and reputational. The latter, often women, are those who have established reputations for problem solving. Their influence may cross several categories.

References

Achor, Shirley. 1978. *Mexican Americans in a Dallas Barrio.* Tucson, Ariz.: University of Arizona Press.

Ackelsberg, Martha. 1984a. "Women's Collaborative Activities and City Life: Politics and Policy." In *Political Women: Current Roles in State and Local Government,* ed. Janet Flammang, 242–309. Beverly Hills: Sage Publications.

———. 1984b. Communities, Resistance, and Women's Activism: Some Implications for Democratic Theory." In *My Troubles Are Going to Have Trouble with Me,* ed. Karen Brodkin Sacks and Dorothy Remy, 297–313. New Brunswick, N.J.: Rutgers University Press.

Acuña, Rodolfo F. 1996. *Anything But Mexican.* New York: Verso.

———. 1988. *Occupied America.* New York: Harper and Row.

———. 1984. *Community under Siege: A Chronicle of Chicanos East of the Los Angeles River, 1945–1975.* Los Angeles: Chicano Studies Research Center, University of California.

Acuña, Rudy. 1989. "The Fate of East L.A.: One Big Jail." *Los Angeles Herald Examiner,* April 28, A15.

Alhambra City School District. 1986. "Racial and Ethnic Survey Summary." Superintendent's Office, Alhambra (California) City School District.

Alinsky, Saul. 1946. *Reveille for Radicals.* New York: Vintage Books.

Allen, James P., and Eugene Turner. 1997. *The Ethnic Quilt: Population and Diversity in Southern California.* Northridge, Calif.: Center for Geographical Studies.

Anzaldúa, Gloria. 1987. *Borderlands/La Frontera: The New Mestiza.* San Francisco: Spinsters/Aunt Lute.

Apodaca, Linda. 1993. "They Kept the Homefires Burning: Mexican-American Women and Social Change." Ph.D. diss., University of California, Irvine.

Aptheker, Bettina. 1989. *Tapestries of Life: Women's Work, Women's Consciousness, and the Meaning of Daily Experience.* Amherst: University of Massachusetts Press.

Aulette, Judy, and Trudy Mills. 1988. "Something Old, Something New: Auxiliary Work in the 1983–86 Copper Strike." *Feminist Studies* 14, no. 2 (Summer): 227–66.

Baca Zinn, Maxine. 1979. "Field Research in Minority Communities: Ethical, Methodological, and Political Observations by an Insider." *Social Problems* 5, no. 2 (December): 18–24.

———. 1975. "Chicanas: Power and Control in the Domestic Sphere." *De Colores* 2, no. 3: 19–31.

Barnett, Bernice McNair. 1995. "Black Women's Collectivist Movement Organizations: Their Struggles during the 'Doldrums.' " In *Feminist Organizations: Harvest of the New Women's Movement,* ed. Myra Marx Ferree and Patricia Yancey Martin, 199–219. Philadelphia: Temple University Press.

Barth, Frederik. 1969. Introduction to *Ethnic Groups and Boundaries,* ed. Frederik Barth. 9–38. Boston: Little, Brown.

Bayes, Jane M. 1982. *Minority Politics and Ideologies in the United States.* Novato, Calif.: Chandler and Sharp.

Becker, Howard. 1978. "The Relevance of Life Histories." In *Sociological Methods,* ed. Norman K. Denzin. San Francisco: McGraw-Hill.

Bennett, Linda. 1986. "The Gender Gap: When an Opinion Gap Is Not a Voting Bloc." *Social Science Quarterly* 67, no. 3 (September): 613.

Berenson, Harold. 1984. "Women's Occupational and Family Achievement in the United States Class System." *British Journal of Sociology* 35, no. 1 (March): 19–41.

Bernal, Dolores Delgado. 1996. "Grassroots Leadership Reconceptualized: Chicana Oral Histories and the 1968 East Los Angeles School Blowouts." *Frontiers.* Forthcoming.

Bertaux, Daniel, and Martin Kohli. 1984. "The Life Story Approach: A Continental View." *Annual Review of Sociology* 10: 215–37.

Blonian, Rodney J. 1986. "The Los Angeles Crown Coach Prison Site—A Superior Location." *Americas 2001* (March): 2.

Blumberg, Louis, and Robert Gottlieb. 1989. *War on Waste: Can America Win Its Battle With Garbage?* Covelo, Calif.: Island Press.

Bonder, Gloria. 1989. "Women's Organizations in Argentina's Transition to Democracy." In *Women and Counter Power,* ed. Yolanda Cohen, 65–85. New York: Black Rose Books.

Bookman, Ann, and Sandra Morgen, eds. 1988. *Women and the Politics of Empowerment.* Philadelphia: Temple University Press.

Bourque, Susan, and Donna Robinson Divine. 1985. Introduction to *Women Living Change,* ed. Susan Bourque and Donna Robinson Divine. Philadelphia: Temple University Press.

Bouvard, Marguerite Guzman. 1996. "Juana Beatrice Gutiérrez and the Mothers of East Los Angeles." In *Women Reshaping Human Rights.* 179–197. Wilmington, Delaware: SR Books.

Boyte, Harry C. 1989. *Common Wealth.* New York: The Free Press.

Briggs, Vernon M., Walter Fogel, and Fred Schmidt. 1977. *The Chicano Worker.* Austin: University of Texas Press.

Broder, John M. 1990. "EPA Stops Letting Polluters Set Cleanup Terms." *Los Angeles Times,* 22 June, A25.

Brown, Judith K. 1985. Introduction to *In Her Prime: A New View of Middle Aged Women,* ed. Judith K. Brown, Virginia Kerns, et al., 1–11. South Hadley, Mass.: Bergin and Garvey Publishers.

Brown, Linda Keller, and Kay Mussell. 1984. Introduction to *Ethnic and Regional Foodways in the United States,* ed. Linda Keller Brown and Kay Mussell. 3–15. Knoxville: University of Tennessee Press.

Brownil, Sue. 1984. "From Critique to Intervention: Socialist Feminist Perspectives on Urbanization." *Antipode* 16, no. 3: 21–34.

Brownstein, Ronald. 1990. "Catholicism a Political Issue Again." *Los Angeles Times,* 22 June, A1.

Bunche, Lonnie G. 1990. "A Past Not Necessarily Prologue: The Afro-American in Los Angeles." In *Twentieth Century Los Angeles,* ed. Norman M. Klein and Martin J. Schiesl, 100–130. Claremont, Calif.: Regina Books.

Burns, Jeffrey M. 1994. "The Mexican Catholic Community in California." In *Mexican Americans and the Catholic Church, 1900–1965,* eds. Jay P. Dolan and Gilberto M. Hinojosa, 129–233. Notre Dame: University of Notre Dame Press.

Cadena, Gilbert R., and Lara Medina. 1996. "Liberation Theology and Social Change: Chicanas and Chicanos in the Catholic Church." In *Chicanas and Chicanos in Contemporary Society*, ed. Roberto M. De Anda, 99–111. Needham Heights, Mass.: Allyn and Bacon.

Calderón, José Zapata. "Mexican American Politics in a Multi-Ethnic Community: The Case of Monterey Park, 1984–1990." Ph.D. diss., University of California, Los Angeles.

————. 1990. "Latinos and Ethnic Conflict in Suburbia: The Case of Monterey Park." *Latino Studies Journal* 1, no. 2 (May): 23–32.

Čapek, Stella. 1993. "The 'Environmental Justice' Frame: A Conceptual Discussion and an Aplication." *Social Problems* 40, no. 1: 5–25.

Carlessi, Carolina. 1989. "The Reconquest." *NACLA Report on the Americas* 13, 4 (November/December): 14–21.

Carrillo, Victor. 1996. "The Politics of Language." *Ahora/Now!* Labor Strategy Community Center Newsletter (Los Angeles) (Fall): 1.

Castells, Manuel. 1983. *The City and the Grassroots*. Berkeley: University of California Press.

Caulfield, Mina Davis. 1974. "Imperialism, the Family, and Cultures of Resistance." *Socialist Revolution* 29: 67–85.

Cerrell Associates, Inc. 1984. "Political Dificulties Facing Waster-to-Energy Conversion Plant Siting." Report Prepared for Caliirnia Waste Management Board, State of Caliornia, Los Angeles.

Chavez, Ernesto. 1994. "Creating Aztlan: The Chicano Movement in Los Angeles, 1966–1978." Ph.D. diss., University of California, Los Angeles.

Christiansan-Ruffman, Linda. 1995. "Women's Conceptions of the Political: Three Canadian Women's Organizations." In *Feminist Organizations: Harvest of the New Feminist Movement*, ed. Myra Marx Ferree and Patricia Yancey Martin, 372–93. Philadelphia: Temple University Press.

Christrup, Judy, and Robert Schaeffer. 1990. "Not in Anyone's Backyard." *Greenpeace* 15, no. 1 (January/February): 14–19.

Chuchryk, Patricia M. 1989. "Subversive Mothers: The Women's Opposition to the Military Regime in Chile." In *Women, The State, and Development*, ed. Jana Everett, Kathleen Staudt, and Sue Elen M. Charleton, 130–51. Albany: State University of New York Press.

Clifford, James, and George E. Marcus. 1986. *Writing Culture: The Poetics and Politics of Ethnography.* Los Angeles: University of California Press.

Cockburn, Cynthia. 1977. "When Women Get Involved in Community Action." In *Women in the Community*, ed. Marjorie Mayo. Boston: Routledge and Kegan Paul.

Collins, Patricia Hill. 1991. *Black Feminist Thought: Knowledge, Consciousness, and the Politics of Empowerment.* New York: Routledge.

Compean, Guadalupe. 1983. "The Los Angeles Corporate Center: Its Probable Impact on North East Los Angeles." Master's thesis, University of California, Los Angeles.

Coyle, Laurie, et al. 1980. "Women at Farah: An Unfinished Story." In *Mexican Women in the U.S.: Struggles Past and Present,* ed. Magdalena Mora and Adelaida del Castillo, 117–43. Los Angeles: Chicano Studies Research Center, University of California.

Curry Rodríguez, Julia E. 1988. "Labor Migration and Familial Responsibilities." In *Mexicanas at Work in the United States*, ed. Margarita B. Melville, 47–63. Houston, Texas: Mexican American Studies Program, University of Houston.

Dabrowski, Irene. 1983. "Working-Class Women and Civic Action: A Case Study of an Innovative Community Role." *Policy Studies Journal* 11, no. 3 (March): 427–35.

Darnovsky, Marcy, Barbara Epstein, and Richard Flacks. 1995. *Cultural Politics and Social Movements.* Philadelphia: Temple University Press.

Davis, Mike. 1987. "Chinatown, Part Two? The Internationalization of Downtown Los Angeles." *New Left Review* 164 (July/August): 64–86.

de Lauretis, Teresa. 1986. "Feminist Studies/Critical Studies: Issues, Terms and Contexts." In *Feminist Studies/Critical Studies*, ed. Teresa de Lauretis, 1–19. Bloomington: Indiana University Press.

Díaz, David. Forthcoming. "Environmental Logic and Minority Communities." In *Asian and Latino Immigrants in a Restructuring Economy: The Metamorphosis of Los Angeles,* ed. Marta López-Garza and David Díaz. Palo Alto, Calif.: Stanford University Press.

Dietz, Mary. 1987. "Context Is All: Feminism and Theories of Citizenship." *Daedalus* 116, no. 4 (Spring): 1–24.

di Leonardo, Micaela. 1987. "Female World of Cards and Holidays: Women, Families and the Work of Kinship." *Signs* 12, no. 3 (Spring): 440–53.

Dill, Bonnie Thornton. 1987. "The Dialectics of Black Womanhood." In *Feminism and Methodology,* ed. Sandra Harding. Bloomington: Indiana University Press.

Dolan, Jay P., and Gilberto M. Hinjosa, eds. 1994. *Mexican Americans and the Catholic Church 1900–1965.* Notre Dame: University of Notre Dame Press.

Durning, Alan B. 1989. "Saving the Planet." *The Progressive* 53, no. 4 (April): 35–59.

Eisenstein, Sarah. 1983. *Give Us Bread But Give Us Roses.* Boston: Routledge and Kegan Paul.

Emerson, Robert M. 1983. *Contemporary Field Research.* Boston: Little, Brown.

Epstein, Cynthia Fuchs. 1981. "Women and Power: The Roles of Women in Politics in the United States." In *Access to Power: Cross Cultural Studies of Women and Elites,* ed. Cynthia Fuchs Epstein and Ross Laub Coser. Boston: Allen and Unwin.

Escobar, Edward. 1993. "The Dialectics of Repression: The Los Angeles Police Department and the Chicano Movement, 1968–1971." *Journal of American History* 74, no. 4 (March): 1483–1504.

Escobedo, Raúl. 1979. *Boyle Heights Community Plan.* Los Angeles: Department of City Planning.

Evans, Sara M. 1989. *Born for Liberty.* Philadelphia: Temple University Press.

Fanon, Frantz. 1969. "Algeria Unveiled." In *The New Left Reader,* ed. Carl Oglesby, 161–85. New York: Grove Press.

Feijoo, María del Carmen. 1984. "Women in Neighborhoods: From Local Issues to Gender Problems." *Canadian Woman Studies* 6, no. 1 (Fall): 86–89.

Feldberg, Rosylyn, and Evelyn Nakano Glenn. 1984. "Male and Female: Job versus Gender Models in the Sociology of Work." In *Women and the Public Sphere,* ed. Janet Siltanen and Michelle Stanworth. London: Hutchinson.

Ferree, Myra Marx. 1984. "Sacrifice, Satisfaction, and Social Change: Employment and Family." In *My Troubles Are Going to Have Trouble with Me,* ed. Karen Brodkin Sacks and Dorothy Remy, 61–79. New Brunswick, N.J.: Rutgers University Press.

Fincher, Ruth, and Jacinta McQuillen. 1989. "Women in Urban Social Movements." *Urban Geography* 10, no. 6: 604–13.

Fisher, Jo. 1989. *Mothers of the Disappeared.* Boston: South End Press.

Flammang, Janet A. 1985. "Female Officials in the Feminist Capital: The Case of Santa Clara County." *Western Political Quarterly* 38, no. 1 (March): 94–118.

———. 1997. Women's Political Voice: *How Women Are Transforming the Practice and Study of Politics*. Philadelphia: Temple University Press.

Flores, Henry. 1989. "The Selectivity of the Capitalist State: Chicanos and Economic Development." *Western Political Quarterly* 42, no. 2 (June): 377–95.

García, John, and Rudolfo de la Garza. 1985. "Mobilizing the Mexican Immigrant: The Role of Mexican American Organizations." *Western Political Quarterly* 38, no. 4 (December): 551–64.

García, Philip. 1985. "Immigration Issues in Urban Ecology: The Case of Los Angeles." In *Urban Ethnicity in the United States,* ed. Lionel Maldonado and Joan Moore, 73–100. Beverly Hills, Calif.: Sage Publications.

Garland, Anne Witte. 1988. *Women Activists: Challenging the Abuse of Power.* New York: Feminist Press.

Geiger, Susan N. G. 1986. "Women's Life Histories: Method and Content." *Signs* 11, no. 2 (Winter): 334–51.

Gilkes, Cheryl Townsend. 1982. "Successful Rebellious Professionals:

The Black Woman's Professional Identity and Community Involvement." *Psychology of Women Quarterly* 6, 32 (Spring): 289–311.

———. 1980. "Holding Back the Ocean with a Broom." In *The Black Woman,* ed. Frances Rodgers-Rose. Beverly Hills: Sage Publications.

Gittell, Marilyn, and Teresa Shtob. 1980. "Changing Women's Roles in Political Volunteerism and Reform of the City." *Signs* 5, no. 3 Supplemental: S67–68.

Gluck, Sherna Berger. 1987. *Rosie the Riveter Revisited.* New York: New American Library.

———. 1977. "What's So Special About Women? Women's Oral History." *Frontiers* 2, no. 2: 3–13.

Goffman, Erving. 1951. "Symbols of Class Status." *British Journal of Sociology* 2 (December): 294–304.

Gómez, James M. 1988. "Incinerator Foes Enlist New Allies." *Los Angeles Times,* 13 November, II:1.

Goodman, Michelle. 1990. "Picketers Say Office Must Go." *Post-Advocate,* 1 March, 1A.

Grebler, Leo, Joan W. Moore, and Ralph C. Guzmán. 1970. *The Mexican-American People.* New York: Free Press.

Gutiérrez, Gabriel. 1994. "Mothers of East Los Angeles Strike Back." In *Unequal Protection, Environmental Justice, and Communities of Color,* ed. Robert D. Bullard. San Francisco: Sierra Club Books.

———. 1989. "The Founding of Mothers of East Los Angeles." Los Angeles: Gabriel Gutiérrez, December.

Hamilton, Luann. 1984. "The Evolution of Neighborhood Identities: Competing Images of a Chicago Community." *Urban Resources,* 1, no. 4 (Spring): 3–8.

Hardy-Fanta, Carole. 1993. *Latina Politics, Latino Politics: Gender, Culture and Political Participation in Boston.* Philadelphia: Temple University Press.

Harley, Sharon. 1990. "For the Good of Family and Race: Gender, Work, and Domestic Roles in the Black Community, 1880–1930." *Signs* 15, no. 2: 336–49.

Harris, Mary. 1988. *Cholas: Latino Girls in Gangs.* New York: AMS Press.

Hayden, Dolores. 1995. *The Power of Place: Urban Landscapes as Public History.* Cambridge, Mass: MIT Press.

Hayes-Bautista, David, and Jorge Chapa. 1987. "Latino Terminology: Conceptual Bases for Standardized Terminology." *American Journal of Public Health* 77, no. 1 (January): 61–68.

Heer, David M., and Pini Herman. 1990. *A Human Mosaic: An Atlas of Ethnicity in L.A. County, 1980–1986.* Panorama City, Calif.: Western Economic Research Co.

Hernández, Patricia. 1980. "Lives of Chicana Activists: The Chicano Student Movement in the United States." In *Mexican Women in the United States,* ed. Magdalena Mora and Adelaida R. Del Castillo, 17–25. Los Angeles: Chicano Studies Research Center, University of California.

Hewitt, Nancy A. 1987. *Women's Activism and Social Change.* Ithaca, N.Y.: Cornell University Press.

Hirschman, Albert O. 1979. "The Search for Paradigms as a Hindrance to Understanding." In *Interpretive Social Science,* ed. Paul Rabinow and William M. Sullivan, 163–79. Los Angeles: University of California Press.

Hochschild, Arlie. 1992. "The Second Shift: Employed Women Are Putting in Another Day's Work at Home." In *Men's Lives,* ed. M. S. Kimmel and M. A. Messner. New York: Macmillan.

Hondagneu-Sotelo, Pierrette. 1994. *Gendered Transitions: Mexican Experiences of Immigration.* Berkeley: University of California Press.

hooks, bell. 1990. *Yearning: Race, Gender, and Cultural Politics.* Boston: South End Press.

Horowitt, Sanford D. 1989. *Let Them Call Me Rebel: Saul Alinsky—His Life and Legacy.* New York: Alfred A. Knopf.

Horowitz, Ruth. 1987. "Community Tolerance of Gang Violence." *Social Problems* 34, no. 5 (December): 437–50.

———. 1983. *Honor and the American Dream: Culture and Identity in a Chicano Community.* New Brunswick, N.J.: Rutgers University Press.

Horton, John. 1995. *The Politics of Diversity.* Philadelphia: Temple University Press.

———. 1990. *Changing Relations, Newcomers and Established Residents in U.S. Communities: The Case of Monterey Park, California.* Ford Project Report. Department of Sociology, University of California, Los Angeles, February.

———. 1989. "The Politics of Ethnic Change: Grass-root Responses to Economic and Demographic Restructuring in Monterey Park, California." *Urban Geography* 10, no. 6: 578–92.

Horton, John, and José Calderón. 1992. "Language Struggles in a Changing California Community." In *Language Loyalties: A Source Book on Official English Controversy,* ed. James Crawford. Chicago: University of Chicago Press.

Hunter, Floyd. 1953. *Community Power Structure.* Chapel Hill, N.C.: University of North Carolina Press.

Johnson-Odim, Cheryl. 1991. "Common Themes, Different Contexts: Third World Women and Feminism." In *Third World Women and the Politics of Feminism,* ed. Chandra Mohanty. Bloomington: Indiana University Press.

Jones, Jacqueline. 1985. *Labor of Love, Labor of Sorrow.* New York: Basic Books.

Kalcik, Susan. 1984. "Ethnic Foodways in America: Symbol and the Performance of Identity." In *Ethnic and Regional Foodways in the United States,* ed. Linda Keller Brown and Kay Mussell, 37–65. Knoxville: University of Tennessee Press.

Kaplan, Temma. 1981. "Female Consciousness and Collective Action: The Case of Barcelona, 1910–1918." In *Feminist Theory: A Critique of Ideology,* ed. Nannerl O. Keohane et al., 55–76. Chicago: University of Chicago Press.

Katz, Jack. 1983. "A Theory of Qualitative Methodology: The Social System of Analytic Fieldwork." In *Contemporary Field Research,* ed. Robert M. Emerson. Boston: Little, Brown.

Katznelson, Ira. 1981. *City Trenches.* New York: Pantheon.

Klein, Julie Thompson. 1996. *Crossing Boundaries: Knowledge, Disciplinarities and Interdisciplinarities.* Charlottesville: University Press of Virginia.

Kornblum, William. 1974. *Blue-Collar Community.* Chicago: University of Chicago Press.

Lamphere, Louise. 1987. *From Working Daughters to Working Mothers.* Ithaca, N.Y.: Cornell University Press.

Larana, Enrique, Hank Johnston, and Joseph R. Gusfield. 1994. *New Social Movements: From Ideology to Identity.* Philadelphia: Temple University Press.

Lawson, Ronald, Stephen Barton, and J. W. Joselit. 1980. "From Kitchen to Storefront: Women in the Tenant Movement in New York City." In *New Space for Women,* ed. Gerda R. Wekerle et al. Boulder, Colo.: Westview Press.

Light, Ivan. 1974. "From Vice District to Tourist Attraction: The Moral Career of American Chinatowns, 1880–1940." *Pacific Historical Review* 43 (August): 367–94.

Lin, Cynthia. 1989. "Child Care Task Force." *West San Gabriel Valley* (California) *News Digest,* 7 June, 1.

Lipsky, Michael. 1963. "Protest as a Political Resource." *American Political Science Review* 62, no. 4 (December): 1144–58.

Lofland, Lyn. 1975. "The 'Thereness' of Women: A Selective Review of Urban Sociology." In *Another Voice: Feminist Perspectives on Social Life and Social Science,* ed. Marcia Millman and Rosabeth Moss Kanter. Garden City: Anchor Books.

Logan, John. 1978. "Growth, Politics, and the Stratification of Places." *American Journal of Sociology* 84: 404–14.

Logan, John R., and Harvey L. Molotch. 1987. *Urban Fortunes: The Political Economy of Place.* Los Angeles: University of California Press.

López-Garza, Marta. 1986. "Toward a Reconceptualization of Women's Economic Activities." In *Chicana Voices: Intersections of Class, Race, and Gender,* ed. Teresa Cordova, 66–75. Austin, Texas: Center for Mexican American Studies.

López-Garza, Marta, and David Diaz, eds. *Asian and Latino Immigrants in a Restructuring Economy: The Metamorphosis of Los Angeles.* Palo Alto, Ca: Stanford University Press. Forthcoming.

Lugones, María C., and Elizabeth Spelman. 1983. "Have We Got a Theory for You! Feminist Theory, Cultural Imperialism and the

Demand for the Woman's Voice." *Women's Studies International Forum* 6, no. 6: 573–81.

Mackenzie, Suzanne. 1987. "Women's Responses to Economic Restructuring: Changing Gender, Changing Space." In *The Politics of Diversity: Feminism, Marxism and Nationalism,* ed. Roberta Hamilton and Michelle Barrett. London: Verso.

MacManus, Susan A., et al. 1986. "A Longitudinal Examination of Political Participation Rates of Mexican American Females." *Social Science Quarterly* 67, no. 3 (September): 604–12.

March, Kathryn S., and Rachelle L. Taqqu. 1986. *Women's Informal Associations in Developing Countries: Catalysts for Change?* Boulder, Colo: Westview Press.

Marin, Chris. 1985. "La Asociación Hispano-Americana de Madres y Esposas: Tucson's Mexican American Women in World War II." In *Renato Rosaldo Lecture Series 1: 1983–1984,* ed. Renato Rosaldo. Tucson: Mexican American Studies Center, University of Arizona, 1985.

Marin, Marguerite V. 1991. *Social Protest in an Urban Barrio: A Study of the Chicano Movement, 1966–1974.* New York: University Press of America.

Marshall, Barbara. 1994. *Engendering Moderneity, Feminism, Social Theory and Social Change.* Boston: Northeastern University Press.

Martin, Biddy, and Chandra Mohanty. 1986. "Feminist Politics: What's Home Got to Do with It?" In *Feminist Studies/Critical Studies,* ed. Teresa de Lauretis, 191–212. Bloomington: Indiana University Press.

Martínez, Diana, and Mary Pardo. 1990. "Mothers of East Los Angeles." *Hispanic* (April): 18–19.

Mascia-Lees, Frances E., Patricia Sharpe, and Colleen Ballerino Cohen. 1989. "The Postmodernist Turn in Anthropology: Cautions from a Feminist Perspective." *Signs* 15, no. 1 (Autumn): 7–33.

Maxwell, Bruce, and Michael Jacobson. 1989. *Marketing Disease to Hispanics.* Washington, D.C.: Center for Science in the Public Interest.

McAdam, Doug. 1982. *Political Process and the Development of Black Insurgency, 1930–1970.* Chicago: University of Chicago Press.

McCourt, Kathleen. 1977. *Working-Class Women and Grass-Roots Politics.* Bloomington: Indiana University Press.

McDougal, Gerald S., and Harold Bunce. 1986. "Urban Services and the Suburbanization of Blacks." *Social Science Quarterly* 67, no. 3 (September): 596–603.

McFadden, Margaret, ed. 1997. *Women's Issues.* Pasadena, Calif.: Salem Press.

McNamara, Patrick Hayes. 1957. "Mexican Americans in Los Angeles County: A Study in Acculturation." Master's thesis, St. Louis University.

Melucci, Alberto. 1989. *Nomads of the Present.* Philadelphia: Temple University Press.

Melville, Margarita, ed. 1988. *Mexicanas at Work in the United States.* Houston, Texas: Mexican American Studies Program, University of Houston.

———, ed. 1980. *Twice a Minority.* St. Louis, Mo.: C. V. Mosby Company.

Miller, Alan S. 1987. "Saul Alinsky: America's Radical Reactionary." *Radical America* 21, no. 1 (January/February): 8.

Minault, Gail. 1981. "Introduction: The Extended Family as Metaphor and the Expansion of Women's Realm." In *The Extended Family: Women and Political Participation in India and Pakistan,* ed. Gail Minault, 3–18. Delhi, India: Chanakya Publications.

Mirande, Alfredo, and Evangelina Enríquez. 1979. *La Chicana: The Mexican American Woman.* Chicago: University of Chicago Press.

Mishler, Elliot G. 1979. "Meaning in Context: Is There Any Other Kind?" *Harvard Educational Review* 49, no. 1 (February): 1–19.

Molina, Gloria. 1986. "Response to Department of Corrections from Assemblywoman Gloria Molina." *Americas 2001* (March): 6.

Mollenkopf, John. 1983. *The Contested City.* Princeton: Princeton University Press.

Molotch, Harvey. 1976. "The City as a Growth Machine: Toward a Political Economy of Place." *American Journal of Sociology* 82, no. 2: 309–30.

Moore, Joan W. 1985. "Isolation, Stigmatization in the Development of an Underclass: The Case of Chicano Gangs in East L.A." *Social Problems* 33, no. 1: 1–12.

———. 1966. *Mexican Americans: Problems and Prospects*. Madison: Institute for Research on Poverty, University of Wisconsin.

Mora, Magdalena. 1981. "The Tolteca Strike: Mexican Immigrant Workers and the Struggle for Union Representation." In *Mexican Immigrant Workers in the U.S.*, ed. Antonio Ríos-Bustamante, 111–117. Los Angeles: Chicano Studies Research Center, University of California.

Mora, Magdalena, and Adelaida Del Castillo. 1980. *Mexican Women in the United States: Struggles Past and Present*. Los Angeles: Chicano Studies Research Center, University of California.

Morales, Armando. 1972. *Ando Sangrando (I Am Bleeding): A Study of Mexican American–Police Conlict*. LA Puente, Calif: Perspectiva Publications

Morales, Rebecca, and Paul Ong. 1993. "The Illusion of Progress: Latinos in Los Angeles." In *Latinos in a Changing Economy*, ed. Rebecca Morales and Frank Bonilla, 55–84. Newbury Park, Calif.: Sage Publications.

Morgen, Sandra. 1995. "It Was the Best Times and the Worst Times: Emotional Discourse in the Work Cultures of Feminist Health Clinics." In *Feminist Organizations: Harvest of the New Feminist Movement*, ed. Myra Marx Ferree and Patricia Yancey Martin. Philadelphia: Temple University Press.

———. 1988. "It's the Whole Power of the City against Us!" In *Women and the Politics of Empowerment*, ed. Ann Bookman and Sandra Morgen, 97–115. Philadelphia: Temple University Press.

Morris, Aldon. 1984. *The Origins of the Civil Rights Movement*. New York: Free Press.

Morris, Aldon, and Carol Mueller, eds. 1992. *Frontiers in Social Movement Theory*. New Haven: Yale University Press.

Muñoz, Carlos. 1989. *Youth, Identity, Power: The Chicano Movement*. London: Verso.

Naples, Nancy A. 1992. "Activist Mothering: Cross-Generational Continuity in the Community Work of Women from Low-Income Urban Neighborhoods." *Gender and Society* 16, no.3 (September): 441–63.

Noriega, Chon. 1988. "Chicano Cinema and the Horizon of Expectations: A Discursive Analysis of Film Reviews in the Mainstream, Alternative, and Hispanic Press, 1987–1988." *Aztlán* 19, no. 2 (Fall): 1–30.

Oakley, Ann. 1981. "Interviewing Women: A Contradiction in Terms." In *Doing Feminist Research,* ed. Helen Roberts. Boston: Routledge and Kegan Paul.

Oboler, Suzanne. 1995. *Ethnic Labels, Latino Lives: Identity and the Politics of (Re)Presentation in the United States.* Minneapolis: University of Minnesota Press.

Oliver, Melvin, and James Johnson, Jr. 1984. "Inter-Ethnic Conflict in an Urban Ghetto: The Case of Blacks and Latinos in Los Angeles." In *Research in Social Movements, Conflict, and Change,* ed. Richard Ratcliff. Greenwich, Conn.: JAI Press.

Ong, Paul. 1989. *The Widening Divide: Income Inequality and Poverty in Los Angeles.* Los Angeles: Research Group on the Los Angeles Economy, University of California, Los Angeles.

Orozco, Cynthia. 1992. "Beyond Machismo, La Familia, and Ladies Auxiliaries: A Historiography of Mexican-Origin Women's Participation in the United States, 1870–1990." Renato Rosaldo Lecture Series monograph vol. 10. Tucson: Mexican American Studies and Research Center, University of Arizona.

Ortiz, Isidro D. 1984. "Chicano Urban Politics and the Politics of Reform in the Seventies." *The Western Political Quarterly* 37, no. 4 (December): 565–77.

Pardo, Mary. 1995."Doing It for the Kids: Mexican American Community Activists, Border Feminists?" In *Feminist Organizations: Harvest of the New Women's Movement,* ed. Myra Marx Ferree and Patricia Yancey Martin, 356–71. Philadelphia: Temple University Press.

———. 1993. "Creating Community: Mexican American Women in Eastside Los Angeles." *Aztlán* 20, nos. 1–2 (Spring 1991): 39–71.

———. 1990. "Mexican American Grassroots Community Activists: Mothers of East Los Angeles." *Frontiers* 11, no. 1, 1–7.

Parson, Don. 1983. "Los Angeles' Headline-Happy Public Housing War." *Southern California Quarterly* 55, no. 3 (Fall): 251–85.

———. 1982. "The Development of Redevelopment: Public Housing and Urban Renewal in Los Angeles." *International Journal of Urban and Regional Research* 6, no. 4 (December): 392–413.

Pateman, Carole. 1970. *Participation and Democratic Theory.* Cambridge: Cambridge University Press.

Pesquera, Beatríz M. 1993. "In the Beginning He Wouldn't Lift Even a Spoon: The Division of Household Labor." In *Building With Our Hands,* ed. Adela de la Torre and Beatríz M. Pesquera, 181–95. Los Angeles: University of California Press.

Phillips, Bruce A. 1986. "Los Angeles Jewry: A Demographic Portrait." In *American Jewish Year Book 1986,* ed. Hilton Himmelfarb et al., 126–95. Philadelphia: Jewish Publication Society of America.

Pitt, Leonard, and Dale Pitt. 1997. *Los Angeles A to Z: An Encyclopedia of the City and County.* Berkeley: University of California Press.

Press, Sylvia Peña. 1992. "Hispanic Women in Suburbia." In *Latina Women in Transition,* ed. Ruth E. Zambrana. New York: Hispanic Research Center, Fordham University.

Radell, David Richard. 1961. "Mom 'n' Pop Grocery Stores in the Boyle Heights Section of Los Angeles, California: A Study of Site and Situation." Master's thesis, California State University, Los Angeles.

Randall, Vicky. 1982. *Women and Politics: An International Perspective.* Chicago: University of Chicago Press.

Reitzes, Donald C., and Dietrich C. Reitzes. 1987. *The Alinski Legacy: Alive and Kicking.* Greenwich, Conn.: JAI Press.

Reynoso, Raymundo. 1989. "Juana Beatrice Gutiérrez: La incansable lucha de una activista comunitaria." *La Opinión,* 6 August.

Reynoso, Raymundo, and Josefina Vidal. 1986. "Las Madres del Este de Los Angeles se proponen seguir luchando por sus hijos y su barrio." *La Opinión,* 28 August, 1.

Ries, Paula, and Anne J. Stone, eds. 1992. *The American Woman: A Status Report, 1992–1993.* New York: W. W. Norton & Co.

Rocco, Raymond. 1990. "The Theoretical Construction of the 'Other' in Postmodernist Thought: Latinos in the New Urban Political Economy." *Cultural Studies Special Issue: Chicana/o Cultural Representations* 4, no. 3 (October): 321–30.

————. 1970. "The Chicano in the Social Sciences: Traditional Concepts, Myths, and Images." *Aztlán* 1 (Fall): 75–98.

Rodríguez, Néstor, and Rogelio T. Núñez. 1986. "An Exploration of Factors That Contribute to Differentiation between Chicanos and Indocumentados." In *Mexican Immigrants and Mexican Americans: An Evolving Relation,* ed. Harley L. Browning and Rodolfo O. de la Garza, 138–56. Austin: Center for Mexican American Studies, University of Texas at Austin.

Romano-V., Octavio I. 1970. "Social Science, Objectivity and the Chicanos." *El Grito: A Journal of Contemporary Mexican American Thought* 4, no. 1 (Fall): 4–16.

Romero, Mary. 1992. *Maid in the U.S.A.* New York: Routledge.

Romo, Harriett. 1984. "The Mexican Origin Population's Differing Perceptions of Their Children's Schooling." *Social Science Quarterly* 69, no. 2 (June): 635–50.

Romo, Ricardo. 1983. *East Los Angeles: History of a Barrio.* Austin: University of Texas Press.

Root, Maria P. P., ed. 1992. *Racially Mixed People in America.* Knobbier Park, Calif.: Sage Publications.

Rosaldo, M. Z. 1980. "The Use and Abuse of Anthropology: Reflections on Feminism and Cross-Cultural Understanding." *Signs* 5, no. 3 (Spring): 389–417.

Rosaldo, Renato. 1989. *Culture and Truth, The Remaking of Social Analysis.* Boston: Beacon Press.

Rose, Margaret. 1994. "Gender and Civic Activism in Mexican American Barrios in California: The Community Service Organization, 1947–1962." In *Not June Cleaver: Women and Gender in Postwar America 1945–1960,* ed. Joanne Meyerowitz. Philadelphia: Temple University Press.

————. 1990. "Traditional and Nontraditional Patterns of Female Activism in the United Farm Workers of America, 1962–1980." *Frontiers: A Journal of Women Studies* 11, no. 1: 26–32.

Roy, William G. 1984. "Class Conflict and Social Change in Historical Perspective." *Annual Review of Sociology* 10: 483–506.

Rubenstein, Jonathan. 1973. *City Police.* Toronto: Doubleday Canada Ltd.

Ruiz, Vicki L. 1987. *Cannery Women, Cannery Lives: Mexican Women, Unionization, and the California Food Processing Industry, 1930–1950.* Albuquerque: University of New Mexico Press.

Russell, Dick. 1989a. "The Air We Breathe: Viva Las Madres!" *Parenting,* November, 127–28.

———. 1989b. "Environmental Racism: Minority Communities and Their Battle against Toxics." *Amicus Journal* 11, no. 2 (Spring): 22–32.

Sacks, Karen Brodkin. 1989a. "Toward a Unified Theory of Class, Race, and Gender." *American Ethnologist* 16, no. 3 (August): 534–50.

———. 1989b. "What's Life History Got to Do with It?" In *Interpreting Women's Lives,* ed. Personal Narratives Group, 85–95. Bloomington: Indiana University Press.

———. 1988. *Caring by the Hour.* Chicago: University of Illinois Press.

Saegert, Susan. 1989. "Unlikely Leaders, Extreme Circumstances: Older Black Women Building Community Households." *American Journal of Community Psychology* 17, no. 3: 295–316.

Saito, Leland. Forthcoming. "The Politics of Adaptation and the 'Good Immigrant': Japanese Americans and the New Chinese Immigrants." In *Asian and Latino Immigrants in a Restructuring Economy: The Metamorphosis of Los Angeles,* ed. Marta López-Garza and David Díaz. Palo Alto, Calif.: Stanford University Press.

———. 1993. "Asian Americans and Latinos in San Gabriel Valley, California: Ethnic Political Cooperation and Redistricting, 1990–1991." *Amerasia Journal* 19: 55–68.

Salter, Christopher. 1984. "Urban Imagery and the Chinese of Los Angeles." *Urban Resources,* 1, no. 4 (Spring): 15–21.

Sánchez, Jesús. 1988. "The Environment: Whose Movement?" *California Tomorrow* 3, nos. 3–4 (Fall): 13.

Sandoval, Chela. 1991. "U.S. Third World Feminisms: The Theory and Method of Oppositional Consciousness in the Postmodern World." *Genders* 10, 1–24

Sapiro, Virginia. 1995. "Feminist Studies and Political Science and Vice-Versa." In *Feminisms in the Academy,* ed. Domna C. Stanton and Abigail J. Stewart. Ann Arbor: University of Michigan Press.

Sassen, Saskia. 1988. *The Mobility of Labor and Capital.* Cambridge: Cambridge University Press.

Schoenberg, Sandra Perlman. 1980. "Some Trends in the Community Participation of Women in Their Neighborhoods." *Signs.* 5, no. 3: S261–S268.

Scott, Joan Wallach. 1988. "On Language, Gender, and Working-Class History." In *Gender and the Politics of History,* 53–67. New York: Columbia University Press.

Segura, Denise. 1988. "Familism and Employment among Chicanas and Mexican Immigrant Women." In *Mexicanas at Work in the United States,* ed. Margarita Melville, 24–32. Houston, Texas: Mexican American Studies Program, University of Houston.

Sekul, Joseph D. 1988. "Communities Organized for Public Service: Citizen Power and Public Power in San Antonio." In *Latinos and the Political System,* ed. F. Chris García. Notre Dame, Ind.: University of Notre Dame Press.

Sen, Gita. 1980. "The Sexual Division of Labor and the Working Class Family: Towards a Conceptual Synthesis of Class Relations." *Review of Radical Political Economics* 12, no. 2 (Summer): 76–86.

Serros, Michele. 1993. *Chicana Falsa and Other Stories of Life, Death, Identity, and Oxnard.* Valencia, Calif.: Lalo Press.

Shorris, Earl. 1989. "Sanctuary for L.A. Homeboys: The Priest Who Loved Gangsters." *The Nation* 249, no. 21 (18 December): 1.

Shuit, Douglas. 1990. "L.A. Prison Fight Revived by Assembly Budget Move." *Los Angeles Times,* 18 April, B4.

Simmel, George. 1904. "Fashion." *International Quarterly* 10: 130–55.

Simon, Richard, and Frederick M. Muir. 1990. "L.A. Supervisor Districts Illegal." *Los Angeles Times,* 5 June, A1.

Skerry, Peter. 1984. "The Resurrection of Saul Alinsky, Neighborhood COPS." *The New Republic,* 6 February, 21–23.

Smith, Dorothy. 1977. "A Sociology for Women." In *The Prism of Sex,* 135–187, ed. Julia Sherman and Evelyn Beck. Madison: University of Wisconsin Press.

———. 1990. *The Conceptual Practices of Power.* Boston: Northeastern University Press.

Soja, E. W., Rebecca Morales, and Goetz Wolff. 1983. "Urban Restruc-

turing: An Analysis of Social and Spatial Change in Los Angeles." *Economic Geography* 59, no. 2 (April): 195–229.

Soja, E. W. 1986. "Economic Restructuring and the Internationalization of Los Angeles." In *The Capitalist City*, ed. Michael Smith and
Joe Feagin. New York: Basil Blackwell.

Soldatenko, María. 1992. "The Everyday Lives of Latina Garment
Workers in Los Angeles: The Convergence of Gender, Race,
Class, and Immigration." Ph.D. diss, University of California,
Los Angeles.

———. 1991. "Organizing Latina Garment Workers in Los Angeles."
Las Obreras: The Politics of Work and Family (special thematic issue), *Aztlán* 20, nos. 1–2: 74–96.

Sowell, Thomas. 1981. *Ethnic America: A History.* New York: Basic
Books.

Spelman, Elizabeth V. 1988. *Inessential Woman.* Boston: Beacon Press.

Spring, Greg. 1992. "Opposition Builds to Prison." *L.A. Downtown
News,* 24 August, 1.

Stanley, Liz, and Sue Wise. 1993. *Breaking out Again: Feminist Ontology
and Epistemology.* New York: Routledge.

Stansell, Christine. 1986. *City of Women.* New York: Alfred A. Knopf.

State of California. 1995. *Vital Statistics of California, 1993.* Sacramento:
Department of Health Services, Vital Statistics Section.

Steger, Mary Ann E., and Stephanie L. Witt. 1989. "Gender Differences in Environmental Orientations." *Western Political Quarterly,* 42, no. 4 (December): 627–49.

Steinberg, L. S. 1980. "The Role of Women's Social Networks in the
Adoption of Innovations at the Grass-roots Level." *Signs* 5, no. 3
Supplement 2.

Stern, Gwen Louise. 1976. "Ethnic Identity and Community Action in
El Barrio." Ph.D. diss., Northwestern University.

Stone, Gregory P. 1962. "Appearance and the Self." In *Human Behavior and Social Processes*, ed. Arnold M. Rose, 86–118. Boston:
Houghton Mifflin.

Sturgeon, Noël. 1995. "Theorizing Movements: Direct Action and Direct Theory." In *Cultural Politics and Social Movements*, ed. Marcy
Darnovsky, Barbara Epstein, and Richard Flacks, 35–51. Philadelphia: Temple University Press.

Suad, Joseph. 1983. "Working Class Women's Networks in a Sectarian State: A Political Paradox." *American Ethnologist* 10, no. 1: 1–22.

Susser, Ida. 1988. "Working-Class Women, Social Protest, and Changing Ideologies." In *Women and the Politics of Empowerment,* ed. Ann Bookman and Sandra Morgen, 257–71. Philadelphia: Temple University Press.

Suttles, Gerald D. 1972. *The Social Construction of Communities.* Chicago: University of Chicago Press.

Swerdlow, Amy. 1993. *Women Strike for Peace: Traditional Motherhood and Radical Politics in the 1960s.* Chicago: University of Chicago Press.

Takash, Paule Cruz. 1993. "Breaking Barriers To Representation: Chicana/Latina Elected Officials." *Urban Anthropology,* 22, nos. 3–4: 325–60.

Tarrow, Sidney. 1994. *Power in Movement: Social Movements, Collective Action and Politics.* Cambridge: Cambridge University Press.

Thiele, Beverly. 1986. "Vanishing Acts in Social and Political Thought: Tricks of the Trade." In *Feminist Challenges, Social and Political Theory,* ed. Carole Pateman and Elizabeth Gross. 30–43. Boston: Allen and Unwin.

Thompson, Paul. 1978. *The Voice of the Past.* New York: Oxford University Press.

Tilly, Louise. 1981. "Paths to Proletarianization: Organization of Production, Sexual Division of Labor, and Women's Collective Action." *Signs* 7, no. 2: 400–417.

Tirado, Miguel David. 1970. "Mexican American Community Political Organization." In *Ethnic Tenacity: A Reader in Mexican American Studies,* ed. Ralph Guzmán, 62–64. Palo Alto: Cummings Publishing Company.

Tobar, Hector. 1990. "Growing Voter Discontent Felt by Incumbents." *Los Angeles Times,* 12 April, 1.

Tseng, Yen-Fen. 1994. "The Chinese Ethnic Economy: San Gabriel Valley, Los Angeles County." *Journal of Urban Affairs* 16 (1994): 169–89.

UCLA Ethnic Studies Centers. 1987. *Ethnic Groups in Los Angeles: Quality of Life Indicators.* University of California, Los Angeles.

Vaca, Nick C. 1970. "The Mexican American in the Social Sciences,

1936–1970, Part II." *El Grito: A Journal of Contemporary Mexican-American Thought* 4, no. 1 (Fall): 17–51.

Valdivia, Steve. 1993. "Covering Gangs and Gang Violence." In *Covering L.A.'s Majority,* ed. Diana Martínez and Andrés Chávez. Los Angeles: L.A. Media and the County of Los Angeles Commission on Human Relations.

Verba, Sidney, and Norman Nie. 1972. *Participation in America.* New York: Harper and Row.

Vigil, James Diego. 1983. "Chicano Gangs: One Response to Mexican Urban Adaptation in the Los Angeles Area." *Urban Anthropology* 12, 1 (Spring): 45–75.

Villalobos, Frank. 1988. "No Prison in East L.A." *Americas 2001* 1, no. 8 (October/November): 11.

Waldinger, Roger, and Mehdi Bozorgmehr. 1990. *Ethnic Los Angeles.* New York: Russell Sage Foundation.

Wallerstein, Immanuel. 1983. *Historical Capitalism.* London: Verso.

Weber, Devra Ann. 1990. "Mexican Women on Strike: Memory, History and Oral Narratives." In *Between Borders: Essays on Mexicana/Chicana History,* ed. Adelaida R. Del Castillo, 175–200. Encino, Calif.: Floricanto Press, 1990.

Weintraub, Daniel M. 1988. "$10,000 Fee Paid to Lawmaker Who Left Sickbed to Cast Vote." *Los Angeles Times,* 13 March, I:3.

Wekerle, Gerda R. 1980. "Women in the Urban Environment." In *Women and the American City,* ed. Catherine R. Stimpson et al. Chicago: University of Chicago Press.

West, Guida, and Rhoda Lois Blumberg, eds. 1990. *Women and Social Protest.* New York: Oxford University Press.

Williams, Brett. 1988. *Upscaling Downtown: Stalled Gentrification in Washington, D.C.* Ithaca, N.Y.: Cornell University Press.

———. 1984. "Why Migrant Women Feed Their Husbands Tamales." In *Ethnic and Regional Foodways in the United States,* ed. Linda Keller Brown and Kay Mussell, 113–26. Knoxville: University of Tennessee Press.

Wong, K. Scott. 1995. "Chinatown: Conflicting Images, Contested Terrain." *Journal of the Society for the Study of Multi-Ethnic Literature of the United States* 20, no. 1 (Spring): 3–15.

Ybarra, Lea. 1982. "When Wives Work: The Impact on the Chicana." *Journal of Marriage and the Family* 44, no. 1 (February): 169–78.

Yudelman, Sally W. 1987. *Hopeful Openings: A Study of Five Women's Development Organizations in Latin America and the Caribbean.* West Hartford, Conn.: Kumarian Press.

Zavella, Patricia. 1987. *Women's Work and Chicano Families.* Ithaca, N.Y.: Cornell University Press.

Index

United Neighborhood
organization (UNO): in Boyle
Heights, 26–27, 34–39, 50; card
club controversy, 159
urban planning: community
identity and, 68–69;
downzoning and, 95–96,
268n.6; politics of, 68–69,
266nn. 11–12
urban politics: women in sociology
of, 244–47

V

Vernon, California, 133–35
Vigil, Diego, 264n.40
Vigil, James Jr., 55, 264n.40
Villalobos, Frank, 108, 137, 167
Villaseñor, Rosa, 73–74, 165–67,
177–78, 194–95
Virgin Mary, devotion to, 190, 275n.21

W

War on Poverty programs, 87–88
Water Conservation Project, 138
*West San Gabriel Valley News
Digest*, 213
wetbacks *(mojados)*, new
immigrants stereotyped as,
165, 273nn.3
Wilson, Pete (Governor), 56
"window monitoring" in
Monterey Park, 202–205
Wissman, Marijune, 152–53, 217
women activists: affirmation of,
247–52; barrio/suburban
comparisons, 49–51, 223–25,
234–36; in Boyle Heights,
26–39, 261n.14; in Chicano
movement, 31–34, 262n.24,
263n.25; community
mobilization by, 139–41,
172–82; comparative

prison/parole office con-
troversies, 59–60; in CSO,
29–31, 262n.24; demographic
comparisons, Boyle Heights/
Monterey Park, 102–104;
driver's training initiative
and, 182–86; of Eastside Los
Angeles, 105–41, 229–33;
ethnic identity issues, 76–81;
household management by,
23, 128–31, 144–45, 167,189–95,
271n.4, 273n.9, 275nn.20;
immigrants *vs.* established
residents, 165–72; language
barriers in Monterey Park
and, 147–52; lobbying activities, 125–28; long-time residents as, 69–75; Monterey
Park parole office controversy
and, 143–62, 272n.5; parish
networks and, 173–78; personal empowerment of,
122–25, 158–62, 218–22; po-
liticization of motherhood
and, 112–18, 140–41; private/
public dichotomies, 236–38;
Recreation Center initiative
and, 187–89; sociology of
urban politics, 244–47, 280n.12;
transformation of political by,
226–52; in UNO, 35–39
Wyvernwood housing project,
71–75, 166–67, 169–70,
273n.4

Y

Yee, Cindy, 99–100, 146, 211–12,
218–22, 227
Yen Fen Tseng, 277n.6

Z

Zavella, Patricia, 249